Jossey-Bass Teacher

Jossey-Bass Teacher provides educators with practical knowledge and tools to create a positive and lifelong impact on student learning. We offer classroom-tested and research-based teaching resources for a variety of grade levels and subject areas. Whether you are an aspiring, new, or veteran teacher, we want to help you make every teaching day your best.

From ready-to-use classroom activities to the latest teaching framework, our value-packed books provide insightful, practical, and comprehensive materials on the topics that matter most to K–12 teachers. We hope to become your trusted source for the best ideas from the most experienced and respected experts in the field.

The Complete Learning Disabilities Handbook

Ready-to-Use Strategies & Activities for Teaching Students with Learning Disabilitces

Third Edition

Joan Harwell
Rebecca Williams Jackson

JOSSEY-BASS
A Wiley Imprint
www.josseybass.com

Contents

Acknowledgments

Bill Jackson, my first and foremost supportive partner and computer specialist, is an excellent editor, English professional, and computer instructor, all specialties that helped me get this book finished.

Rebecca Smith, my illustrator, worked on a tight deadline, produced beautiful work, and literally drove through snowstorms to help me.

Catherine Elgin, my Harvard adviser. Kate was the first adviser who told me to write and keep writing, that my work would be published. I will always be grateful for that.

Margie, my editor, has been supportive from the start. She has faithfully guided me through the steps of publishing and offered good advice and opportunities all the way around.

Nancy Mindick has been instrumental in providing information on visual processing and has been a sounding board for many of my ideas.

Dr. Rachel M. Williams has offered advice from a medical perspective and helped me work through the medical approach to learning disabilities.

St. Mary's School teachers helped preview the book and give feedback during the writing process.

St. Peter's School teachers helped gather information and let me look over student work to help solidify concepts and work samples.

Riverview School teachers reviewed the book and offered their feedback and support in rewriting this text.

Tiffany Winters graciously offered help in structuring the legal debates occurring in the field of special education and school districts.

I want to thank my family for all their support and belief in my writing: my husband and my daughter, Victoria; Mom, Dad, Rachel, Adam, Edward, Eric, Mary, Elizabeth, and Josh. Gratitude goes to Mary and Edward Milanowski and Kay and Paul Williams, my grandparents, who have spread the word about my book and work.

—RWJ

This is dedicated to my daughter Jakki, who encourages me.

—JH

I dedicate this book to my family, my rock.

—RWJ

About the Authors

Joan Harwell has more than 40 years of experience as a regular classroom teacher and a special education teacher for students with learning disabilities in San Bernardino, Calif. She was also a special education mentor teacher. After retirement from full-time teaching, she served as a field work supervisor for student teachers and intem.

Rebecca Williams Jackson is an educational specialist who received her master's degree in education from Harvard University. She has guided parents and students for over ten years, in the classroom and in private practice. She currently works as an educational consultant and advocate.

About This Book

The Complete Learning Disabilities Handbook, Third Edition, covers the field of learning disabilities from research to practice, including summaries of important laws, recent research in the field, and dozens of reproducible worksheets. This book is a collaboration of two experts in the field of education: a master teacher with over forty years of experience and an educational specialist who graduated from the Harvard Graduate School of Education. The book covers many aspects of working with children with learning disabilities, from causes and assessment to classroom management and lesson planning.

Equally useful for special educators or general education teachers, the book includes practical information that all teachers need in order to address the increasingly diverse needs of the students in their classroom.

Topics covered include the following:

- An overview of learning disabilities

- Tips for teaching at-risk students

- Classroom management strategies

- Solutions to specific problems (including attention deficits, dyslexia, poor social skills, low self-esteem, and other common classroom problems related to learning disabilities)

- Guidelines for interventions in specific academic areas

- Advice for working with learning disabled adolescents and adults

- Tips for successful collaboration with parents

Chapter 1

An Overview of the Field of Learning Disabilities

Leonardo da Vinci (1452–1519)

Italian sculptor, painter, architect, engineer
Was believed to be learning disabled; used "mirror writing"

Contributions:

Painting: *Last Supper*
             Mona Lisa
             The Adoration of the Magi

Drawing: Illustrated his anatomical observations; designed helicopters, bicycles, pumps, and military weaponry

---

Learning disability (LD) is a term currently used to describe a group of neurological conditions that interfere with a person's learning. Under the umbrella called LD, there are disorders related to listening, speaking, reading, reasoning, and mathematical calculation. Individuals with LD have intelligence in the near average, average, or above-average range. Because these individuals do not appear to be different, difficulties are not expected. The impact of the conditions may range from mild to severe. As we expand our knowledge of learning disabilities, we have come to realize that learning disabilities may also include an attention-deficit component, a socioemotional component, and perhaps emotional issues.

Unlike physical disabilities, learning disabilities are not so obvious and have been referred to as the "hidden handicap." Sometimes these disabilities go unrecognized by parents, teachers, and physicians. As a result, individuals with learning disabilities may be thought of as "underachievers," "lazy," or "weird."

Learning disabled individuals have to work harder to succeed. They receive more negative feedback regarding their work. They may experience feelings of frustration, anger, depression, anxiety, and worthlessness.

Individuals with LD need early identification, sound remedial teaching appropriate to their needs, personal and family counseling, continuous training in social skills, vocational guidance, and on-the-job coaching.

History of Learning Disabilities

The field of learning disabilities is relatively young. Historically, the learning disabled person may not have been singled out in school; perhaps those with learning difficulties dropped out of school or went to work. With the technological revolution of the 1950s came a demand for an educated workforce that is adept at working with technology, machinery, and scientific study. Geographic mobility, an increase in international exposure, and the sudden spurt in technology are among many factors that have changed the scope of the education and work prospects for people with learning disabilities.

Dynamic social changes in society are putting pressure on schools to do a better job educating all students, especially as different tracking systems and measurement agents have demonstrated the numbers of students graduating from high school and other schools. Numerous studies point to the fact that almost a quarter of students who enter high school don't graduate.

Prior to 1937, there was no recognition of learning disabilities. In 1937, Samuel Orton, a neuropathologist, used the term "strephosymbolia" to describe a problem he had observed in children with reading difficulties, namely, the reversals of symbols, such as *b* and *d,* or words, such as *saw* and *was.* He thought that this might be caused by the failure of one hemisphere of the brain to establish dominance over the other, which he assumed resulted in mirror images of words and symbols. He noted that there seemed to be a continuum of reading disability ranging from mild cases to severe cases. The Orton Dyslexia Society was named for him.

The look-say method of learning to read in the early 1940s resulted in a high degree of failure to acquire reading skills. Samuel Orton, Anna Gillingham, Bessie Stillman, Romalda Spalding, and Grace Fernald responded to the need by developing alternative methods to teach students who couldn't learn to read by memorizing sight words. Despite their pioneering efforts from 1940 to 1960, most students with learning disabilities were thought to be slow learners. It was rare that they received any special help. If they did, they were usually put into classes for the educably retarded.

Research findings in the 1960s were disturbing. Many children who had been classified as retarded were found to have normal intelligence when tested in a nonverbal format. William Cruickshank suggested that their progress was being hindered by deficits in perception and deficits in attention.

A group of concerned parents of children who had difficulty reading met in Chicago in 1963 to discuss the needs of their children. At that time, doctors referred to these children as being "minimally brain damaged" (MBD). These parents objected to the use of that label. Samuel Kirk, who was at this meeting, suggested a new term, "learning disabled." The parents adopted the new term and established the parent organization Association of Children with Learning Disabilities (ACLD) and began to demand services for their children.

Shortly thereafter, the International Council for Exceptional Children created a division of the organization to address the needs of children with learning disabilities. By the late 1960s, education responded. Special education resource rooms were opened. Students were grouped for instruction according to their needs. Special educators tried to work on children's perceptual deficits and to help them reduce their distractibility. Research in animal and human behavior by B. F. Skinner and others led to a very different approach, behavior modification, which became very popular in education during the 1960s.

Attempts to classify learning disabilities into LD subtypes began in the 1970s with the works of Elena Boder, Byron Rourke, and Linda Siegel, and have continued since. The most significant event of the 1970s was the passage of Public Law 94-142 (the Education of All Handicapped Children Act) by Congress in 1975. It guaranteed that each handicapped child, age three to twenty-one, would receive a "free and appropriate" education in the "least restrictive environment" possible. This law became known as the "mainstreaming" law. Children with LD were to be educated in regular classrooms unless the nature and severity of their disability was so great that it could be demonstrated that they could not make progress in regular classes. Each school was given the services of a resource specialist.

Public Law 94-142 had one enormous shortcoming: it did not provide school districts with adequate monies to provide the services it mandated. At the time of its passage, it was presumed that approximately 2 percent of schoolchildren would require services. By 1987, almost 5 percent of schoolchildren qualified for services under the LD category.

Early in the 1980s, educational endeavors changed focus. Less effort was devoted to remediating perceptual deficits, and the focus shifted to skills development. About the same time, there was resurgence in research interest in learning disabilities. New technologies, such as magnetic resonance imaging (MRI) and positron emission tomography (PET), were making it possible, for the first time, to map electrical activity and blood flow in the brains of living subjects as they performed various educational tasks.

In the late 1980s, the Regular Education Initiative (REI) encouraged special education and regular education to join resources. The initiative said that students who had been served in pullout programs would be better served by their general education teachers in regular classrooms, if their teachers had help from special education personnel. "Inclusion" was the buzzword. In classes where inclusion was a success, it attests to the flexibility and cooperation of the two teachers involved, because this is truly team teaching. Resource specialists were encouraged to spend more time with regular teachers consulting and collaborating about students' special needs.

Late in the 1980s, researchers suggested that the true causes of reading disability were deficits in phonological awareness, phonological encoding, and phonological retrieval abilities. (See the work of J. K. Torgesen and Paula Tallal.) This research states that training in phonemic awareness and systematic phonics instruction are necessary for at-risk and reading disabled students.

In 1990, Public Law 94-142 was retitled and expanded. It is now called the Individuals with Disabilities Education Act (IDEA), Public Law 101-476. IDEA further refined the definition of a learning disability:

> *"Specific learning disability" means a disorder in one or more of the basic psychological processes involved in understanding or in using language, spoken or written, which may manifest itself in an imperfect ability to listen, think, speak, read, write, spell or to do mathematical calculations. This term includes such conditions as perceptual handicaps, brain injury, minimal brain dysfunction, dyslexia and developmental aphasia. The term does not include children who have learning problems which are primarily the result of visual, hearing, or motor handicaps, of mental retardation, of emotional disturbance, or of environmental, cultural, or economic disadvantage.*

(U.S. Office of Education, Federal Register)

This definition reflects the historical development of the field. The definition also states who is included and who will be excluded from special education services under the label "learning disabled."

Many educators argue that the excluded child is being unfairly deprived of essential services. For example, there are children whose IQs fall between 75 and 85 who desperately need and would benefit from more help, but do not get it because they do not fall into any category of special education. Likewise, the child whose parents move every few months is in desperate need of remedial help, but many schools have no programs available to address such needs.

Although IDEA requires that a child fit a standard profile in order to receive additional services, Section 504, a civil rights act, was designed to help students who might not qualify under IDEA regulations. (See Chapter Three for a more in-depth discussion of legislation.)

Nationwide, school performance statistics are mixed. Arguing for continued funding, the September 2007 NCLB Report Card to Congress indicated "continued growth and gains by America's schoolchildren, particularly among younger and minority students." The report lists increased reading scores for fourth graders and higher math scores for both fourth and eighth grades. However, the report does not detail, or even address, students with special needs. In fact, the researcher must be clever and diligent to find government data for the learning disabled child. For instance, in 2005 the Department of Education's testing arm (the National Assessment of Educational Progress) published the *NAEP 2004 Trends in Academic Progress: Three Decades of Student Performance in Reading and Mathematics*. This report follows reading and math scores since the early 1970s. Their findings, again not breaking out learning disabilities, show a relatively flat line of scores: "the average reading score at age 9 was higher in 2004 than in any previous assessment year [9 points higher on a 500-point scale]. The average reading score at age 13 was not significantly different in 2004 from the average score in 1999 (the most recent previous assessment year), although it was higher than the average score in 1971. At age 17, there was no statistically significant difference between the average score in 2004 and the average score in 1971 or 1999." (National Assessment of Educational Progress, 2005, data added.)

Other key points indicate the need for serious attention:

- Only 70 percent of students in the United States graduate from high school in four years.

- One in ten schools fail to graduate 60 percent of their entering freshmen.

- 50 percent of adults who had below-basic reading skills were unemployed in 2003.

The status of education in the United States was the subject of a government report titled *A Nation at Risk*, published in 1983. Following this report, parents blamed teachers, and teachers blamed parents. The length of the school day and school year were slightly increased, but achievement scores continued to be poor through the 1990s.

At the turn of the century, a number of distinct trends have emerged:

- Reexamination of our educational theories and practices. One example of this is the movement toward combining the Whole Language reading approach with phonemic awareness training and phonetic skills development into a program called Balanced Literacy.

- A proposal for the development of a uniform, national achievement testing program.

- Stricter credentialing standards for teachers.

- An end to the practice of social promotion and tightening of the standards for promotion and graduation.

- Recognition by industry that it has a responsibility to provide parents with more family leave time, child care on work premises, and compensated time off for parents to help in their children's classrooms.

- The demand for reduction in class size has begun to be translated into action.

- Questions about the wisdom of the "severe discrepancy clause," which prevents earlier remediation for all students who need it.

- A growing awareness that we need to provide more vocational training services in high schools for students who do not wish to pursue academic goals or cannot meet the standards for promotion.

In the year 2000, the No Child Left Behind (NCLB) legislation was introduced to help hold schools accountable for their governance practices and levels of student performance. Schools now must submit yearly "progress reports" to government entities to demonstrate that they are performing at an acceptable level. NCLB legislation allowed the government to step in and take action if a school does not show adequate yearly performance. If a school continues to flounder, the NCLB legislation allows the government to remove funding for the school or take over its leadership and governance by appointed personnel.

Causal Factors

Current literature and research reveal that a number of causes of learning disabilities are under study. Among them are the following:

1. There is a strong familial factor. It is not uncommon to find that several members of the same family have the condition. LD can be inherited.

2. The incidence of learning disabilities increases when there is a difficult pregnancy or delivery, or prematurity.

3. Certain prenatal conditions can harm the fetus, including any condition that interferes with the fetus receiving adequate oxygen or nutrition, and maternal use of cigarettes, drugs, or alcohol during pregnancy.

4. Postnatal or birth trauma, such as high and sustained fever, head trauma, or near-drowning, may cause learning problems.

5. Early childhood exposure to lead, aluminum, arsenic, mercury, and other neurotoxins have been linked to and, in some cases, shown to cause learning impairment. In fact, recent data show a definitive link between lead and a host of learning disorders. Exposure to even low levels of environmental lead and cigarette smoking during pregnancy can cause ADHD (Braun, Kahn, Froehlich, Auinger, and Lanphear, 2006).

Research shows that what happens during the years from birth to age four is critically important to later learning. The role of infant stimulation and cultural deprivation is being studied. We know that early in life, the brain starts to pare away brain cells that are not being used. We have learned that for language to develop properly, young children, birth to age three, need to be sung to, talked with, and read to. In many homes, there is little interactive conversation (soliciting and receiving both a verbal and physical response), which may contribute to phonological awareness deficits. This lack of interactive communication may in turn lead to reading failure.

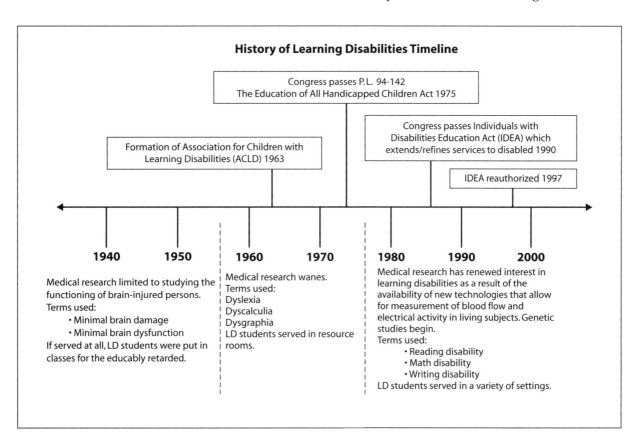

History of Learning Disabilities Timeline

Congress passes P.L. 94-142
The Education of All Handicapped Children Act 1975

Congress passes Individuals with Disabilities Education Act (IDEA) which extends/refines services to disabled 1990

Formation of Association for Children with Learning Disabilities (ACLD) 1963

IDEA reauthorized 1997

1940   1950   1960   1970   1980   1990   2000

Medical research limited to studying the functioning of brain-injured persons.
Terms used:
• Minimal brain damage
• Minimal brain dysfunction
If served at all, LD students were put in classes for the educably retarded.

Medical research wanes.
Terms used:
Dyslexia
Dyscalculia
Dysgraphia
LD students served in resource rooms.

Medical research has renewed interest in learning disabilities as a result of the availability of new technologies that allow for measurement of blood flow and electrical activity in living subjects. Genetic studies begin.
Terms used:
• Reading disability
• Math disability
• Writing disability
LD students served in a variety of settings.

Incidence

How many people have learning disabilities? We really don't know. Estimates range from 5 percent to more than 30 percent. It depends on whom you count. According to the U.S. Office of Education, 5 to 15 percent of the school population is identified as being LD, but data from twenty-six countries show that the incidence of dyslexia ranges from a low of 1 percent in Japan and China to a high of 33 percent in Venezuela. In the United States, 20 percent or more of students have trouble learning to read. Many children are evaluated and found to have a learning disability, but they do not qualify for special education services because they do not show a severe discrepancy between ability (intelligence) and performance. What constitutes a severe discrepancy varies from state to state—a child can qualify for service in one state but not qualify in another state. Even with such variation across states, national incidence rates break down as follows:

Between 3 and 8 percent of children in the United States have ADHD.

Approximately 1 in 150 children have autism, and 1 in 94 boys is diagnosed with autism.

Currently, more boys than girls are identified as being LD. The ratio is about 3 to 1. Many explanations have been offered for this, including that males seem to be more susceptible to brain damage, both prenatally and postnatally, and that males may be more disruptive in the classroom and therefore garner more attention from the teacher than females.

Primary Characteristics of Learning Disabilities

One indication of a learning disability is a perceptual deficit, and they are very common. Perceptual deficits are not caused by deficits in visual or hearing acuity. While glasses and hearing aids will help with acuity problems, they do not help persons who have perceptual problems. Perceptual deficits occur because the brain misinterprets sensory information. (Symptoms of perceptual deficits are discussed in Chapter Ten, and suggestions are given for helping students to cope with these deficits.)

Eighty percent of students identified as being LD have problems in the area of reading. It appears that deficits in phonological processing underlie difficulties learning to read. Research has shown that children who do not develop phonemic awareness will have reading difficulty later. (See the works of Stanovich, 1988, and Mann, 1991.) It has also been found that intervention programs that provide instruction in phonemic awareness and supply ample opportunities for decoding practice have been successful with at-risk and reading disabled children.

Phonological processing skills include our awareness and ability to "tease out" sounds (phoneme discrimination) within words, our ability to learn these symbols of the language and to recall their sounds quickly (phonological memory), and our ability to generalize this information to a variety of oral, written, and reading tasks.

Comorbid or Co-occurring Conditions

An individual with LD may be further handicapped by the simultaneous existence of other conditions. Three prevalent conditions are Attention Deficit Hyperactivity Disorder (ADHD), Conduct Disorder (CD), and Tourette Syndrome (TS).

Attention Deficit Hyperactivity Disorder

ADHD co-occurs with LD in approximately one out of every three individuals identified for special education services. Symptoms of ADHD include the following:

- Impulsivity; acting without consideration of consequences
- Inability to complete routine (or what are considered "boring") tasks
- Distractibility
- Inability to sit or stand still
- Blurting out
- Low frustration tolerance or short fuse
- Overreaction to stimuli
- Sleep disturbances
- Disorganization or a tendency to be messy or to lose things
- Inability to plan ahead
- Inability to mind one's own business
- Intrusiveness
- Incessant talking
- Inattention
- Forgetfulness
- Problems with planning
- Difficulty carrying out directions from start to finish

It was once believed that children with ADHD outgrew their problems. Although some children may outgrow the symptoms of the disorder, others do not.

Conduct Disorder

Conduct Disorder (CD) is sometimes a co-occurring condition with ADHD. In addition to the primary symptoms of inattention and impulsivity, those with CD exhibit a lack of respect for the rights of others. There may be cruelty to others or animals, lying, fire-setting, intentional breaking of rules, and denial of responsibility for acts. Children with CD may have been abused, neglected, or both. They may not have received logical and reasonable consequences for improper actions, and they may have been raised in an environment where the previously mentioned actions are not perceived as unusual and, in some cases, are even encouraged.

Tourette Syndrome

Tourette Syndrome (TS) is an inherited neurological disorder. The condition is characterized by involuntary motor tics or vocal tics or both these types of tics. Symptoms begin in childhood, increase in adolescence, and improve in adulthood. The condition occurs in about one out of one thousand children and more often in boys. The tics may vary from mild to severe and may include excessive eye rolling or blinking, twitches, finger tapping, sniffing, and throat clearing. More serious tics include squealing; barking; echolalia (repeating what someone says); bursts of profanity, racial slurs, or sexually inappropriate words or actions. There may be obsessive behaviors, such as a need for symmetry or evening things up; anxiety related to germs; and ritualistic behaviors. On Individual Education Plans (IEPs), a diagnosed TS student should be labeled "Other Health Impaired." The symptoms are part of their handicapping condition. Tourette Syndrome is frequently accompanied by ADHD and LD.

• • •

When referring a child to a physician for diagnosis, a teacher's or parent's careful observations of symptoms may help the physician delineate which disorders the child manifests.

Prognosis

Whenever a child is diagnosed as being LD, invariably the question arises, What is the prognosis for the child? That is hard to predict because it depends on many factors, such as the following:

1. The nature and severity of the disability

2. Whether ADHD, CD, or both are also present

3. The intellectual potential of the child

4. The quantity and quality of the intervention

5. When the intervention is begun (earlier is better)

6. The quantity and quality of the parental relationship (Does the parent talk with the child, supervise homework, provide a tutor, expose the child to wholesome experiences, work on social skills, and/or use effective parenting skills?)

7. The temperament of the child

8. The maturity and social skills of the child

9. The quality of communication between school and parent

10. The stability of the home

11. The persistence of the child (the most revealing factor in this list)

Having a learning disability does not doom a person to failure. Historians have postulated that a number of successful and famous persons have had the condition: Thomas Edison, Albert Einstein, Winston Churchill, Woodrow Wilson, George Bernard Shaw, Cher, Tom Cruise, and Charles Schwab. All these individuals found ways to maximize their strengths rather than concentrate on their weaknesses. Persistence pays off. As teachers and parents, we can hinder or help. In general, students with high IQs who come from homes in which education is valued and where parents engage the help of tutors tend to have better prognoses.

Programs and Settings for the Learning Disabled

Public schools provide a variety of programs to assist children with LD. If a baby is born at risk for a disabling condition, the local public school system may be asked to provide help to the parents—counseling, locating needed services, and parenting advice. Children who are two and younger can be referred to intervention services and specialists through their family doctors, or parents may request that the local Early Intervention Team evaluate their child in their home or at a controlled location. For children between the ages of birth and three years old, state agencies may devise an Individualized Family Service Plan.

For LD children from three to five years old, programs are available through the state's local Early Intervention Team. Parents can be referred to these programs through their pediatricians, day-care providers, or simply by going online to find their own local Early Intervention Specialist.

Each state provides a range of services to parents of children with learning disabilities or even developmental delays. Services can be provided in a child's home, preschool, or day-care center, depending on the ruling of the state Early Intervention Team.

When the child enters elementary school, there are a variety of settings for obtaining service. The least restrictive setting would be for the child to receive special education services within the regular class setting. Providing special education services can be accomplished in a variety of ways:

- Special education personnel could come into the room to assist the child.

- Special educators could meet with the regular teacher in a collaborative or consultative mode to plan the child's program.

- The child could go to a resource room for help for part of the day.

- The child could be placed in an LD special day class for all or part of the day.

It is the job of the IEP team to determine the amount and type of service the child needs to make academic progress. Children may also be qualified for services of other professionals, such as a speech therapist and/or an adaptive physical education teacher. These services are available through secondary school or until age twenty-one.

Although the needs of most children with LD can be handled in the ways just described, occasionally there are students whose needs are so great that they require more restrictive placements—in special day classes for emotionally disturbed students or in special residential schools. Some may be served at home or in a hospital.

Colleges and universities now provide assistance to LD students, such as placing them in classes of sympathetic professors, providing extra tutorial help, granting modification of time limits or testing formats, and furnishing special equipment. In addition, some colleges have departments devoted to helping students with LD coordinate their college responsibilities. These departments may help students arrange for tutoring and help them navigate the technological tools that offer text-reading software and voice recognition software for writing papers. College textbook publishers are increasingly offering digital textbooks for students to purchase and use with any supportive media the student may choose.

Facts About Learning Disabilities

- More boys than girls are identified as learning disabled; the ratio is about 3:1 (Cone, Wilson, Bradley, and Reese, 1985). Recent studies suggest that as many girls as boys may have the condition but are not identified (Shaywitz, Fletcher, and Shaywitz, 1995).

- Students with learning disabilities are usually identified by the time they reach late third or early fourth grade (Bender, 2001).

- More students are identified because of deficits in reading and the language arts than in mathematics (Smith, 1994).

- IQs of identified LD students are typically in the 90 to 95 range (Bender, 2001).

- Students with LD tend to have deficits in short-term memory. In looking at testing results, you will find that short-term memory scores are often below the 25th percentile.

- About one-third of students on Resource Specialist caseloads have attentional deficits, and a somewhat higher percentage of students in special day classes have attentional problems.

- Phonological awareness deficits and poor phonics development are common among the LD population. Phonemic awareness and phonics training will make LD students better readers and spellers (Bradley and Bryant, 1985).

- Studies that measure time-on-task indicate that nondisabled students are on task 60 to 80 percent of the time, whereas students with LD are on task 30 to 60 percent of the time (Bryan and Wheeler, 1972; McKinney and Feagan, 1983).

- Drug therapies are often effective in reducing behaviors that interfere with learning. Current research suggests that psychostimulant medications increase arousal and alertness of the central nervous system (DuPaul, Barkley, and McMurray, 1991) by stimulating the production of chemical neurotransmitters. Psychostimulant medications seem to lengthen attention span, help control impulsivity, and improve ability to stay on task and to sit quietly (Parker, 1992).

- Students with LD are not as socially acceptable as other students when rated by their peers and teachers (Bender, 2001).

- As many as 50 percent of students with LD will drop out of school prior to high school graduation (Levin, Zigmond, and Birch, 1985).

- Students with LD are more likely to encounter trouble with the law (Keilitz and Dunivant, 1986).

- In comparison to other parents, the parents of students with LD expect less of their children in both academics and behavior. (Bryan and Bryan, 1983).

Summary

The history of the field of learning disabilities has been one of great changes and learning, and new strides are continually being made into the fields of study regarding how we speak, learn, and produce information. New studies focus on how well our schools are educating our students, how many children graduate from high school, and how we may continue to help the children who struggle.

As educators and parents, we have a tremendous opportunity to influence children's lives. We have the power to make their days joyous or dreadful because we help determine the environment in which they live.

List of Major Organizations for the Learning Disabled

Children and Adults with Attention Deficit Disorder (CHADD)

(Information on ADD and local support groups)
8181 Professional Place, Suite 201, Landover, MD 20785
Web site: www.chadd.org

• • •

Council for Learning Disabilities (CLD)

(International organization for professionals in the field)
P.O. Box 40303, Overland Park, KS 66204
Web site: www.cldinternational.org

• • •

International Dyslexia Association (IDA)

(Formerly the Orton Dyslexia Society; has state and local branches for anyone interested in language-based learning disorders)
Chester Building, Suite 382, 8600 La Salle Road,
Baltimore, MD 21286-2044
Web site: www.interdys.org

• • •

Learning Disabilities Association (LDA)

(Organization for anyone interested in improving the quality of life for the learning disabled)
4156 Library Road, Reston, VA 22091
Web site: www.ldanatl.org

• • •

National Center for Learning Disabilities (NCLD)
(Information on learning disabilities)
99 Park Avenue, New York, NY 10016
Web site: www.ncld.org

. . .

Reading Rockets
WETA Public Television
2775 S. Quincy Street, Arlington, VA 22206
Phone: 703-998-2001
Fax: 703-998-2060
E-mail: readingrockets@weta.org

. . .

TeachingLD
(Resources about teaching students with learning disabilities)
Web site: www.teachingld.org

. . .

Periodicals on Learning Disabilities

Annals of Dyslexia
Published by the International Dyslexia Association
Chester Building, Suite 382, 8600 La Salle Road,
Baltimore, MD 21286-2044
Web site: www.interdys.org/AnnalsofDyslexia.htm

. . .

Exceptional Children; Teaching Exceptional Children; Learning Disabilities Research and Practice; Exceptional Education Quarterly
All published by the Council for Exceptional Children
1110 North Glebe Road, Suite 300 Arlington, VA 22201
Phone: 703-620-3660
TTY: 866-915-5000
Fax: 703-264-9494
E-mail: service@cec.sped.org
Web site: www.cec.sped.org

. . .

Exceptional Parent
Published by PSY/ED Corporation–Exceptional Parent
555 Kinderkamack Road, Oradell, NJ 07649

• • •

Intervention
Published by the Intervention Foundation
Tulpenburg 31
1181 NK Amstelveen
The Netherlands
Web site: www.interventionjournal.com

• • •

Learning Disabilities Quarterly
Published by the Council for Learning Disabilities
P.O. Box 40303, Overland Park, KS 66204

• • •

Remedial and Special Education; Journal of Learning Disabilities; Journal of Special Education
All published by PRO-ED
5341 Industrial Oaks Blvd., Austin, TX 78735
Web site: www.proedinc.com

• • •

Thalamus
Published by the International Academy for Research in Learning Disabilities
Web site: www.iarld.net/thalamus

Chapter 2

Research in the Field of Learning Disabilities

Michelangelo di Lodovico Buonarroti Simoni (1475–1564)

Italian sculptor, painter, architect, poet
Was described as quick tempered and unable to get along with others, and as a "loner" (possible ADHD); was never interested in going to school, played hooky often, and dropped out at age thirteen

Contributions:
Painting: Ceiling of the Sistine Chapel (including *The Last Judgment*)

Sculpture: *David*
                Pieta

Architecture: Dome of St. Peter's Cathedral

For busy education professionals, it is sometimes hard to find time to keep up with all the latest research on learning disabilities. This chapter summarizes research findings in the LD field in recent years, eliminating details of the research methodology. If you are interested in reading the more detailed account of a research study, refer to the references listed at the end of this book.

Overview of the Brain, Biology, and Behavior

The central nervous system (CNS) is responsible for learning. Nerves all over the body pick up sensory stimuli and send messages via the spinal cord to the brain. The brain interprets what has been seen, heard, felt, smelled, and tasted. It integrates new sensory knowledge with previously stored information and decides what to do with the new information.

FIGURE 2.1.

Neurons.

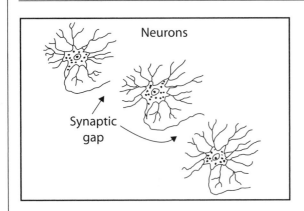

Neurons

Synaptic
gap

Neurons: individual, tiny nerve cells that form the basic structure of the nervous system

Synaptic gap: the microscopic space between two neurons over which neurotransmissions travel

This overview is a very simplified explanation of a very complex function. The CNS is highly influenced by electrical and chemical factors. The smallest unit of the CNS is a single cell called a *neuron.* At birth, billions of neurons lie near each other but do not actually touch (see Figure 2.1). When sensory information is received by a neuron, we say the neuron "fires." An electrical charge is generated, causing the signal to jump across the "synaptic gap" to the next neuron, stimulating it to fire. This stimulates the next neuron to fire (or send along the message). In turn, that neuron signals the next neuron and so on, until the message either reaches its destination or is interrupted.

The CNS produces chemicals that either send the message along its way or inhibit its passage. Chemicals that keep the message flowing are called *neurotransmitters,* and chemicals that interfere with the message are called *neuroinhibitors.* In each category, there are more than one kind of chemical substance, including dopamine, serotonin, and acetylcholine. Each has a different effect on how we feel, behave, and learn.

As a person experiences more exposures to a specific stimulus, the branches of the neurons begin to grow toward the next neuron, eventually closing the synaptic gap. This creates a learning connection, allowing a faster response the next time the same stimulus is received.

The brain stem at the base of the brain is in charge of the automatic functions: breathing, heart rate, and digestion. The cerebellum is just above the brain stem; it controls bodily movements, including posture and balance. The cerebral cortex controls all conscious activity. Figure 2.2 illustrates the anatomy of the brain.

FIGURE 2.2.

Anatomy and Functions of the Brain.

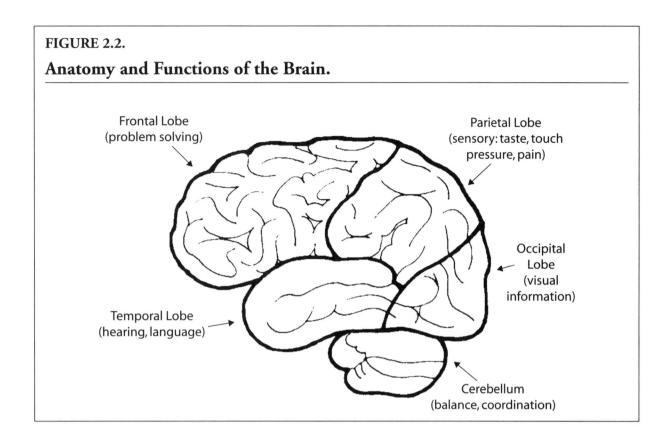

Frontal Lobe
(problem solving)

Parietal Lobe
(sensory: taste, touch
pressure, pain)

Occipital
Lobe
(visual
information)

Temporal Lobe
(hearing, language)

Cerebellum
(balance, coordination)

The cerebral cortex is divided into two hemispheres. Oddly enough, the left hemisphere dictates functioning on the right side of the body. Conversely, the right hemisphere controls body function on the left.

In studies of infants and adults, it has been found that 65 percent of the population have larger left hemispheres, 24 percent have larger right hemispheres, and 11 percent have hemispheres that are the same size. Research has shown that a greater than expected number of people who have reading disabilities have either larger right hemispheres than left or hemispheres of equal size (Hynd, Marshall, and Gonzalez, 1991).

Brain regions don't work in isolation. From computerized tomographic studies, we now know that when a person reads silently, four areas of the cortex are activated. But when the same person reads orally, six cortical regions are activated. Each hemisphere seems to be somewhat specialized in the type of function it performs.

Different parts of the brain work together to complete even the most basic tasks, and in fact, just making a decision about an element of daily life requires multiple regions of the brain to work together. Even when a student decides, for example, how to proceed with a new assignment, the brain must also then create a memory of how this work was done.

Research shows that memories can change based on how the information is stored in the brain. The brain's amazing ability to learn and process new information that can then be applied to what has already been learned is a key component of retaining new information. The brain's ability to alter memories based on new information helps a child when she is learning to spell, for example, because she can take in a correction on a spelling test and replace the incorrect memory (and incorrect word spelling) with the correct memory (correct word spelling).

Brain Injury

Some learning disabled students have brain injuries, which can affect learning and behavior. Brain injuries, including concussion, may be caused by car accidents, falls, and sports accidents. In fact, a growing number of professionals are studying the impacts of concussions and other sports-related brain injuries and the effects that these may have on a child's school performance. Football players and soccer players receive the majority of head injuries, but even getting hit on the head with a basketball, volleyball, or playground ball can cause a closed head injury, especially when the ball is kicked at or thrown at an opponent at close range.

The impact from the ball hitting the skull jars the brain and can cause injury. The brain can be injured from the initial impact that causes the brain to strike the skull, but it can also be injured by the impact when the force of the first impact causes the brain to move and hit another part of the skull (see Figure 2.3).

One study showed that girls tend to get more serious concussions than boys from an impact-related injury due to their smaller body frame size. Boys have larger neck muscles and larger frames that absorb more of the impact. In sports played by both groups, girls sustained more concussions than boys (Gessel, Fields, Collins, Dick, and Comstock, 2007).

It is important to have children evaluated immediately after any type of blow to the head. Since sports injuries often occur at school events and can have negative effects on learning, doctors have basic screening devices to be used at the sidelines of football games in order to ensure prompt treatment of head injuries. This type of screening tool has not been used for playground injuries or other sports injuries, but hopefully as we learn more about sports injuries, the use of a basic screening tool for use at all sporting events will be commonplace.

In cases of multiple concussions, learning and memory attention may be permanently affected. Some children may be permanently removed from a sport, especially if there is recurring damage to the brain from multiple

---

FIGURE 2.3.

Brain Impact Injury.

1. Primary force of impact

2. Secondary force of impact

As the head is hit, the force of the primary impact pushes the brain to hit the back of the skull, causing a secondary impact.

Injury can be caused by basketballs, volleyballs, soccer balls, playground balls, or any blunt-force trauma to the head. The most common type of injury occurs when a ball is kicked at the head.

---

injuries, because the severity of learning disorders associated with the brain trauma increases if the brain is traumatized repeatedly. Sometimes the brain simply cannot handle any more traumas without severely impacting learning, even when students are playing at the grade school or high school level of sports. More information on this issue can be found on the Web site of the American Academy of Pediatrics (www.aap.org).

A particular injury will affect a given child depending on several factors: the location and extent of the injury, the individual's neurological maturity at the time of the injury, and the nature and extent of efforts to retrain the brain. It has been demonstrated that when a brain injury occurs or part of the brain has been surgically removed, remaining areas will try to compensate for lost functions. This compensation is known as *plasticity*, and it tends to decline with age.

At birth, the primary cortical areas appear to be mature, in contrast to the secondary and tertiary areas, which may take months or years to mature (Hynd and Willis, 1988). Children who experience injury to primary cortical areas at birth or in their younger years may have difficulty with higher-order cognitive processes. Early brain damage in one brain area may alter the neuroanatomy, function, neurochemistry, and growth patterns of remaining brain systems (Isaacson and Spear, 1984).

It is helpful for those who work with children with learning disabilities to keep in mind that brain injury may account for a child's inability to grasp a skill or his need to practice that skill numerous times before achieving it. Research has shown that people who have traumatic brain injury may suffer from problems related to diminished working memory and attention. Obviously this affects learning behaviors in the classroom, and teachers should keep in mind that short-term memory, attention-span, and memory-related issues in a person with a brain injury may require that information be presented more than once in the classroom and in shortened, simpler segments.

Traumatic brain injury has been associated with higher rates of depression and sleep problems (Koponen, 2002; Jorge, 2005). For educators, this can mean that during school hours, students may show signs of problems with schoolwork related to depression and fatigue. Traumatic brain injury can cause a myriad of psychiatric conditions, including generalized anxiety disorder and posttraumatic stress disorder in addition to the primary symptom of depression (Rogers and Read, 2007). This may be a long-lasting pattern after traumatic brain injury (Draper, Ponsford, and Schönberger, 2007), and it is an issue teachers may see in the form of lowered academic performance and sleepiness in class. People with injuries to their frontal lobes may show problems with higher-order problem solving, abstractions, and executive functioning (see Figures 2.2 and 2.3). In addition, if the language areas in the brain are injured, reading comprehension, spelling, and receptive and expressive language may be affected.

Structural Brain Differences

Brain injury is not the only cause of learning disabilities. Some children are born with differences in brain structure, and there may be atypical brain tissue, neural circuitry, or brain organization. What causes this? Among the possibilities are genetic predisposition, use of drugs during pregnancy, infections, and exposure to toxins. Dyslexia, autism, and ADHD are all conditions that are involved with the neural circuitry of the brain. They can be caused by brain injury, but they also are genetically predetermined, often occurring in multiple members of a family. These three conditions generally evidence specific structural brain differences that affect learning.

Dyslexia

In autopsy studies of individuals who were dyslexic, anomalies have been found in the left hemisphere (the language area) of the brain. Galaburda (1991) reported finding clusters of neurons in places where they did not occur in nondyslexic adults, as well as odd cell connections. This led him to believe that perhaps the brains of those with dyslexia are not optimally wired for the requirements of learning to read.

Just as our blue eyes, dark hair, or height can be inherited, a number of researchers have established that reading disorders seem to be passed from generation to generation. Researchers have also discovered a genetic link to dyslexia, and it has been shown to run in families (Fagerheim et al., 1999; Nöthen et al., 1999). Scientists found a gap in the gene structure of those with dyslexia that may interfere with the brain pathways that relate to reading (Gruen, 2005). Even more exciting than the studies that prove that dyslexia is a measurable disorder are the studies demonstrating that dyslexia responds to intervention. As shown in Figure 2.4, a study done at the University of

FIGURE 2.4.

Areas of the Brain Activated After Reading Intervention.

Postintervention images show a dramatic increase in left temporoparietal activation, which is associated with improvement in phonological decoding skills.

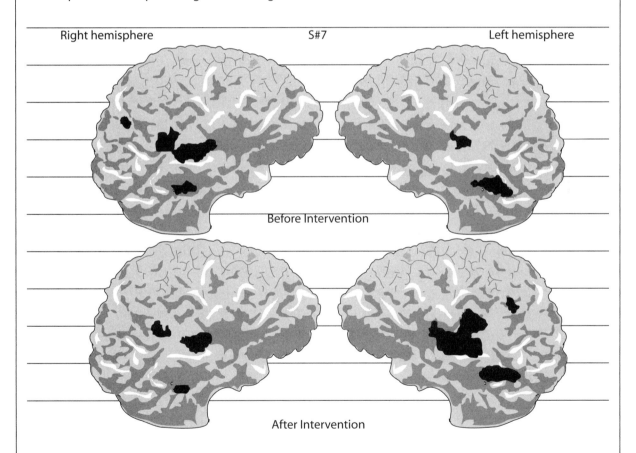

Source: *Used with permission from the Center for Clinical Neurosciences, Children's Learning Institute, University of Texas Houston Health Science Center. (Research coordinated by Andrew Papanicolaou, Panagiotis Simos, Shirin Sarkari, and Rebecca Billingsley-Marshall, in collaboration with Barbara Foorman and Jack Fletcher.)*

Texas Houston Health Science Center demonstrates that intensive remediation programs that help children read more effectively can actually change the way children's brains respond to written language.

Autism

Autism is a neurological disorder that severely affects a child's development. Its primary symptoms arise in the social realm, particularly with language and social interactions. Many children have distinct problems interacting with others, communicating, and maintaining socially appropriate behaviors.

People with autism are not able to read emotions or facial markers as well as their peers and may be severely impaired in this area (Pellicano, Jeffery, Burr, and Rhodes, 2007). Children with autism tend to focus on an individual feature of the face (such as the mouth) in isolation, rather than seeing the global facial expression, with the many features forming an expressive entity (Deruelle, Rondan, Gepner, and Tardif, 2004). In order to read a single expression—surprise, for example—the observer must perceive all the features of the face at the same time. Inability to correctly interpret facial expressions can contribute to communication and social interaction difficulties.

Recent studies have shown that there are structural differences in the brains of children with autism (Sparks et al., 2002). Autism is "strongly heritable," meaning that it follows a genetic pathway (Johnson, Meyers, and the Council on Children with Disabilities, 2007), often showing up as a pattern in families. One study found an abnormally large brain volume in the white cerebellar matter and enlarged cortical gray matter as early as two years of age in boys with autism. By contrast, in adolescence, the same boys had less brain volume in some areas than the normal control group (Courchesne, Karns, et al., 2001; Courchesne, Carper, and Akshoomoff, 2003). Studies that examine how autism might affect the social centers in the brain suggest that the same cerebellar areas that become reduced in the boys with autism may also play a role in social deficits, cognitive deficits, and motor problems (Belmonte et al., 2004).

More information about how to normalize social skills is now on the horizon. New research suggests that the biochemical relationship with autism may be more convoluted than originally realized, as researchers found that children with autistic behaviors improved during the course of a fever (Curran et al., 2007). This points to the fact that we still have a great deal to learn about the brain, its development, and autism. Social skills training aids that help teach appropriate behavior and increase social awareness have also been shown to help children with autism (Gray 2002).

Attention Deficit Hyperactivity Disorder

Attention Deficit Hyperactivity Disorder (ADHD) is one of the few learning disabilities that has a distinct link to an environmental toxin. When young brains and bodies are exposed to even small doses of lead, damage can result, and often shows up in the form of ADHD. Symptoms of ADHD are caused by the brain's inconsistent processing of sensory input; sometimes a message is sent through the nervous system and action is taken, but other times the messages the central nervous system receives are not processed in an organized fashion. When this happens, the person's behavior is disorganized, and his ability to focus on a task for a long period of time are affected. Structural differences in the brains of children with ADHD show that in some instances, there may be an average maturational delay of three years (Shaw et al., 2007).

In other instances, structural anomalies in some areas of the brain of children with ADHD seem to function in a different manner from those in control groups (Ashtari et al., 2005). Although research has demonstrated that there is atypical brain processing during even simple number tasks for persons with ADHD (Hale, Bookheimer, McGough, Phillips, and McCracken, 2007), we still lack a general consensus on the ways in which these differences in brain function cause the symptoms of ADHD.

The biochemistry of the brain may explain some of the symptoms of ADHD: For these children, in which hyperactivity is a major component, evidence shows more of the excitatory chemicals in their brains (Courvoisie, Hooper, Fine, Kwock, and Castillo, 2004). These differences may be part of the reason that some people with ADHD have trouble with impulse control and show impulsive behaviors in the classroom.

One study did note that people with ADHD have less trouble focusing on digital media, or information coming through a computer or digital device, such as computer or video games (Shaw, Grayson, and Lewis, 2005). This knowledge can be used to advantage in the classroom when planning curriculum; teachers could make use of digital media, when appropriate, to supplement or increase interaction with subject material and help students with ADHD in the process.

Biochemical Influences

Brain biochemistry is an area of ongoing research interest. As noted earlier, ADHD and Tourette Syndrome are conditions that may co-occur with learning disabilities, and both are believed to be caused by biochemical irregularities. Medications like Ritalin, Cylert, and Adderall, all stimulants, seem to help persons with ADHD sustain attention for longer periods, and inhibit undesirable behaviors such as temper outbursts, distractibility, and frustration. Improvement is reported in approximately 75 percent of persons treated (DuPaul, Barkley, and McMurray, 1991).

In the classroom, investigators found that medicated students improved in the accuracy and quantity of work produced (Douglas, Barry, O'Neill, and Britton, 1986; Mayo Clinic, 2007). Children who take Ritalin seem to suffer less from the inconsistent messaging in their neurological systems. It is thought that Ritalin helps stimulate the circuitry in the brain. In one study, children who had been on Ritalin for over two years showed fewer anatomical brain differences (Ashtari et al., 2005). In addition, another study that followed a large group of children for a number of years found that the children who received medication for their ADHD had better school performance in the long term (Barbaresi, Katusic, Colligen, Weaver, and Jacobsen, 2007).

Biochemical irregularities can be influenced by pharmaceuticals, substances we eat, and things we drink. Our cells respond on a chemical level to sugar, caffeine, and even chocolate. Our bodies and brains, all the way to the cellular level, are also influenced by stimulants. Stimulants used in the treatment of ADHD are thought to affect the speed at which information is processed and the strength of the connections between neurons. The stimulant forces the message to be sent across neurons, and this may help people with ADHD, who may not have the same neurochemical passageways. Stimulant medication may suppress noncompliant, disruptive, and aggressive behaviors seen in some ADHD individuals (Dykman and Ackerman, 1991).

Methylphenidate, also known as Ritalin, has been used to treat tics in children with Tourette Syndrome. Doctors recently discovered that methylphenidate helps reduce the severity of tics and ADHD behaviors (Goldberg, 2002), as does another medication, Straterra, used also to treat ADHD (Spencer et al., 2008).

Not all information on stimulant medications is positive, and some advocacy groups claim that giving children stimulant medication sets up a pattern of abuse. Side effects of the drugs used to treat ADHD are similar to other stimulant drugs: decreased appetite, shakiness, and trouble sleeping or increased sleepiness, and others related to stimulating the central nervous system (see Figure 10.1 in Chapter Ten for a complete list of potential side effects.) The decision to use medication is always an individual one, and Ritalin is the only medication that has been used long term to treat symptoms of ADHD. It is not appropriate for every child, and the school district cannot mandate that medications be administered to children.

Research on Memory

How do we learn? In order to learn, students must

- Be able to attend to stimuli

- Encode information about that stimuli
- Integrate and store data in memory

- Be able to retrieve the data as they are needed

Learning disabled students may have deficits in one or more of these areas.

We are continually bombarded with data coming in from the senses. The chemicals in our bodies are balanced in such a way that we are able to stay alert but also able to weed out unimportant stimuli. LD students often do not have these abilities. Some have deficits in arousal: they may not be alert to incoming stimuli, or they may only pick up bits and pieces. Others are overwhelmed by the multitude of messages arriving simultaneously. For other students, the problem may lie in remembering the data they receive.

New studies done at Brandeis University point to a protein that the researchers have named the "memory molecule," which influences memory in rats. Memories are "stored" in the hippocampus in the brain, and the chemical messages communicated in the hippocampus change when memory is stored (Brandeis University, 2007). This information is currently being used in research with patients with Alzheimer's and epilepsy, and it holds promise for those seeking to understand how a person learns and whether there is a chemical passage in the nervous system that can be influenced with memory.

Alcino Silva, a professor of neurobiology and psychiatry at the David Geffen School of Medicine at UCLA, states that "[m]aking a memory is not a conscious act." Elaborating on this idea, Silva notes that memories are controlled by chemical signals in the brain that are triggered by learning (University of California, Los Angeles, 2007). Researchers have proven that there is a biochemical link to memory, and although it may be difficult to understand why some students have such a difficult time with recall and memory, we may one day be able to understand exactly why they struggle much more than their classmates.

Research has shown that quieter classrooms will benefit all students. Several studies have shown that background noises—particularly voices—bother students, and that distractible students are particularly affected. The ringing of the classroom phone, the opening of the classroom door, or an airplane flying overhead interrupts learning. Many teachers are now using "white music" (soothing instrumental music played softly) to mask some of the incidental noises in the room.

How can educators help students with LD improve memory? Visual supports (writing information on the board, having students take notes) greatly facilitate learning because most auditory information is lost from short-term memory (STM) within a few seconds. Teachers can help students make connections between new information and their prior experiences. If we connect new information to old information, it is more likely to be remembered.

Teachers need to provide sufficient practice for students to learn to move information from STM to long-term memory (LTM). Most students with LD have normal LTM and will retain information once it is mastered. How many times does one have to be exposed to a given piece of information in order to retain it? This varies greatly among individuals. For the average child, it might take twenty-two exposures. For the child with LD and with STM deficits, it may take many more exposures than that or require other techniques. Once the information is in LTM, periodic reinforcement through use will usually maintain it in working memory. Of course, motivation plays an important role in learning. Students tend to learn information more quickly and retain it more easily if they have reason or motivation to do so.

Retrieval refers to the mental operations we go through to extract a given piece of information from memory. Researchers have found that the LD individual (even in adulthood) require a longer time to retrieve known information—about 300 milliseconds longer if retrieving a known word (Manis, 1985). LD individuals require more time to do sorting tasks (Copeland and Reiner, 1984). Researcher at Tufts University have shown that in addition to having dyslexia, some students may also have a much slower processing speed than other children (Wolf and Bowers, 1999). It is worthwhile to note that when individuals with LD are given unlimited time to show what they know, they can sometimes match the performance of their nondisabled peers (Runyan, 1991). Giving students with LD extra time to complete their work may not only be helpful but may also be necessary.

Research on Metacognition

Metacognition refers to the knowledge and control individuals have over their own thinking and learning (Brown, 1980). It is the ability to think about what one is thinking about. It is an active process whereby the individual examines information and makes a decision regarding the best way to learn it. Because metacognition requires an ability to think abstractly, strategies requiring metacognition are best taught to children over the age of seven. Young children do not have a repertory of methods or strategies from which to choose. Teachers and parents are advised to teach children various strategies for learning new information or processes.

Young children seldom use metacognitive strategies to learn because they think concretely, rather than abstractly. At ages five, six, and seven, children benefit when the teacher uses *rote drill* to help them memorize poems, the alphabet, and sight words. Children with LD do not seem to transfer the practice of verbal rehearsal from one activity to another—they must be reminded what to do.

Beginning in first grade, children can be taught to *make predictions* about what might happen when given a series of events. Anticipating what will happen next helps focus student attention, which can lead to greater learning.

By age eight, children can be taught *visualization* and *verbalization* techniques. (These activities will be described in further detail in Chapter Eleven.) Texts for young children are illustrated with numerous pictures. By the age of eight, however, children can generate their own mental images through a visualization process (Pressley, 1982). Reading activities that require students to read a portion of descriptive text and draw a picture to illustrate what the words said allow the teacher to evaluate whether they are converting words into mental images, thus constructing meaning from text.

Teachers can use *think-alouds* to

- Model the thinking process that good readers use to help them understand what they are reading

- Guide students through a series of steps in a process

- Demonstrate to students how they can decide on strategies to help them comprehend and better remember what they have read

- Help students through the thinking process when they encounter an unfamiliar word while reading or when meaning has broken down

Let's say, for example, that during a guided reading, a teacher wants to help students understand how they might make an inference based on what an author says about a story character. A teacher could provide a think-aloud similar to the one that follows.

• • •

The author gives me clues about the characters. For example, although the author never says directly that the story character Peter is generous, I know that he is because he is always doing things for others, and, in one instance, he gave his brother a book that was one of Peter's favorites. Based on what Peter does and says, I can infer that Peter is a generous person.

• • •

Teaching students to use this technique can help them gain insights into their own cognitive and metacognitive processes.

Note-taking is a skill that helps increase information storage. To build the skill, beginning in late third or early fourth grade, teachers can ask students to copy board notes or tell students what to record, then have them reread their notes daily for several days before taking a quiz. In sixth grade and junior high, students need to learn how to locate key words in a question and how to find information in an index. As students increase their understanding, they learn to locate information and take their own notes. In the beginning, however, they need to learn the skills through carefully prepared guided practice. A note-taking graphic organizer can be helpful to students (see Worksheet 2.10 later in the chapter).

Verbal self-mediation is a useful organizational strategy. It involves "talking to yourself" about the steps you need to go through to get something done. Some people do it out loud; other people make written lists. Thinking a task out step-by-step saves time and effort. For example, if someone starts out with a list of errands to run but hasn't thought through a logical order, she will waste time and gas to complete her tasks.

Mnemonics instruction has been found to be extremely helpful to students with LD (Mastropieri and Scruggs, 1991). This technique assists the student in memorizing new vocabulary and facts by hooking new information to known information, thus facilitating retrieval. For example, after hearing a stock market report on the car radio, one might remember a stock symbol—BTGI—by making up the sentence "Big toe got infected" using visual imaging to assist memory.

Mapping and graphic organizers are useful visual means of helping students organize information acquired from a text. Students can use graphic organizers before, during, or after reading. Charts and graphs can help students better remember what they have read. Students can also use graphic organizers to help them gather their thoughts before writing. It is important to introduce the use of graphic organizers directly—offering examples, ample practice, and numerous opportunities for students to apply their understandings. Several maps and graphic organizers are provided at the end of this section. These include the following:

> **Story Maps** can be used by students to identify the important parts of a story—that is, its title and author, its characters and setting, the story problem, events, and the resolution of the problem. Story maps can be modified, depending on grade level and student ability. For example, in the early grades, students might not be asked to identify story events leading up to the resolution of the problem; in later grades, more emphasis might

be placed on how the characters' traits or the setting affected the story's outcome. See Worksheet 2.1.

Word Maps or **Word Webs** can be used for brainstorming ideas about a topic, building vocabulary, or engaging student interest. There are many kinds of word maps or webs that can be used to make connections among ideas. See Worksheet 2.2.

K-W-L Charts can be used to help students identify what they know about a topic, what they want to know, and what they learned. This can be a helpful graphic organizer to use when introducing a new topic or unit. For example, if you were beginning a unit on the solar system with fourth-grade students, you might begin by asking students what they already know about the solar system and what they would like to learn. As students explore the topic, they can record ideas in the "What I Learned" column. See Worksheet 2.3.

Main Idea and Supporting Details and **Summary Charts** are useful when reading nonfiction and content-area curriculum. While reading, students can complete these charts to identify a main idea and supporting details in paragraphs. When finished, students ideas use the main ideas to write a summary of what they read. See Worksheets 2.4 and 2.5.

Making Inferences graphic organizers are especially useful when reading fiction. As students read, they can identify clues the author gives, think about what their own experiences have been, and draw an inference based on those two pieces of information. This can help students in their understanding of their own metacognitive processes. See Worksheet 2.6.

Time Lines and **Sequence Charts** can be used for identifying events in the order in which they happened. These can be useful when students are asked to identify historical facts or are asked to tell the events of a story. See Worksheets 2.7 and 2.8.

Venn Diagrams are useful for comparing and contrasting ideas in either fiction or nonfiction. Students can compare and contrast characters or points of view within a story or across stories. Venn diagrams can be used across content areas—in reading and language arts, mathematics, social studies, and science. See Worksheet 2.9.

Note-Taking graphic organizers can be used when students are reading information that is difficult for them to retain. By identifying key words and important events and ideas as they read, students can increase their comprehension of subject content and better remember what they have learned. Students can review their notes when studying for an exam. See Worksheet 2.10.

Title _____ **Author** _____

Characteristics: **Setting:**

_____   _____

_____   _____

_____   _____

_____   _____

Problem:

_____

_____

_____

_____

Event 1:

_____

_____

_____

_____

Event 2:

_____

_____

_____

_____

Event 3:

_____

_____

_____

_____

How the problem was solved:

_____

_____

_____

_____

_____

_____

_____

_____

WORKSHEET 2.2. WOLD MAP OR WEB.

WORKSHEET 2.3. K-W-L CHART.

What I Know	What I Want to Know	What I Learned

Main Idea Sentence

Detail 1

Detail 2

Detail 3

WORKSHEET 2.5. SUMMARY CHART.

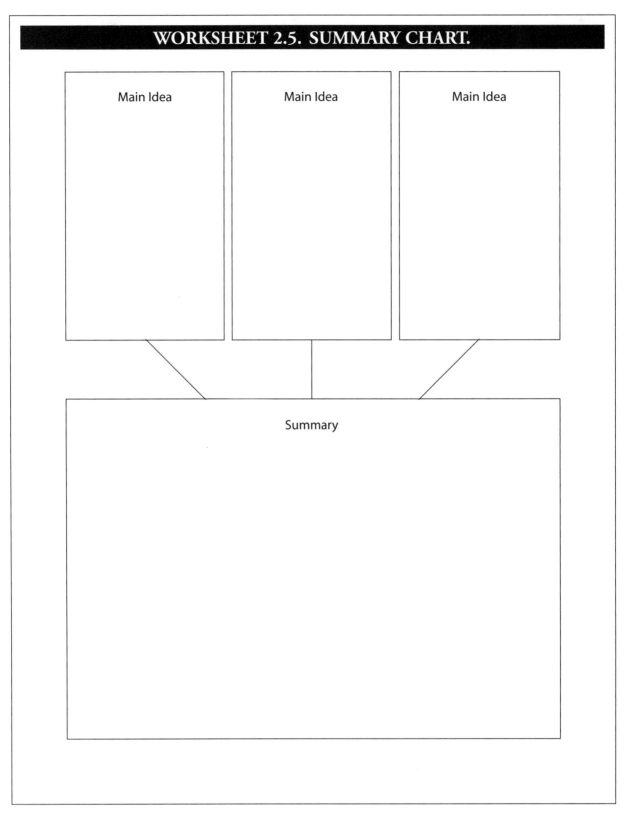

Main Idea

Main Idea

Main Idea

Summary

WORKSHEET 2.6. MAKING INFERENCES.

Clues from the Story

Clues from My Experience

My Inference Is

WORKSHEET 2.7. TIME LINE.

WORKSHEET 2.8. SEQUENCE CHART.

1.

2.

3.

4.

5.

6.

7.

8.

WORKSHEET 2.9. VENN DIAGRAM.

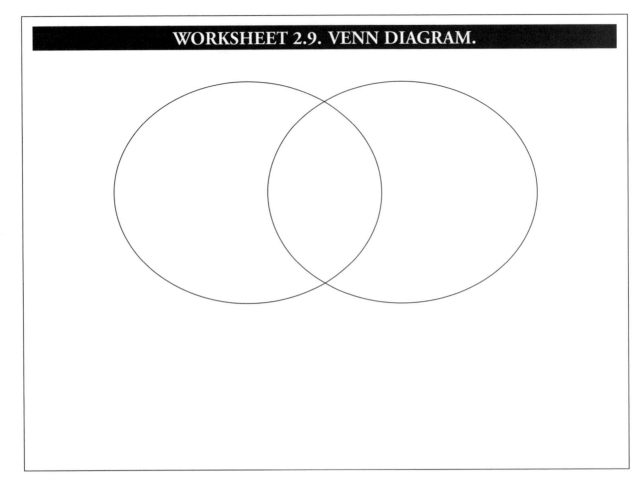

WORKSHEET 2.10. NOTE TAKING.

Key Words	Important Events or Ideas

Research on Phonological Processing Problems

Often the first sign of a phonological processing problem is delayed speech. By age one, a child should be able to say, at the very least, one syllable at a time. By age two, a child should be combining at least two words to make simple sentences. By age three, a child should be able to use pronouns like *I, me, she,* or *he* in a sentence with a more complex structure. Often when there is a speech delay, there is also a corresponding reading and language issue. One main cause of reading and language issues is phonological processing problems—difficulties with the way the brain processes the sounds and order of language.

Phonologically based reading disabilities (PRD) are characterized by difficulties acquiring alphabetic or phonetic reading strategies. Children who have difficulty learning to read tend to be slow to grasp the concept that letters have sounds and slow to encode those sounds. Even after the child knows the sound, he may be slow to recall the correct sound. These children are slow to acquire "sight words" (the print says *look*, child says *see*). These children require more time to develop adequate decoding and reading fluency.

Recent research on children with LD who have reading difficulties indicates that these children have difficulty perceiving the temporal order of speech stimuli. Paula Tallal and her colleagues (1996) have developed a computer-based intervention program that is helping LD students develop sensitivity to the temporal order of sounds within words by markedly slowing down the pronunciation of the word and exaggerating its phonemic components.

Phonological processing problems may cause children to have trouble consistently spelling words correctly. Because the children do not have an encoded memory of a sound referring to a distinct letter, they often have trouble replicating the correct spelling of words. The visual representation of sound, the letter (phoneme), does not always match any memory or instantly recognizable sound for some children with phonological processing problems. Consistent explanation of the letter-sound relationships and repeated phonics instruction are helpful, but some children will still grow up never "learning to spell." This is often the case with some children who grow up with severe dyslexia. In fact, a problem with phonological processing is often a sign of dyslexia.

What causes these processing difficulties? We know that phonological processing occurs in the left temporal area of the brain. Upon microscopic examination, Galaburda (1991) found that the brains of postmortem dyslexic adults had anomalies in this area. The kinds of anomalies found had developed in the brain while babies were in utero during the fifth month of gestation and appeared to be genetically dictated. Studies utilizing newer technologies show that the amount of blood flow in that same area of the brain during performance of the reading task was markedly different in children with phonological processing problems (Flowers, Wood, and Naylor, 1991). In dyslexics, however, it is the right anterior portion of the cerebellum that is anatomically different from the control group (Eckert et al., 2003). As with all processes in the brain, there is still a great deal to learn about how the different areas of the brain work together during tasks of phonological processing.

Fortunately, children with phonological processing problems are able to learn to read when exposed to the right instruction (Torgeson, Wagner, and Rashotte, 1994b). Some school districts provide training to both regular and special education teachers in the Auditory in Depth Program (Lindamood and Lindamood, 1984)—an intensive program of remediation.

One of the most successful ways to remediate phonological processing problems with reading is with explicit and repeated discussion of phonetic principles. The letter-sound correlation must be taught systematically, and in older students, this may not be the only form of remediation. Because some students will fall behind in their subject matter if their classes focus on just repeating phonetic skills, it's wise to use assistive technology for age-appropriate content matter.

Problems with phonological processing may manifest themselves in other ways beyond phonics and reading instruction. Children who have trouble with phonological processing may also have trouble following oral directions, reading aloud in the classroom, and interpreting vocal instructions on assignments. Because problems with phonological processing occur in the regions of the brain that process sound, children with these problems often benefit from visual cues for instructions, directions, and assignments.

Research on Maturation and Retention

Ames (1968) claimed that more than 50 percent of children entering kindergarten are not ready for the curriculum they will encounter. The child with LD falls within the 50 percent who do not do well in kindergarten. Ames has suggested that girls need to be six years old and boys need to be six and a half, as developmental immaturities are more prevalent in boys than girls. In some states, children as young as four years nine months can be admitted to kindergarten. For an immature child, school can turn out to be a very unpleasant and frustrating place.

A quality early childhood program can help children prepare for school, and this may be considered as an alternative to starting kindergarten right at the age of five for children with maturational delays. Research demonstrates that quality early childhood programs can have a positive effect on early school performance (Barnett, 1995). One study links the mother's return to the workforce before her child is nine months old with a delay in maturational readiness for school, even taking into account quality early childhood programs (Brooks-Gunn, Han, and Waldfogel, 2002); however, another study finds that quality early childhood programs can increase test scores in reading, mathematics, and other subjects (Magnuson, Meyers, Ruhm, and Waldfogel, 2004). Additionally, another study indicates that even a small increase in income can boost a child's social skills, because developmental outcomes are affected by a lowering of family income, especially in poor families (Dearing, McCartney, and Taylor, 2001).

The quality of the early childhood program is the key element in this discussion. The National Institute of Child Development states that program quality definitely affects school readiness. Other studies point to the quality of care in the home and the socioeconomic levels of the parents. School readiness and maturation are not simple questions of age or whether parents stay home with their children, but of the quality of interaction children receive in their child care, whether at home or in a child-care setting.

If, after a child enters kindergarten, it becomes evident that the child is not "ready," the teacher should discuss this matter with the parents or caregivers as early in the year as possible. If the child is young and has never attended preschool, the parent may be willing to withdraw the child and enroll him in preschool. If the child is older, retention in kindergarten may be advised.

What does research say about the practice of retention? There have been numerous studies in this area—one involving more than thirty thousand subjects. *It has been shown that children who are young for their grade are far more likely to lag academically in the early school years or to develop learning difficulties than those who are older* (Donofrio, 1977; Maddux, Green, and Horner, 1986; Shephard and Smith, 1986).

Research suggests that retention in the very early grades can be helpful, both socially and academically, if the parents support the retention (Medway, 1985). Retention that is accompanied by special remediation has been shown to have more positive effects than simple retention (Medway, 1985).

Research shows that retention after the sixth grade has little benefit and, in fact, hurts self-image (Medway and Rose, 1986).

Research on Communication Problems

Children with LD often have deficits in expressive language. Some children with LD do not differ from non-LD children in *quantity* of speech, but the *quality* of their speech is significantly poorer (Bryan, Donahue, and Pearl, 1981). In addition, they may talk later as children, have more difficulty expressing themselves verbally, and have trouble building their vocabularies at the same rate as their peers. Adolescents with autism report more loneliness (Bauminger, Shulman, and Agam, 2003) and have a poorer understanding of social rules and interactions.

Some children with LD have no trouble with expressive speech (telling a teacher what they want), but they may have trouble with receptive language, such as when following directions in a sequence. However, I have also met students who have no trouble understanding what I ask of them (receptive language), but they struggle to answer a question about text material in class, even if they know the answer (expressive language). These issues with communication often surface when a child begins writing for meaning and as a way of completing assignments, in the second and third grades. It's intensified by the end of third grade and beginning of fourth grade, when students have to read their textbooks to understand new content material and then write down their responses for their assignments. Individuals with LD find it very difficult to express themselves through written communication. In addition, their difficulties in conceptual thinking, spelling, and grammar make them reluctant to write. Difficulties with these issues can show up in such areas as handing in an incomplete essay or having trouble writing a paper or short answers on test questions.

Research on Self-Concept, Self-Esteem, and Self-Efficacy

Bryan (1991) offers the following definitions:

Self-concept refers to a person's awareness of her own characteristics and the ways she is like and unlike others.

Self-esteem refers to the value a person puts on his own self or behavior.

Self-efficacy refers to a person's judgment of her own competence to deal with prospective situations.

In regard to self-concept and self-esteem, LD students tend to feel they are adequate in nonacademic endeavors, such as in their appearance or in sports, but they rate themselves below their normally functioning peers in academic endeavors.

Research on Teachers' Perceptions

Studies on teachers' perceptions of children with learning disabilities show that teachers felt that these students were more often off task, tended to act out more, and had disturbed relationships with peers (Bryan, 1991). Research has borne out that LD students have a lower rate of time-on-task behavior than do regular students. The time-on-task behavior rate for LD students is between 30 and 60 percent, whereas regular students are on task 60 to 85 percent of the time (McKinney and Feagan, 1983). In the general population, the rate of hyperactivity is between 5 and 10 percent; within the learning disabled population, it is about 37 percent (Cantwell and Baker, 1991). Research shows that many LD students have difficulty establishing relationships with peers and are more likely to be rejected by their peers (Bryan, 1991).

Research on Social Competence and Social Skills Training

By 1991, approximately twenty studies had been done on whether social skills training with children who are learning disabled would improve their social skills. The studies showed that one could improve social skills in children, but that such a change did not necessarily improve the child's social acceptance with non–learning disabled peers (Vaughn, Hogan, Kouzekanani, and Shapiro, 1990). Being aware of what is socially appropriate and what comprises good manners is important for everyone. In some homes, little or no training is provided. Early social skills training can provide a smoother transition for LD individuals when they join adult society.

Some research studies show that children with LD may have more social problems, being more likely to be rejected than the control group, and they may show higher signs of aggression (Swanson and Malone, 1992). Researchers at the University of Georgia hypothesize that in some children who have a "right hemispheric dysfunction," the brain may also have trouble processing nonverbal cues, difficulty with problem-solving tasks, and issues with speech prosody and social skills (Semrud-Clikeman and Hynd, 1990).

When a child has trouble processing nonverbal cues, all his social interactions can be affected. In another study, researchers found a direct correlation between children with LD who have trouble with processing nonverbal information also have trouble with social perceptual functioning (Reiff and Gerber, 1990). For children who have trouble with social rules and social competence, there may be a biological reason they aren't catching on to social and nonverbal cues.

Summary

For the past twenty years, there has been renewed interest in the research of learning disabilities. Technological developments are moving rapidly at the start of the new millennium. Machines are now available that scan a book and read it aloud. Software programs that allow students to interact with the content have become standard learning tools.

Pharmaceutical companies are continually involved in the research and development of new and more effective medications. Universities continue to improve and expand their programs for training educators to work with LD children. Such developments hold great promise for the field of learning disabilities.

Chapter 3

Understanding the Laws

Galileo Galilei (1564–1642)

Italian mathematician, scientist (physicist)
Was believed to have had difficulty with reading; was described as being argumentative and unable to get along with others

Contributions:

Science: Formulated the principle of inertia
        Stated emphatically that the sun, not the Earth, was the center of our solar system

---

The Children with Specific Learning Disabilities Act (P.L. 91-230, 1969) was the first in a series of laws enacted by Congress to help improve the lives of children and adults with learning disabilities.

The Education of All Handicapped Children Act (P.L. 94-142, 1975) marked a major commitment to the nation's disabled. It stated,

> . . . more than half of the handicapped children in the United States do not receive appropriate educational services which would allow them to have full equality of opportunity.
>
> . . . It is in the national interest that the Federal Government assist state and local efforts to provide programs to meet the educational needs of the handicapped children in order to assure equal protection of the law.
>
> . . . It is the purpose of this Act to assure that all handicapped children have available to them a free and appropriate public education which emphasizes special education and related services designed to meet their unique needs.

The intent of P.L. 94-142 was clear: to provide each handicapped child, ages three to twenty-one, with a free and appropriate education (FAPE) in the least restrictive environment (LRE). (The law at that time covered only children deemed handicapped, but the mandates were expanded in 1990 to include a broader range of disabilities).

What is the appropriate "least restrictive environment" for a given student? Can a school district be required to pay for private schooling in a difficult case? If a child requires occupational or physical therapy services, door-to-door transportation, or such equipment as a home computer or wheelchair, is the school district required to provide such items? Can a disruptive student be excluded (suspended or expelled) from school? Are the assessments used to determine eligibility for services appropriate for a particular student? When disputes arise, answers to such questions are settled in due process hearings.

The mandates of P.L. 94-142 were reauthorized in 1990 as part of the Individuals with Disabilities Education Act (IDEA). Under this law, services are available to individuals who are learning disabled, mentally retarded, hearing disabled, speech and language disabled, visually disabled, severely emotionally disturbed, orthopedically impaired, other health impaired, deaf-blind, multiply disabled, or autistic, and those who have traumatic brain injury.

IDEA extended services to young children with disabilities, ages three to five. P.L. 99-457 (1986) extended special services to at-risk and developmentally delayed infants and toddlers from birth through age two.

Since the passage of P.L. 94-142 in 1975, there has been a steady increase in the number of students being identified and served. This has placed enormous strain on school districts' budgets, and in many cases districts are having to encroach on regular education funds to meet the needs of special education students.

Section 504 of the Rehabilitation Act of 1973 addresses issues that have to do with other individuals with special needs. Eligibility under 504 is based on having an "impairment which substantially limits one or more of major life activities such as caring for oneself, performing manual tasks, walking, seeing, hearing, speaking, breathing, learning and working." One of the first cases I encountered that fell under the umbrella of change to "Section 504" was a child who was in a physician's care for severe sleep disturbances. Lack of sleep resulted in irritability, a short fuse, and fighting. Although the child did not qualify for special education services, he certainly required special handling at school. Special accommodations were defined by 504.

Section 504 defines seven conditions that might make a child eligible for modifications of her program or special accommodations to meet her needs:

1. A drug or alcohol dependency.
2. ADD, ADHD.

3. Health needs.

4. Communicable diseases.

5. Social maladjustment.

6. Learning disability but without a severe discrepancy.

7. The student has a disability but has been exited from special education.

P.L. 98-199, Section 626 (1983), provides grants for the development of transition programs to help learning disabled students gain the skills necessary to adequately function in the area of employment. The Americans with Disabilities Act was enacted to provide protections for disabled workers.

Figure 3.1 compares the major tenets of IDEA and Section 504, and Figure 3.2 traces the evolution of federal laws governing the treatment of individuals with disabilities from 1975 through 2000.

Parental Rights

It is the intent of the laws that parents will be involved at every stage in the evaluation and planning process and must be kept informed of their child's progress. It is important that school personnel make every effort to build a trusting relationship with parents in order to promote a two-way exchange of information. This is to be accomplished by actively soliciting parents' input on a regular basis. For example, children frequently go home and claim, "I don't have any homework" or "I can't do this. I don't know how." Regular failure to return homework sends a signal that a conference is needed between parent and teacher. Homework issues are often easily resolved. When the parent has a packet of alternative (reinforcement) homework assignments on hand, such excuses do not work and are soon abandoned. When parent and teacher are working together cooperatively, better results become apparent.

It is a legal requirement that parents be given a copy of their rights. Due to limited space, the following is not a complete statement of parents' rights, but it is a statement of several very basic ones.

Parents Have the Right to . . .

1. Require confidential treatment of their children's records: only a limited group of people within the school should have access to them.

2. Review and inspect records.

3. Have copies of all records and any documentation regarding their child on file with the school.

FIGURE 3.1.

Comparison of IDEA and Section 504.

	IDEA (P.L. 94-142)	SECTION 504
PURPOSE	Federal statute to ensure appropriate services for disabled children	Civil rights law to protect the rights of individuals with handicaps in programs that receive federal financing
SCOPE	All school-age children who fall into these categories: —Specific learning disability —Mental retardation —Speech impaired —Seriously emotionally disturbed —Other health impaired —Multiply handicapped —Orthopedically impaired —Deaf, hearing impaired —Visually impaired —Traumatic brain injury —Autism —Deaf-blind	All school-age children qualified as handicapped who have or have had a physical or mental impairment that substantially limits a major life activity
FUNDING	Provides additional funds for eligible students	Does not provide additional funds
ENFORCEMENT	U.S. Department of Education (Office of Special Education)	U.S. Office of Civil Rights
ACCESS EVALUATION	Requires written notice to parent and informed parent consent (written)	Requires notice to parent—suggests it be written
	Full comprehensive evaluation by a multidisciplinary team	No formal evaluation; decisions made by a group of knowledgeable professionals (may be same people who serve as IEP team)
	Provides for independent evaluation at public expense if parent disagrees with school evaluation	Does not provide for independent evaluation
PLACEMENT	Reevaluation not required for a change of placement; change is an IEP team review decision	Reevaluation is required for a significant change of placement
DOCUMENTATION	Both laws dictate that there should be thorough documentation	
DUE PROCESS	Both laws require impartial hearings for parents or guardians who disagree with the identification, evaluation, and placement of student	

FIGURE 3.2.

Laws for Learning Disabilities.

Education of All Handicapped Children (1975)	Individuals with Disabilities Education Act (IDEA) (1990, 2000)	Section 504 Civil Rights Act	No Child Left Behind (NCLB) (2000)
• Entitled all children to a "free and appropriate education in the least restrictive environment"— including those with disabilities • Protected rights of children with disabilities (and their parents) • Now revised and appropriated under IDEA	Designed to provide government services for those with disabilities in the field of education: • Criteria for receiving services is set at governmental level; child must fit in criteria • Requires an IEP and parental consent • Extended services for children 2–5 years with special needs • Enforced by U.S. Dept. of Education, Office of Special Education	• To prevent discrimination against those with disabilities in programs that receive federal funding • Less specific criteria to receive services • Does not require parental consent • Requires a plan set by individuals in the school district • Enforced by the U.S. Office of Civil Rights	School accountability to governmental entities regarding student progress: • Schools must submit an annual yearly report for public viewing (available on state government's Web site) • Annual assessments for grades 3–8 mandated • Funding can be revoked based on school progress

4. Release records to nonschool personnel when permission is obtained by the school in writing.

5. Be notified in advance (ten days) of any meeting pertaining to their child. They may bring anyone they wish to the meeting, and they may tape-record meetings.

6. Request an assessment for their child.

7. Be apprised of the assessment tools to be used and have the child assessed in his own language.

8. Request an independent evaluation at public expense if they do not agree with the district's evaluation.

9. Have input into the development of the Individual Education Plan (IEP).

10. Refuse services or placement in special education.

11. Have an independent, fully paid private school placement if it is deemed necessary to meet the child's needs.

12. Request and have a fair hearing if disagreements arise in regard to identification, placement, or services.

Parents as Advocates

Usually parents do know their children best; however, using that knowledge to get services to help their children can be very difficult. Parents may find information on how to become an advocate for their child the most quickly online. The Learning Disabilities Association (www.ldonline.com) has information for parents about the types of educational legislation in place, sample form letters to send to schools, and information about different types of learning disabilities. Another organization, Reading Rockets, produced a series of videos that parents can watch online that spell out the advocacy process and how to be successful. A legal group called Wrightslaw puts on training seminars, offers advocacy information sheets online, and has a number of books out that list the legal issues involved in advocating for children with learning disabilities.

Student Rights

The courts and laws have given the student the following rights.

The Student Has the Right to . . .

- Receive due process if she gets in trouble at school. The student shall know the charges.
- Be heard in defense of self and has the right to review all documents that support the charges.
- Be treated at all times with respect and courtesy by all members of the school staff.
- Receive a prompt hearing if he is suspended or faces expulsion or involuntary transfer.
- Expect a safe learning environment.
- Receive a free and appropriate education (FAPE).
- Be provided accommodations for her learning disabilities.

Teacher Rights and Obligations

- Teachers have a right to work in a safe environment.
- Teachers have a right to be treated respectfully by their students.
- Teachers have a right to be able to teach.
- Teachers have an obligation to notify parents before beginning the evaluation process to set up an IEP.

- Teachers have an obligation to follow the guidelines set forth in the IEP.

- Teachers should realize that parents have the right, by law, to access and have copies of anything teachers add to a student's file.

If a student is disrespectful or uses profanity, the best way to handle it is for the teacher to ask the student to sit in the office or another class-room for the balance of the period (a cooling-off and thinking time) until there is time for a follow-up discussion. At that point, the student can be told, "Your behavior was inappropriate. You owe ___ an apology." If the student returns to class and gives the apology to the offended party, the incident can be recorded in a discipline log. If the student refuses, he can be asked again to offer an apology: "You have one more hour to think about it. These are your choices: apologize and return to class, or have your parent or guardian contacted." It is extremely rare that a student will choose to have a parent contacted if she is allowed time to cool off and consider the consequences.

If a student assaults you, this must be reported to the police. Then you can decide whether you wish to proceed with having the student arrested and prosecuted.

Behavioral Goals and Behavioral Improvement Plans

Whenever an IEP is written, it is necessary to consider the student's social, emotional, and behavioral needs. If there are significant problems in any of these areas, the IEP committee should examine ways to help the student. The committee needs to write in the IEP the methods the teacher will use to address these issues. Failure to address these considerations can lead to due process or court hearings and to the awarding of damages. Fines may be—and have been—levied against districts or against the teacher responsible for that student.

If a student has difficulties following school or class rules, the school's psychologist should be advised to evaluate the child's behavioral needs. A meeting should then be scheduled with the parents for the purpose of writ-ing a Behavioral Improvement Plan (BIP). (See Figure 3.3 for a sample BIP.) Once a BIP is signed by the parent, each person who is involved in the plan should receive a copy of it. It is a legally binding contract; the procedures outlined therein must be followed.

FIGURE 3.3.

Sample Behavior Improvement Plan (BIP).

Meeting Date 2-31-09   Date of Next Meeting 4-09

San Bernardino City Unified School District
Student Conduct/Behavior Improvement Plan
(E.C. 56520; Title 5, 3001, 3052)

MIS No:	000 000	Current Placement:	LH-RSP	Type of Plan:
Name:	John Doe	Last IEP Date:	6-08	General Education:
Birth Date:	1-17-97	Last Assessment:	6-08	Special Education: ✓
Grade	6th	Date:		Section 504:
School:	Liberty School	Primary Handicap:	LH	

BEHAVIOR OF PRIMARY CONCERN: Name calling/hitting

1. Will the student be subject to standard disciplinary procedures (District/School Policy)?   (Yes) No

For Special Education Students Only:

2. Is the current Special Education placement appropriate?   (Yes) No
3. Are the IEP and last assessment current?   (Yes) No
4. Is there a causal relationship between the student's handicap and the behavior?   Yes (No)

STUDENT'S RESPONSIBILITIES:

1. Student will refrain from name calling
2. Student will keep hands and feet to himself
3. Student will observe class rules/school rules
4.

SCHOOL'S RESPONSIBILITIES (including positive interventions):

1. School will involve student in token economy (one ticket per 6 hours of good behavior)
2. Daily note to parent re: student's behavior
3. Teacher will give praise for good behavior
4.

PARENT/GUARDIAN'S RESPONSIBILITIES (including positive interventions):

1. Parent will sign and return daily note
2. Parent will reward student with 50 cents for each good daily note
3. Parent will contact teacher if problems arise
4.

NOTES AND COMMENTS:

The undersigned agree with the above plan:

Margaret Doe   2/31/09   Constancia Florez   2/31/09
Parent/Date   Teacher/Date

John Doe   2/31/09   John G. Cramer   2/31/09
Student/Date   Administrator/Date

Other (Please specify job title)/Date   Other (Please specify job title)/Date

SE-44 (Rev. 1/98)   (Please attach a copy of the BIP with the IEP or Section 504 Plan if applicable.)

Note: The names used in this sample BIP are fictitious and in no way resemble actual people.

Student and Parental Rights Regarding Suspension or Expulsion

In order to understand policies regarding suspension and expulsion, it is necessary to know the intent of the policymakers. Foremost is that students need to be in school. Lawmakers felt that some of the LD students were being suspended indiscriminately and were, therefore, being deprived of the free and appropriate education (FAPE) guaranteed by P.L. 94-142.

To require schools to work on improving a difficult student's behavior, the regulations now allow a school to suspend a student for a cumulative period of up to ten days a year. Before a district can suspend a student for an eleventh day, the IEP team must meet either to write a BIP and behavioral goals or to review the existing BIP to see if it is still appropriate. For every day a district suspends a student beyond twenty days in any given year, it becomes increasingly more unlikely that due process review teams will support the school's actions and more likely that parents may be awarded damages.

In deciding whether a suspension is justified, the due process officer looks not only for the total number of suspension days but also at how the school dealt with each infraction:

- Were teachers actually working with the student on behavioral goals? If so, how, and how often? It is critical that teachers keep documentation logs.
- When the student was referred to the principal for action, what action was taken?
- Were the nature and severity of the offense considered before suspension was invoked?
- Would another alternative have been more appropriate?

When a student has repeated problems at a school, sometimes she might benefit from a change of school. It is acceptable to suggest to the parents that they might want to request that their child be moved to another campus, but it is not acceptable to pressure them to do so.

When expulsion is being considered for a student, a Pre-Expulsion IEP Meeting is held. At this IEP meeting, three questions must be answered:

1. Is the student appropriately placed?
2. Is all FAPE paperwork up-to-date?

3. Is there a link between the behavior and the disability? The decision requires a functional behavioral assessment (FBA) by a specifically trained team.

What happens when a student's behavior involves very serious consequences, such as possession of drugs or a weapon? School districts can unilaterally place a student with a disability in an interim alternative educational setting for up to forty-five days without parent agreement if the student commits a drug or weapons offense. Such a move may also take place if a hearing officer determines that the student is likely to cause injury to self or others if he remains in the present placement. This forty-five-day period may be extended by court order if safety remains an issue. The teacher at the Interim Alternative Educational Setting should be apprised in writing of the student's history.

Summary

The laws affecting special education all move toward a single-minded intent: that we will provide students with the opportunity to develop whatever potential they have. Should specific equipment or services be required in order for the student to actualize that potential, these will be provided at public expense if necessary.

IDEA has been a great help to students with mild disabilities, including those who are learning disabled. It has encouraged teachers to include these students to the maximum extent possible. It has moved children out of special schools and into regular classes for all or part of the school day. It has also provided increased learning opportunities for students who have learning disabilities but are still capable of learning and competing with their peers.

Such forward-thinking initiatives give us reason to take great pride. New technology, such as computers, calculators, PDAs, spelling tools, digital voice recorders, scanners, text recognition software, and online publications of lectures and class content continue to be developed to help students with disabilities.

Chapter 4

Early Childhood Education for At-Risk Students

Sir Isaac Newton (1642–1727)

English scientist, mathematician, physicist
Was believed to have been learning disabled; had poor performance in grade school

Contributions:

Science: Formulated the theory of gravity

              Formulated the three fundamental laws of mechanics

              Published *Opticks*, which discussed optical theory

Mathematics: Invented calculus

Why are early childhood assessments and referrals important? One Harvard researcher who has been studying human development, Kathleen McCartney, will tell you why they are a good investment: "Economists have demonstrated that investments early in childhood pay off. For every dollar spent, society saves between four and six dollars. Here's why: early childhood programs result in lower rates of special education, kids are less likely to be retained in a grade, and they're more likely to graduate from high school" (Hough, 2007).

The years from birth to age five are known as "the formative years." This is a period when extraordinary learning takes place. The infant pays attention to sounds and sights and soon distinguishes her mother from other women. Within a few months, the baby begins to make the sounds required by our language, even eliminating sounds not needed in the spoken language. Motor skills develop in a fairly predictable sequence. When these predictable events do not happen on schedule, doctors, parents, preschool teachers, and others make referrals to local school districts' early childhood learning programs. Even if a parent is simply concerned about an aspect of her child's development, the parent may request that her child be evaluated by an early development team with the school district, from birth up until five years of age.

The earlier these referrals are made, the better. There are optimal periods for various kinds of development, such as speech at age two. If a child is not speaking by age two, it generally indicates a learning disability. In general, the sooner remediation is undertaken, the better the results. When a child's problems go unaddressed until third or fourth grade, the child generally never catches up and, consequently, never reaches his full potential.

According to No Child Left Behind legislation, the state has the responsibility to find children who may be at risk for disabilities or in need of special services, and the state must evaluate the child whether or not she is in a public school program. This system is designed to make sure all children, regardless of where they attend school, receive necessary services if evaluations show developmental delays.

A table of normal developmental milestones follows. When a child is not achieving the skills listed by the age indicated, a referral is in order.

Normal Development Milestones

	Expected Behaviors	Suggested Toys
At 3 months	• Follows movement with eyes • Looks at an object or person • Coos and smiles • Rolls from side to side • Holds head upright	• Mobiles • Rattles • Small, child-safe animals
At 6 months	• Reaches for a desired object • Makes babbling noises and laughs • Bangs objects in play • Holds bottle • Rolls over	• Small, colorful balls • Mirrors • Large spoon

(*continued*)

Normal Development Milestones

	Expected Behaviors	Suggested Toys
At 9 months	• Gets up on hands and knees • Sits unsupported • Tracks and follows falling object • Feeds self with hands • Stands with support	• Bell and noise toys • Blocks • Nests of cups • Set of plastic keys • Push toys
At 12 months	• Crawls • Looks at pictures in a book • Makes marks on paper with crayon • Plays pat-a-cake and waves good-bye • Pulls self up • Stops when told "No"	• Water toys • Washable books • Thick crayons • Bucket and sand pail • Pop-up toys • Drum
At 18 months	• Walks • Stacks objects • Recognizes shapes • Removes simple garments • Follows simple commands • Uses toys appropriately • Says a few words	• Large ball and pull toys • Doughnut stacking toy • Wood puzzles (6 pieces) • Rocking horse • Plastic cups and blocks • Small table and chairs • Toy piano or keyboard
At 24 months	• Pretends • Enjoys nursery rhymes • Points to pictures • Jumps in place • Attends to other children • Makes two- to three-word sentences • Runs	• Plastic zoo animals • Mother Goose books • Beginning books • Climbing equipment • Sandbox • Dolls and trucks • Puzzles (15 pieces)

Normal Development Milestones

	Expected Behaviors	Suggested Toys
At 36 months	• Sorts objects by category	• Toys about shapes
	• Walks up and down stairs	• Tricycle
	• Joins in singing and rhythm	• More complex books
	• Makes simple cuts in paper	• Safety scissors
	• Speaks understandably	• Toy buildings (for example, barn, airport)
	• Uses toilet with help	• Paper, easel, paint, and large brush
	• Makes simple pictures	
	• Feeds self and dresses self	
At 48 months	• Tells a simple story	• More difficult books
	• Climbs a slide	• Slide
	• Catches and kicks ball	• Balls
	• Colors within lines	• Coloring books
	• Classifies pictures into groups	• Sorting activities
	• Copies an oval or square	• Easel, paint, brushes, paper
	• Laces shoes	• Lacing toys
	• Hops on one foot	• Building blocks
	• Counts to five	
	• Names four colors	
	• Talks in sentences	
	• Shares and plays cooperatively	
At 60 months	• Cuts and pastes	• Paper and glue
	• Copies a bead pattern	• Beads and string
	• Taps and claps rhythms	• CDs and cassettes
	• Plays simple games	• Cards
	• Prints some letters	• Crayons and colored pencils
	• Follows three simple directions	• Paper and coloring books

(continued)

Normal Development Milestones		
	Expected Behaviors	**Suggested Toys**
	• Counts sets to 4; rote counts to 10	
	• Copies a triangle	
	• Skips and catches a bounced ball	
	• Buttons and ties shoes	
	• Learns to repeat nursery rhythms verbatim	
	• Draws a person with head, body, some facial features	
	• Sees likenesses and differences (comparing two objects)	

Special Education Services from Birth Through Age Two

In recent years there has been an increase in the number of young children receiving services in state infant programs. More states have infant programs, and there is a growing awareness that these programs are available. Infants and children from birth to age two receive services under the IDEA Part C legislation (www.idea.ed.gov). Universal Infant and Newborn Hearing Screening and Child Find, part of the IDEA legislation, mandates that all states must have a system that "finds," or locates and evaluates, all children from birth to twenty-one months who may need early intervention services. You can also call the National Information Center for Children and Youth with Disabilities (NICHCY) at 800-695-0285 (voice/TT) to find services in your area.

According to IDEA (34 *Code of Federal Regulations*, sec. 303.16), infants and toddlers (from birth to age two) with disabilities qualify for services if they (1) "are experiencing developmental delays, as measured by appropriate diagnostic instruments and procedures, in one or more of the following areas": cognitive, physical (including vision and hearing), communication, social or emotional, or adaptive development; or (2) "[h]ave a diagnosed physical or mental condition that has a high probability of resulting in developmental delay."

Assessment of infants relies heavily on observation, parent questionnaires, and the opinions of members of the multidisciplinary team, usually involving a speech pathologist, a physical or occupational therapist, and a psychologist or developmental specialist. Once eligibility for services is verified, an Individual Family Service Plan (IFSP) is developed. This document should address and prioritize the family's concerns and identify the family's resources.

Service to the child may take place in a wide variety of environments. Many times, services are brought directly to the child's home. Other times, children may attend centers that are designed by the school district to help infants and toddlers with established disabilities or delays. There may even be therapy sessions set up in the form of early preschools for children who need extra help before attending school.

If in-home visits are recommended, the educational specialist visits on a regular basis, working with the parents to implement ways to reach the goals set forth in the IFSP. The early childhood specialists can also provide services in the child's day-care center or setting. Typically, goals include such things as feeding skills, toileting, mobility, speech/language development, bonding between caregiver and infant, discipline, and self-help skills. Parents of a deaf child, for example, are taught to sign. The IFSP must be reviewed and updated every six months. As the child approaches age three, a meeting must be held to determine whether there is need for continuing services and, if so, to plan for that transition.

Special Education Services for Children Ages Three Through Five

If a parent or teacher suspects that a child between three to five years of age needs an evaluation or is just not performing at the same level as his peers, the first place to call to find out about government services is the local public school district. If that is not helpful, the next place to check is with the state's listing of Early Childhood Specialists. You can call the National Information Center for Children and Youth with Disabilities (NICHCY) at 800-695-0285 (voice/TT) to find out more about services and referrals in your area.

In order for a three- to five-year-old child to receive services, the child must have one of the following qualifying conditions:

- Hearing impairment
- Deafness
- Blindness
- Speech impairment
- Mental impairment
- Serious emotional disturbance
- Traumatic brain injury

- Specific learning disability
- Show a significant delay below the average for her peer group in one or more basic psychological processes

Eligibility is determined by a multidisciplinary team using observation, parent questionnaires, and standardized tests. Current policy is to try to place eligible children in an inclusive classroom whenever possible, with additional resources provided. Itinerant educational specialists generally provide consultation services to the regular teacher or direct services to the child within the preschool setting. The Individual Education Plan (IEP) spells out the goals, and services may vary widely. As the child approaches age five, the team meets and plans for transitioning the child to a regular school.

Assessment of Young Children

There are many rating scales, questionnaires, and tests that can be used to assess a young child. Here are a few that are used widely:

1. *The Bayley Scales of Infant Development (BSID-III)* is a test that can be given to children ages one to forty-two months. Administered by a qualified psychologist with a parent present, it requires about an hour. This norm-referenced test consists of a mental scale, a motor scale, and an infant behavioral rating scale. It is published by Harcourt Assessment (Web: http://harcourtassessment.com; phone: 800-211-8378).

2. *The Batelle Developmental Inventory Test, Second Edition (BDI-II)* can be administered in the home by qualified professionals, such as a psychologist, special education teacher, speech-language therapist, or occupational therapist. It is appropriate for use with a child from birth to age eight. Through structured interactions with the child in a controlled setting, and interviews with caregivers, this test assesses the areas of personal-social adaptive behavior, motor functioning, communication, and cognitive development. Results are given as age-equivalent scores, percentiles, and standard scores. Information about the test is available through Riverside Publishing (Web: www.riverpub.com; phone: 800-323-9540).

3. *The Denver Developmental Screening Test—Revised*, which takes about twenty minutes to administer, is an easy and quick individual screening test. It is designed to be administered to children ages one month to six years. The test measures personal-social development, fine and gross motor development, and language. Results are given as age-equivalent scores. This test, too, can be administered by qualified personnel, such as a psychologist, special education teacher, speech-language therapist,

or occupational therapist. It is available from Denver Developmental Materials (Web: www.denverii.com; phone: 800-419-4729).

4. *Ages & Stages Questionnaires (ASQ), Second Edition* is a "Parent-Completed, Child-Monitoring System," used by some state agencies and recommended by First Signs (an autism advocacy and information organization) to evaluate and flag normal developmental milestones. Results are compiled by an educational professional, psychologist, or an early intervention team. More information is available through Brookes Publishing (Web: www.brookespublishing.com; phone: 800-638-3775).

The Components of an Effective Early Childhood Education Program

When an early childhood education program is functioning effectively, the following attributes should be evident:

1. An adult-to-child ratio of 1:4 or 1:5

2. Adults who communicate well with the parents

3. Staff charting or documentation of weekly or daily activities completed with the children, as well as some sort of weekly schedule of events

4. Attention paid to age-appropriate and developmentally appropriate play activities

5. Careful planning of play activities that allow for small time periods of structured play, along with lots of unstructured play opportunities

6. Specific curricular guidelines that support language development through stories, songs, language-play games, books, and vocabulary development

7. Staff-guided activities that allow children to experiment with numerical concepts with blocks, counting aids, sorting, and shapes games

8. Curricular guidelines and activities determined by a certified instructor (many states now mandate a four-year college degree for early childhood instructors, as of 2006) or educational professional

9. Staff that recognizes and attends to signs of stress in children, such as thumb sucking, crying, regression, or avoidance of activities and instructions

10. Encouragement of indoor and outdoor play each day

11. Both individualized and group instruction from the teacher or lead caregiver

12. Happy children at the center who engage with both their peers and the adults involved in the program

Maturation and "Readiness" for Kindergarten

Children mature at varying rates. Girls generally mature faster than boys. A few children are ready for kindergarten at four years nine months, but most children are not. There is nothing that can be done to hurry up neural maturation; the brain requires time to develop. Pressuring children to acquire academic skills when they are not ready can cause future difficulties. This is especially true of the child with learning disabilities. The decision as to whether the child is ready for kindergarten is an individual one. When a child is confused and "lost" all the time, he has not been properly placed. Giving that child another year to mature can be a good solution.

Age-Appropriate Activities for Parent-Child Interactions

Age-appropriate activities parents might engage in with their children include the following:

Birth to 6 Months	6 to 12 Months
• Talk and sing to the baby daily. • Cuddle and stroke the infant's skin. • Hold the baby up to a mirror so he can look at himself. • Provide age-appropriate toys, such as small stuffed animals, rattles, mobiles, a baby swing.	• Use names for things, such as "spoon," "ball," "cup." • Speak in short sentences like "Roll the ball." • Read simple books to the child, beginning at 12 months.
13 Months	**30 to 36 Months**
• Introduce the child to paper and big crayons. • Begin giving the child names for colors—for example, "The ball is blue." • Take the child for short walks; stop to look at things like rocks, leaves, and bugs. • Talk, talk, talk. • Furnish the child with toys and books.	• Consider enrolling your child in a preschool. • Help at the school. • Teach "please" and "thank you." • Have your child "help" clean up after self and dress self. • Allow the child to experience some frustration—gently encourage the child to keep trying, with words such as "You are making progress" and "Good."

Summary

A child's early environment plays a crucial role in determining later success in life. By providing a quality early childhood education experience and monitoring and remediating developmental delays, we can greatly improve a child's ability to succeed in school. Parents can have their children evaluated if they suspect delays. When early intervention increases a child's chances of success, all of us in society reap the benefits.

Chapter 5

The Student Study Team Process

Charles Darwin (1809–1882)
_____

English biologist and naturalist
Was believed to be learning disabled because of poor school performance, but enjoyed watching birds, studying plants and animals, and collecting fossils

Contributions:
Science: Formulated the theory of evolution
            Published such works as *On the Origin of Species* and *Variation in Animals and Plants Under Domestication*

Chapter Four discussed children who are identified for services between birth and age five. It is more common, however, for a child's problems to be recognized when she enters kindergarten or first grade. There, observant teachers note that the child is not performing at the same level as other children of the same age.

Children with moderate learning disabilities are usually identified in their primary school years, and children with milder disabilities are identified later, or sometimes not at all. I have worked with numerous college students who have made it through high school, only to find out that they can't make it through their college courses due to a learning disability. Some students go for testing so that they can get the extra help they need to make it through school, but there are others who simply drop out or never go; school in their early years was an endless array of failures and embarrassments.

Some students progress through the school system labeled as "underachievers" because they are able to meet minimum standards for promotion. Teachers sometimes see obvious abilities in LD students and attribute their poor performance in other areas to laziness or lack of motivation. I frequently see LD students labeled as "lazy," and in fact, I have not yet met one student with LD who was not labeled as "lazy" before being diagnosed with a disability. This can have far-reaching consequences. Some students continue to fear risk taking and often go through later life being underemployed and not living up to their potential.

The Case for Early Intervention

We know that early intervention is key to minimizing these concerns. When we provide the child with enough assistance early—especially in kindergarten and first grade—we can usually bring that child up to grade level within a short time. When children do not get the necessary quantity and quality of help needed until third or fourth grade, they rarely catch up. They become special education students for the balance of their school careers. This lapse in diagnosis allows the student to continue to flounder in school, and experience a large amount of failure and perhaps stigma when they are unable to complete their work. Providing early assistance turns out to be cost efficient for schools. It also is the most effective.

Recognizing the Need

Within the first few weeks of school, some teachers are able to see which children in class are not at grade level. It is important to inform parents as early as possible. When a teacher suspects that a child is working below grade level, basic assessments should be done to determine where the student needs help catching up. Some children begin acting out as a defense mechanism; others may cry or declare they don't like school.

Even falling behind half a grade level can affect the way a child feels about her ability to succeed in school. Immediate intervention should be the priority with the teacher and parents. Sometimes all a child needs is additional practice at home for a few weeks to move up to the next skill level.

Talking with Parents

Once a child is identified as needing special help, a conference should be scheduled with parents or guardians.

Page 70 shows a sample of the type of letter that might be sent.

When you talk with parents, **be factual, not emotional.** Be honest but not brutal. "I've observed that Sabrina has a hard time focusing her attention. For example, she loses a lot of time and looks around to see what others are doing before getting started on her work. When she reads aloud to me, she misses about two out of every five words. Have you noticed this kind of behavior at home?"

September 21, 2009

Dear Mrs. Martin,

I am Sabrina's teacher. I would like to talk with you at your earliest convenience. You may already be aware that Sabrina is having trouble with her reading. If you and I can sit down and talk about it, I feel we can find ways to help her. I am available to meet with you at 8:00 AM on Monday, September 30th, or at noon Tuesday, October 1st, or at 4:00 PM on Friday, October 4th.

We will need about an hour to get acquainted, share ideas, and work out a plan for assisting your daughter. Please feel free to bring a friend or relative with you to the appointment.

Please call me to let me know which day you are able to meet with me. If none of these times are good, let me know, and we'll try to determine another time that will work for you.

Sincerely,

Try to get parents to listen to the child read at home for ten minutes a day. Give her a grade-level book to use. Ask the parents about the reading experience at home. Sometimes it is helpful to make notes of the things parents share with you. You may want to give parents a copy of those notes.

Ask the parents or guardians about their expectations for their child. Some parents expect too much; others expect too little. Do they expect their child to excel in particular areas? Are these academic? Behavioral? Social? Are their expectations reasonable given the capabilities of their child?

Ask about homework. Where and when does the child complete homework? Does she do her homework on her own, or does the parent have to force it? How long does it take the child to do homework, and does she require help to get it done? Which parent (or guardian) is available to help with homework in the evening? Is there a designated time set aside for homework with an adult each evening?

Ask parents to participate as part of a Student Study Team. Explain to parents that you are going to request that a student study be done, and that you hope they will participate by coming to another meeting. Explain that the purpose of a student study is to help teachers and parents find ways to help and support children in their academic, social, and behavioral progress. You might say, "You probably know more about your child than anyone else, and your input will be helpful in determining our plan."

Parent and Student Preparation for the Student Study Team (SST)

At this time, give the parents a Parent Preparation Sheet (Figure 5.1). Offer to help the parents fill it out. Also give them either the Elementary or Secondary Student Worksheet (Figure 5.2 and Figure 5.3) as a way to obtain relevant information from their child. Ask that both forms be brought to the initial SST meeting.

FIGURE 5.1.

Parent Preparation Sheet.

Please complete and bring to the SST meeting. This step will help you be a part of the team.

1. **Strengths my child has (include interests, hobbies, possible career potentials, anything your child does that you appreciate and/or enjoy):**

   _____

   _____

   _____

   _____

2. **Concerns for my child:**
   At school _____

   _____

   At home _____

   _____

3. **I help my child be more successful by:**

   _____

   _____

4. **Things that motivate my child:**

   _____

   _____

5. **Goals or expectations I have for my child:**

   _____

   _____

   _____

Source: Student Success Teams—Supporting Teachers in General Education, *1997. Reprinted by permission of the California Department of Education.*

FIGURE 5.2.

Elementary Student Worksheet.

A supportive teacher or a parent explains the purpose of the team meeting and the value of being pre-pared with good information, then assists the student as needed while he or she thinks through his or her responses.

The student brings this completed worksheet to the meeting (fourth grade and up).*

1. **At school, activities I really like are** _____

    _____

2. **I am really good at** _____

    _____

3. **I want to know more about (activities, hobbies, vocations)** _____

    _____

4. **I learn best when** _____

    _____

5. **I would like help with** _____

    _____

6. **When I do things well, I like to do or get** _____

    _____

7. **One of my strengths is** _____

    _____

8. **I am concerned (worried) about** _____

    _____

*Students in third grade and younger would be asked these questions as appropriate, and the answers would be shared at the meeting by the parent or teacher.

Source: Student Success Teams—Supporting Teachers in General Education, *1997. Reprinted by permission of the California Department of Education.*

FIGURE 5.3.

Secondary Student Worksheet.

The student brings this completed worksheet to the meeting. A supportive teacher or counselor explains the purpose of the team meeting and the value of being prepared, then assists the student as needed while he or she thinks through his or her responses.

AT SCHOOL

1. **I really enjoy** _____

   _____

2. **One of my strengths is** _____

   _____

3. **I want to know more about (activities, hobbies, vocations)** _____

   _____

4. **Things I like about school are** _____

   _____

5. **My concerns are** _____

   _____

6. **Changes I would make at school are** _____

   _____

AT HOME

1. **My family (the people who live in my home) are** _____

   I get along best with _____

2. **The person I like to talk to most is** _____

   _____

3. **The person who helps me learn is** _____

   _____

MY FUTURE

1. **When I finish high school, I plan to (work? go to college? where?)**

   _____

   _____

2. **Jobs that I would enjoy are** _____

   _____

3. **The things that I am doing right now to get myself ready for a job or a career are**

   _____

   _____

4. **Two important goals that I have for this year are**
   1. _____
   2. _____

5. **To achieve these goals, I plan to** _____

   _____

Source: Student Success Teams—Supporting Teachers in General Education, *1997. Reprinted by permission of the California Department of Education.*

Predictable Parental Feelings and Reactions

When parents first learn that their child is having problems at school, they may show some of the following reactions. These reactions vary in intensity and duration and may or may not be voiced.

Feelings	Reactions/Response
1. *Shock, Denial* Parent denies there is a problem.	"All kids fight." "She reads fine at home." "He's just going through a phase."
2. *Anger, Guilt, Blaming* Parent admits there is a problem, but …	"It's the teacher's/school's/ex's fault." "If only … hadn't occurred."
3. *Resignation*	"It runs in the family." "He's always been like that."
4. *Depression*	"I can't bear this." "What will people think?"
5. *Acceptance*	"I believe I understand the issues and would like to work on a plan to resolve them." "This is difficult for us to hear, but we want to find ways to support and encourage our child."

Once a family achieves a state of acceptance, it can function and begin to resolve the problem at hand.

Initiating a Request for a Student Study Meeting

To schedule a meeting of the Student Study Team, the classroom teacher generally submits a written request similar to the one shown in Figure 5.4.

The Student Study Team Process

The Student Study Team (SST) does the following:

1. Gathers student data

2. Plans strategies to assist the student within the resources of the general educational program

3. Monitors student progress

4. Builds trust between parent and school

5. Makes referrals for formal evaluation when needed

Every school needs one or more SSTs. It is wise to have a sufficient number of teams so that requests can be scheduled within three weeks.

FIGURE 5.4.

Sample Request for Student Study Team.

Student's Name ___Sabrina Martin___   Grade __2__

Date of Birth ___4-7-02___   Age ___7.0___

Parent's/Guardian's Name ___Mrs. J. Martin___

Address _____345 Cedar Lane_____
_____Sunrise, California_____

Referring Teacher: _____Mr. Keen, Rm. 5_____

Reason for Referral:

Sabrina is behind in both her reading and spelling skills. Her decoding skills are poor—she is unsure of sounds for c, g, q, x, y, and all vowels. She cannot blend sounds into words. Sabrina needs 1:1 help to complete writing tasks.

Date and Data Regarding Academic Functioning:

Achievement score: 6-00
Reading total: 5th percentile
Spelling total: 5th percentile
Math total: 10th percentile

Relevant Personal Information:

Sabrina's mother reports Sabrina does not want to read and often claims she has no homework.

Mrs. Martin says Sabrina's father had problems in school and was in a special class.

[Be sure to attach interventions logs and/or work samples.]

J. Keen
Submitted 4-28-09

Form used with permission of San Bernardino City Unified School District. The names in this form are fictitious and in no way resemble actual people.

You might want to explain to or remind parents that the purpose of the SST is to help teachers and parents find ways to keep the child who has academic, social, health, behavioral, or attendance problems in regular education. Referral for formal assessment and possible special education services is made after a concerted effort has been made to help the child make steady progress within the regular program without satisfactory results; however, parents may request that the school district perform an assessment at any time during the process. The school district has a set amount of time to reply.

The first meeting of the SST is a time for staff and parent to share the data they have. It is a child study process, which involves gathering as much relevant data as we can. Participants prioritize their concerns, make a list of interventions that will be tried, and specify who will do what. A follow-up meeting is planned for three to six weeks later so that the team (parent included) can evaluate the effectiveness of the interventions. See How to Use an SST Summary Sheet (Figure 5.5) and the Sample SST Summary Sheet (Figure 5.6). A blank SST Summary Sheet is also included and may be duplicated (Worksheet 5.1).

Over several weeks of working together, parents usually see that the school is truly dedicated to helping children, and trust is built. As this trust develops, anger, blaming, and so on usually subside.

Figure 5.7 is an SST Process Flowchart. Note the time frame shown on the left side.

The Roles of the SST Members

1. The *Facilitator,* who is the principal or designee, greets and introduces the participants, states the purpose of the meeting, and appoints someone to act as timekeeper so that the meeting moves along quickly.

2. The *Referring Teacher* leads off with a list of the student's strengths. Starting on a positive note allays parental anxiety. Next, the referring teacher lists briefly her concerns. Comments of an emotional nature should be avoided—instead of "He's driving me nuts," try "We need to improve his on-task behavior."

3. The *Student Study Chairperson* schedules meetings and acts as scribe, recording information on a large visual-memory sheet during the meeting. The chairperson ensures that information is transferred to a smaller sheet for storage in the student's permanent record, and files it in that record. The large visual-memory sheet can be rolled up and

FIGURE 5.5.

How to Use an SST Summary Sheet (Typical Column Topics).

NAME OF STUDENT _____

TEACHER _____ SCHOOL _____ GRADE _____ TEAM _____

PRIMARY LANGUAGE _____ BIRTH _____ PARENTS _____

MALE _____ FEMALE _____

DATES OF MEETINGS

_____

_____

_____

_____

Strengths	Known		Concerns (Prioritized)	Questions	Strategies (Brainstorm)	Actions (Prioritized)	Responsibility	
	Information	Modifications					Who?	When?
Academic	School background	Changes in program	Academic	Questions that can't be answered at this time	Team brainstorms multiple creative strategies to address top concerns	Two to three actions chosen from strategies brainstormed	Any team member, including the parent and student	Specific dates
Social	Family composition	Reading specialist	Social/emotional					
Physical	Health	Tutoring	Physical					
What student likes	Performance levels	Counseling	Attendance					
		Repeating grade					FOLLOW-UP DATE: 3–6 WEEKS	

Source: *Marcie Radius, Pat Lesniak Student Study Team Manual, California Department of Education, 1987.*

FIGURE 5.6.
Sample SST Summary Sheet.

NAME OF STUDENT Martin, Sabrina

TEACHER Mr. Keen   SCHOOL Liberty Elementary   TEAM B

PRIMARY LANGUAGE English   GRADE 2   BIRTH 4-7-02   PARENTS Ms. J. Martin

MALE _____ FEMALE _____

DATES OF MEETINGS

5/22/09

| Strengths | Known | | Concerns | Questions | Strategies | Actions | Responsibility | |
	Information	Modifications	(Prioritized)		(Brainstorm)	(Prioritized)	Who?	When?
likes art	Achievement scores 6100	sits near front	achievement	Does anyone in family have a learning problem?	Aide will read 1:1 w/child 15 min./day	→	aide	5-23-09 to 6-18-09
draws well	read 5% tile spell 5% tile	incomplete work is sent home (mother helps complete it)	work production					
quiet	math 10% tile			Father was a poor student	Parent → will help w/homework (spell/math)	Teacher will give parent additional strategies for spelling	parent	
well-behaved	seems immature							
has friends	lacks confidence						FOLLOW-UP DATE: 8-15-09	

Source: *Marcie Radius, Pat Lesniak Student Study Team Manual, California Department of Education, 1987.*

Copyright © 2008 by John Wiley & Sons, Inc.

WORKSHEET 5.1. SST SUMMARY SHEET.

DATES OF MEETINGS

_____
_____
_____
_____

NAME OF STUDENT _____

TEACHER _____ SCHOOL _____ TEAM _____

PRIMARY LANGUAGE _____ GRADE _____ BIRTH _____ PARENTS _____

MALE _____ FEMALE _____

Strengths	Known		Concerns (Prioritized)	Questions	Strategies (Brainstorm)	Actions (Prioritized)	Responsibility	
	Information	Modifications					Who?	When?
							FOLLOW-UP DATE:	

Source: *Marcie Radius, Pat Lesniak Student Study Team Manual, California Department of Education, 1987.*

FIGURE 5.7.

SST Process Flowchart.

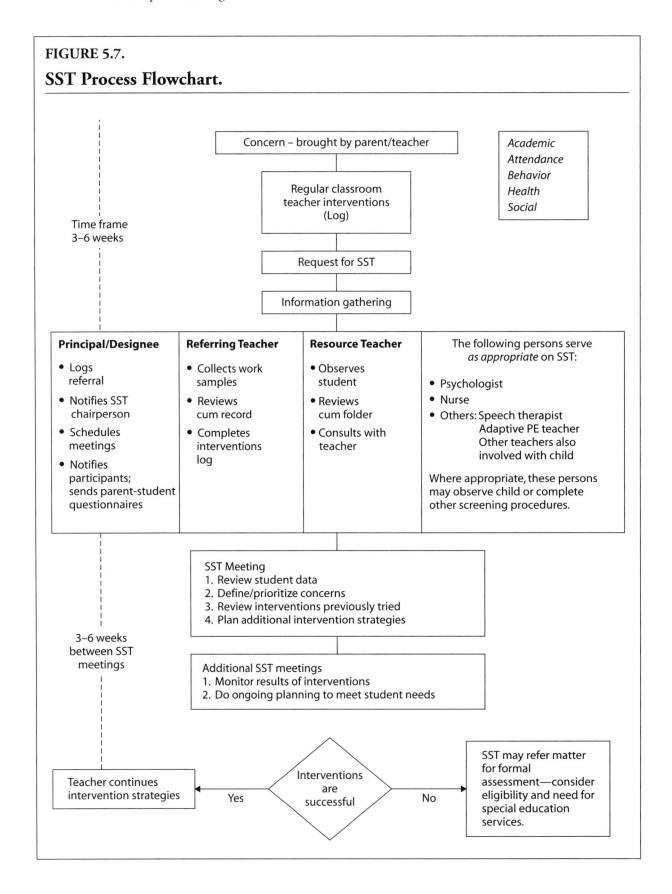

stored until the next meeting, when it is brought out as a reminder of the issues from the last meeting and is used to record results of the interventions that were tried.

4. The *Timekeeper* tries to hold the meeting to thirty minutes by keeping members on task. Approximately fifteen minutes are needed to cover strengths, known information, concerns, and questions. Allow fifteen minutes for brainstorming and planning time. Important issues should be summarized at the end with clearly stated next steps.

5. It often is helpful to have *one other teacher* on the team. This could be a resource teacher or, if the meeting takes place late in the second semester, perhaps a teacher for the next grade.

6. The *parent* is the most important person at the meeting, and every effort should be made to encourage a parent to attend. In general, parents know more about the child than anyone else, and their input is valuable. If they have not been involved in the child's education, we want them to become involved.

7. The *student* who is in fourth grade or higher should attend the meeting unless the parent is adamant that the child not attend.

SST meetings are a function of regular education. Psychologists, resource specialists, speech therapists, or other specialists are not usually part of the team at the initial meeting.

The purpose of the first meeting, and probably at least one or two more meetings, is to brainstorm and to attempt to find ways to use the resources of regular education more efficiently so that the student begins to progress. Ideally the need for special education services can be avoided. The earlier these meetings begin, the better the chance of a successful outcome for the student.

Kindergarten and first-grade teachers should be encouraged to start the study process promptly if they have concerns about a child. The earlier we begin, the more likely it is that we can avert the need for formal assessment and special education services.

While brainstorming during the SST meeting, team members may use the List of Accommodations and Modifications shown in Figure 5.8. Some teams are very creative in finding local resources to help, such as retired teachers willing to work with a child. Some localities have grandparent or church tutoring programs they can tap into. Also provided here are a Sample Documentation Log (Figure 5.9) and a reproducible log for your review and use (Worksheet 5.2).

FIGURE 5.8.

List of Accommodations and Modifications.

There are many possible instructional modifications and accommodations to consider:

__ Change seating.

__ Assign preferential seating near teacher.

__ Provide an individual carrel out of the traffic pattern.

__ Furnish written directions.

__ Limit number of directions.

__ Assign student buddy to help with directions.

__ Sit with child to initiate work.

__ Monitor student's progress.

__ Prioritize tasks to be done.

__ Shorten the assignments.

__ Give extra time at recess, at lunch, or after school for completion of assignments.

__ Allow student a choice of assignments.

__ Provide alternative assignment, at a lower level.

__ Increase student–teacher time.

__ Increase student–aide time.

__ Recruit student's parent to help child in classroom.

__ Assign peer tutor or cross-aged tutor to help child.

__ Modify assignments by breaking them into short tasks.

__ Enroll students in remedial program in school.

__ Encourage remedial program outside school.

__ Use special materials—calculator, computer, spell-check, tape recorder.

__ Use rewards to stimulate work completion.

__ Use high-interest material of student's choosing when possible.

__ Provide immediate feedback of results.

__ Keep daily parent–teacher notes.

__ Reassign classroom.

__ Allow student to use larger-print books.

__ Give parent set of texts and papers to use at home with child if homework is not taken home.

__ Counsel student so that your expectations are clearly understood.

__ Test orally.

*__ Use multiple-choice or matching tests instead of full recall.

__ Give open-book study sheets to student and parent two weeks before major test so that parent can review information several
    times with student.

*__ Allow student extra time on timed tests if they are not standardized tests.

*__ Provide student a quiet setting free of distractions in which to take tests.

__ Talk with student to determine prior knowledge and begin instruction at the appropriate level of understanding.

__ Use assignment calendar to give student a clear idea of due dates.

__ If student cannot read text, use tape-recorded books in a listening center or assign a peer to read to the student.

__ Use videos, demonstrations, and concrete materials.

*__ Really get to know the student. Target his strengths and help him shine in these areas. Assure him that you care how
    he feels.

__ Set up expectations for behavior. Give positive feedback when behavior is satisfactory. "I like it when you …" When behavior
    is not satisfactory, request compliance: "I want you to …"

__ If attendance is a problem, adjust level of work so that the child succeeds. Relate with the child one-on-one, letting him know you
    are glad when he is present.

*These accommodations are especially beneficial for students with LD.

FIGURE 5.9.

Sample Documentation Log.

| Student | Sabrina Martin |

Date/Time	No. of Minutes/ Size of Group	Activity	Comments
5-25-09 11:15	20 min 1:1	Check knowledge of sounds	Sabrina knows sounds of consonants except for c, g, q, x, y Does not know any vowel sounds
6-1-09 11:30	20 min 1:1	Check knowledge of sight vocabulary with Dolch list	List 1 "look" called "see" "work" not recognized
6-2-09 11:30	15 min 1:2	Begin dictation practice	Words covered: boy, girl, mother, the, can, help, to, read Sabrina cannot spell girl (gril), mother, hlpe (help), read (ride)
	20 min 1:2	Decoding practice	While Sabrina has most consonant sounds, blending cvc words will require daily practice

If after a period of six months the child still shows difficulties, a formal assessment is warranted.

Digital Classroom Accommodations

There are many kinds of digital programs, hardware, software, and accommodation options available. There are computer games that help children practice basic skills, such as math, phonics, and reading skills. Some children respond readily to computer-based instruction methods, especially if there is an instant visual reward associated with completion of a task. Some computer games show a big star or ribbon, or use music to cue children on to the next part of the assignment or to give a reward.

Other types of in-class accommodations include giving the student a laptop to type up notes, record lectures, or complete assignments. There are specialized types of digital communications, including picture boards, writing boards, and digital text readers that can be made available to students as well. Some students may use voice recognition software to write papers or take notes. There are many kinds of classroom aids available

WORKSHEET 5.2. DOCUMENTATION LOG.

Student _____

Date/Time	No. of Minutes/ Size of Group	Activity	Comments

to students now, and the technology makes schooling more accessible to many students with disabilities.

Sensory Accommodations

For students who have sensory issues that make functioning in the classroom difficult, there are many types of seats, sensory feedback mats, manipulatives, headphones, and types of clothing that are designed to help manage sensory information sent to the brain. Some types of physical therapists specialize in sensory integration disorders, and they often can direct teachers to products that may be helpful in the classroom.

I have seen some students perform extraordinarily well with seat wedges that are specially designed for sensory integration. Other students tend to do well with a specially fitted vest that has weights. Yet other students like a vest with many pockets in it. Sometimes checking with a physical therapist or occupational therapist (or one who specializes in sensory integration) within the school district can lead to amazing results in the classroom.

Chapter 6

Formal Assessment and Identification of the Student with Learning Disabilities

---

Louis Pasteur (1822–1895)

French chemist, microbiologist
Was believed to be learning disabled; struggled throughout school, despite being a "hard worker"

Contributions:
Science: Formulated the germ theory as the cause of most illness
           Developed the process for pasteurizing milk
           Developed immunization for anthrax in sheep and the treatment for rabies in humans

---

The Multidisciplinary Team Process

Diagnosing a child with learning disabilities involves a multistep process within the school system. Usually a teacher or educational professional notes problem areas for a student and schedules a meeting with the child's caregivers to review the diagnostic process. If the caregiver agrees to have his or her child evaluated by the school district and grants permission in writing, the evaluation begins.

The evaluation of a child's progress and abilities is designed to examine multiple aspects of the child's performance, and is carried out by a team of professionals. Utilizing a team approach ensures that the child's evaluation is more complete. As discussed in Chapter Five, some school districts form a Student Study Team, or a group of school professionals who monitor and increase student performance, before calling for a formal evaluation with the Multidisciplinary Team. The Student Study Team may be a formal grouping of individuals brought together to help the student or a less formal group approach to getting a student on track without in-depth psychoeducational testing.

If it's determined that a student needs further help or if the child's parents request additional testing, a formal evaluation is begun. The formal evaluation also follows the team approach, and the teacher, as well as other school personnel, may be involved. When a formal student evaluation is called for, psychoeducational testing, observations, and samples of student work or test scores are all included in a report created by a psychologist or educational professional. The members of the Multidisciplinary Team each contribute information to the report that will be used as the basis for forming an educational plan customized for the student.

As noted, referrals for formal assessment can come to the Multidisciplinary Team directly from parents or through the SST process. Either way, the district must move within clearly specified time limits to assess the child.

The Multidisciplinary Team includes the following individuals:

1. The school psychologist

2. The classroom teacher

3. The special education specialist

4. The nurse (who works for the school district)

5. The parents

6. A school administrator

Sometimes other persons, such as an adaptive physical education teacher, speech therapist, occupational therapist, social worker, or the child's physician, participate in the Multidisciplinary Team.

Roles of the Members of the Multidisciplinary Team

The *School Psychologist* obtains the parent's permission to assess a child. She gathers information regarding family history, as well as social and cultural information. She is also responsible for measuring intelligence, either through standardized tests or adaptive behavior scales. The psychologist tries to get a clear picture of the child's strengths and weaknesses.

The *Special Education Specialist* generally does the academic assessment by using various individualized tests, observing the student in the learning situation and on the playground, looking at work samples, and discussing the child's performance with the classroom teacher.

The *School District Nurse* may help manage medication or may help accommodate health issues related to a disability.

When a student has deficits in written or oral language, the *Speech Therapist* may be asked to assess language development. The *Adaptive PE Teacher* may assess motor development or may evaluate whether there is a health issue that precludes the child from participating in the regular education program.

The *Classroom Teacher* and *parents* have a valuable understanding of the child's maturity level, skills, motivation, attention span, social acceptance, and emotional adjustment. They may be asked to fill out rating scales regarding the student's attention or adaptive behavior.

The *School Administrator* (site principal or special education services administrator) can act as a facilitator during the meeting. This person's signature is required for the release of necessary funds.

Guidelines for Assessment

Assessment involves both formal and informal procedures. In conducting any assessment, schools are bound by legal and ethical considerations. Legal considerations include the following:

1. Parental permission (written consent) must be obtained before the psychologist or special education personnel can administer any assessment device to the student.

2. Parents have a right to an explanation in their native language of the types of interventions that will be used.

3. Parents have a right to a copy of the findings of the assessment.

4. Parents have a right to obtain an independent educational assessment at public expense and to have the results of that independent assessment considered in planning for the student.

5. Any student whose native language is not English and who does not speak fluent English must, by law, be tested in the native language through the use of an interpreter.

6. Parents of a nonpublic school student may request an assessment for their child.

7. Parents must be involved in the assessment process and in the ongoing education planning for the student.*

8. Even if the child is eligible for special education, the parent may refuse that service.

9. If the parents elect to place the child in any special education services, the child's classroom teacher must be involved in planning the goals.*

It is important to give careful attention to the words used in reports and in talking about children. Because the purpose of the assessments is to help

---

*These requirements are part of the 1997 reauthorization of IDEA.

children, the language of the report should focus on how to use each child's strengths to greater advantage. Assessments should go beyond recognizing a student's limitations to seeking ways to help the student overcome or compensate for areas of deficit. Written goals for the student should be attainable but not too easy. A goal that is too high will result in yet another failure for the child. A goal in which the expectation is too low does not advance the child's skills. If a child accomplishes a given goal sooner than anticipated, it is appropriate to ask for parental consent to add additional goals.

It is important to keep in mind that tests are samples of behavior and that scores can be adversely affected by student fatigue and anxiety. Test scores alone should never be used to assess a student's performance. These scores must be considered in relation to other indicators.

Intellectual Assessment

The psychologist may choose from a variety of devices to measure the student's intellectual functioning.

As a result of a decision in a court case in California, *Larry P.* v. *Riles, California,* 1979, controversy arose over whether IQ tests are racially and culturally discriminatory. The court ruled that the intellectual functioning of a black child must be gauged by his adaptive behaviors, personal history and development, classroom performance, and academic achievement—not by IQ tests.

Intelligence Quotient (IQ)

The instrument chosen to assess IQ should be appropriate to the age of the individual being tested and should be free of cultural bias. The following are some of the most popular IQ tests:

- Wechsler Intelligence Scales for Children (WISC-IV)
- Stanford-Binet Intelligence Scale, Fifth Edition (SB-5)
- Kaufman Assessment Battery for Children, Second Edition (KABC-II)
- Slosson Intelligence Test–Revised (SIT-R3)
- Test of Nonverbal Intelligence, Third Edition (TONI-3)

The Wechsler Scales of Intelligence are perhaps the most widely used individualized measures of intelligence. There are three tests in the series:

- *Wechsler Preschool and Primary Scale of Intelligence (WPPSI-R)* for ages 4.0 to 6.5 years of age

- *Wechsler Intelligence Scale for Children—WISC-IV (2003)* Revised for ages 6.0 to 16.11 (more recent)
- *Wechsler Adult Intelligence Scale, Third Edition (WAIS-III)* for ages 16 and up

The WISC-IV contains several subtests to measure verbal and performance skills. These tests are individually administered and yield very useful information for educationally prescriptive planning. Among the *verbal tests* in the Wechsler are the following subtests:

Information: measures the individual's fund of general knowledge and alertness to the everyday world

Similarities: measures abstract and concrete reasoning, logical thought processes, associative thinking, and memory

Arithmetic: measures arithmetic reasoning, knowledge of computational facts, and ability to concentrate and work under time pressure

Vocabulary: measures the quality of expression and thought, and knowledge of spoken words

Comprehension: measures social judgment and common-sense reasoning

Digit span: measures short-term memory and attention

The Wechsler *performance tests* include:

Picture completion: measures awareness and memory for visual details and ability to separate essential from nonessential detail

Picture arrangement: measures ability to logically sequence events and see cause-and-effect relationships

Block design: measures a person's ability to perceive, analyze, synthesize, and reproduce designs; measures visual-motor integration and manual coordination

Object assembly: measures perceptual speed, and ability to take parts and assemble the whole

Coding: measures eye-hand control, short-term visual memory, flexibility, and speed in learning tasks

Symbol search: measures visual discrimination

Mazes: measures attention, organization, planning, and eye-hand coordination

When the test is scored, a profile emerges. The scores that follow demonstrate the wide fluctuations in the subtest scores that are rather typical of an LD individual:

Verbal		Performance	
Information	7	Picture Completion	13
Similarities	10	Picture Arrangement	10
Arithmetic	13	Block Design	10
Vocabulary	9	Object Assembly	10
Comprehension	10	Coding	10
Digit Span	9	Symbol Search	7

Verbal IQ = 94   **Performance IQ = 100**

Full Scale IQ = 97

The child in the previous example has an IQ that falls in the average range of intelligence (90–100), but there is a wide scatter (7–13) among the scores. On any given test, a score of 10 is average. On the tests where the child scored above 10, we see the child's strengths. Where the child scored below 10, we see her weaknesses. The lower the score, the greater the weakness.

The *Stanford-Binet, Fifth Edition (SB-5)* is another individual standardized IQ test. It can be used with persons from age two to adulthood. Subtests measure verbal reasoning, quantitative reasoning, abstract and visual reasoning, and short-term memory.

The *Kaufman Assessment Battery for Children Mental Processing Scales-II* is an individual standardized IQ test for children ages 2½ to 12½. The test provides clues regarding the strengths and weaknesses of the subject and gives valuable information for educational programming. Scores are reported in percentiles, stanines, and age equivalents.

The *Slosson Intelligence Test–Revised-III* is a norm-referenced individualized test that can be given to persons ages 4 to 65. It is quick to administer, and no reading or writing is required. It covers vocabulary, general information, similarities and differences, comprehension, auditory memory, and quantitative ability. It produces standard scores, age-equivalent scores, percentiles, and stanine scores.

Test of Nonverbal Intelligence, Third Edition (TONI-3) is a norm-referenced individual IQ test that is designed to measure the nonverbal intelligence of persons ages 5 to 85 who are bilingual, speak a language other than English, are socially or economically disadvantaged, deaf, language disordered, or motor or neurologically impaired. No reading, writing, speaking, or listening skills are required.

Visual Perception

Many individuals with learning disabilities have deficits in the area of visual perception. Perception is not to be confused with visual acuity. Visual acuity is how well the eyes see, whereas visual perception refers to how the brain interprets what is seen. The acuity of the eyes may be perfect, but if the brain misinterprets what is seen, learning is more difficult. Some people who have visual perceptual difficulties report that the print "swims" on the page. Others report that some letters look darker than others. For example, the word *mother* may appear to them as **mother**. Because so much information comes through the visual channel, disturbances in this area can have a very negative impact on learning. When a child shows several of the symptoms in the list that follows, we must suspect a visual perceptual deficit:

- Messy work that exhibits poor legibility and spatial planning with many erasures
- Reversal or inversion of letters and numbers, such as *b* and *d*, *p* and *q*, *n* and *u*, and 6 and 9, or turns 3, 5, 7, and 9 backwards
- Awkwardness and clumsiness
- Transposition of numbers or letter sequences, such as *saw* for *was*, 17 for 71
- Difficulty with comprehension of pictures
- Poor spelling
- Poor memory for what was seen only seconds before
- Slowness and inaccurate copying
- Poor directional sense
- Itchy eyes, tearing, blurry vision
- Complaints of print "swimming" on a page or being out of focus
- Loss of place, skipping or rereading of lines
- Difficulty remembering faces, names, and places
- Problems differentiating between colors or shades of color

The following are two popular tests for visual perceptual deficits:

- *The Developmental Test of Visual Motor Integration, Fifth Edition (VMI-5)* for ages 3–18
- *The Bender Visual Motor Gestalt Test (BVMGT-II)* for ages 3 years and older

Both of these tests involve showing the subject a set of stimulus cards, one at a time. The student is asked to reproduce the design on paper. The stimulus cards may be borrowed from the school psychologist, and each card compared with the child's perception of the card. Marked distortions of the designs are common, including rotation, perseveration, shape distortion, and incorrect directionality.

Auditory Perception

The ability to process information received through the auditory channel is critical to learning; many students with LD have deficits in this area. The following are some of the symptoms that students exhibit that suggest auditory perceptual deficits:

- When spoken to, often responds with "Huh?" or "What?"
- Follows written directions better than oral directions
- Has a poor receptive vocabulary
- Fails to hear sounds accurately
- Does not enjoy being read to
- Looks at speakers' lips as they talk
- Mispronounces common words, such as "spaghetti," "chimney," "particular"
- Omits endings to words
- Relies heavily on picture clues
- Has difficulty with rote memory tasks, such as the alphabet, numbers, addresses, phone numbers, poems
- In a noisy setting, is not able to distinguish and follow conversation
- Cannot follow oral directions without visual cues
- Has trouble repeating oral directions or cues, such as songs, phrases, or verses for memorization and recitation

The classroom observation gives many clues as to whether a student can process auditorially.

Does he look at the speaker?

Can he answer questions about the information just presented orally?

Can he repeat words or phrases he has just heard?

Lecture is a primary teaching method in our secondary schools. It is wise for secondary teachers to support their lectures with written materials, board notes, questioning to check understanding, and hands-on experiences.

The following are three popular tests for auditory perception:

- *The Goldman-Fristoe-Woodcock Test of Auditory Discrimination (G-F-WTAD)* for ages 2 to 21 years. The G-F-WTAD consists of two tests of the person's auditory discrimination ability. First the student is tested under ideal conditions in a quiet setting. Then the student is tested when there is distracting background noise on a tape.

- *The Lindamood Auditory Conceptualization Test, Third Edition (LAC-III)* for preschool to adult. The LAC-III tests a person's knowledge of various concepts such as *first* and *last* and *same* and *different* and her auditory discrimination of isolated sounds.

- *Tests of Auditory Perceptual Skills–Revised (TAPS-III)* for ages 4 to 13. The TAPS-III tests auditory memory for digits, words and sentences, ability to discriminate sounds, and ability to use auditory processing to think and reason.

All three tests may be administered by psychologists, special education specialists, or speech and language specialists.

Memory

Many of the tests already described have subtests—for example, the Wechsler digit span and coding subtests—that tease out a measure of the student's memory.

When a person displays several of the following behaviors, we must suspect memory deficits:

- Does not know personal information such as his own birth date or the kind of work his parent does

- Knows only part of a nursery rhyme

- Makes mistakes counting

- Cannot remember three oral directions

- Loses things; forgets things

- Knows something one day but not the next

- Cannot spell frequently used words

- Has not learned arithmetic facts, such as $3 + 5 = 8$

Academic Assessment

Customarily, the special education specialist will conduct the academic assessment. This assessment ordinarily involves the use of two or more norm-referenced, criterion-referenced, or standardized tests in reading, math, spelling, and written expression; examination of student's daily work; and several classroom and playground observations.

Commonly Used Tests

The following are some of the most widely used academic assessments:

- The Brigance Diagnostic Inventory of Basic Skills–Revised (CIBS-R)

- Kaufman Test of Educational Achievement (KTEA-II)

- The Peabody Individual Achievement Test–Revised (PIAT-R)

- The Wide Range Achievement Test–4 (WRAT-4)

- The Woodcock-Johnson Psychoeducational Battery–III (WJ-III)

- The Wechsler Individual Achievement Test–II (WIAT-II)

All these tests are given to individual students and can be administered by a teacher.

The *Brigance Diagnostic Inventory of Basic Skills–Revised (CIBS-R)* is appropriate for use with children in kindergarten through grade 9. It tests "readiness," reading, language arts, and mathematics. This test pinpoints specific skills the child has not learned and therefore is very helpful in writing goals for the IEP.

The *Kaufman Test of Educational Achievement (KTEA-II)* is a norm-referenced, standardized test that measures decoding skills, reading comprehension, spelling, mathematics computation, and applications. This test can be used with students in grades pre-K–12.

The *Peabody Individual Achievement Test–Revised (PIAT-R)* is norm-referenced and standardized. It comes in two levels: Level 1 is used with children in kindergarten and grade 1; Level 2 is used with students in grades 2 through 12. The tests measure the student's general knowledge fund, reading recognition (decoding), reading comprehension, spelling, written expression, and knowledge of mathematics.

The *Wide Range Achievement Test–4 (WRAT-4)* is a norm-referenced test for use with individuals ages 5 to 75. It tests decoding, spelling, and arithmetic. The primary advantage of this test is its quickness and reliability.

The *Woodcock-Johnson Psychoeducational Battery–III* is a norm-referenced test for ages 2 to 90. The achievement battery provides extensive testing of reading decoding and comprehension and of mathematical calculation and the ability to understand math concepts and apply them. It yields samples of dictation and writing. It measures the person's understanding of content in science, social studies, and humanities.

Finally, the *Wechsler Individual Achievement Test–II (WIAT-II)* is a norm-referenced test for ages 5 to 19. It measures decoding and reading comprehension, spelling, mathematical reasoning and calculation, listening comprehension, and oral and written expression.

In planning for testing, keep in mind that Mondays and Fridays are not usually good testing days. Days that precede or follow a holiday also are poor testing days.

With experience, people who administer tests can gain additional information from observing the student's behavior during testing. They learn

1. How to evaluate the student's perceptual speed

2. How to read body language

3. How to use information garnered from tests to develop realistic IEP goals

It is typical for many new resource specialists and special-day-class teachers to have had no experience giving these tests. If an educator's training did not include instruction on administering academic tests, a local program specialist or special education director can help arrange such training.

Read the test manuals carefully and completely. They provide essential information about what can and cannot be done. An effective tester has given tests to numerous people before feeling comfortable and proficient. Scoring the tests properly can be tedious, but it is necessary.

Avoid expressions or movements that might reveal anything about test answers. Some students will watch your expression and body language. If they sense that they have responded incorrectly, they will change their answer.

Classroom and Playground Observations

Observations are usually done by the special education specialist. An observation can be as short as ten minutes. Two in-class observations are necessary; three are preferred. A student's performance often varies from day to day, according to time of day.

Here are three observations of Robert, a student in grade 6.

Sample Observation Summaries

Date: 2-1-2009   *10:00 AM*

I arrived before class began. The teacher had a warm-up activity on the board. It said, "Think about the story we began reading yesterday. Write the following in your reading journal:"

     Name of story:

     Author:

     Setting:

     Main characters:

Most of the students entered quietly and took out their books and journals. Robert sat down, slouched in his seat, looked around. After two minutes, he got out his pencil and went to the pencil sharpener. Upon returning, he took out his book and began turning pages. At the end of five minutes, he had not written anything. Most students had answered the first two questions. Robert located the page, wrote two words (left-handed) before breaking the pencil lead, then returned to the sharpener. At the end of eight minutes, he had written three words. Half the students in the class had all questions answered after eight minutes.

Date: 2-2-2009   *12:15 PM*

Robert and another student were sent to the back of the lunch line by the lunch supervisor for pushing a student who was cutting out of line. He argued with her about fairness, and she had to tell him to leave several times before he followed through. He then pouted. The lunch supervisor says she has trouble with him frequently. He does not stand still.

Date: 2-3-2009   *9:20 AM*

When I arrived, the teacher was having the students read the story. After she read a few paragraphs, students would chorally read a few paragraphs. She drew name sticks from a can for people to read individually. At appropriate intervals she asked questions to check comprehension. Robert was again slouching in his seat. His book marker was not being moved, so the teacher moved it to the right place and asked him to read. He was able to read frequently used words at grade 2 level but relied on her to supply words that were more advanced (for example, vccv patterned words that have prefixes). Finally, Robert said, "This is a dumb story." The teacher let him off the hook but with the comment that if he would follow along, she would give him a satisfactory grade for the day. Later I asked the teacher if he had done so; she said he had.

Observations should be scheduled ahead of time with the teacher, preferably through a face-to-face meeting rather than a note or message. If the student is aware that she is being observed, the process is unlikely to reveal a true picture of her everyday performance. The teacher can acknowledge the observer's presence by saying, "I invited Ms./Mr. X to come see what we are doing today." By placing a hand on the shoulder of the student or calling on a student by name, the teacher can identify the student slated for observation. The student's name should not be entered on the observation sheet until the observer leaves the room. The observer should circulate around the room to watch other students as well, so that the observed student does not feel singled out and know she is being watched.

The observation write-up (as shown in Figure 6.1) should do the following:

- Tell what the lesson was.

- Tell what the student's responsibility was during the lesson.

- Detail the student's degree of participation in the lesson, and state how his participation compared with that of other class members.

- Stick to the facts. For example, if a student tears up his paper and throws it on the floor, the write-up should say, "Student tore up his paper and threw it on the floor" (a fact), rather than, "Student became frustrated and tore up his paper" (an opinion).

- Record verbatim any answers, questions, or comments made by the student.

- Ask the teacher to evaluate or "grade" the student's work and to give you a copy of the student's paper to attach to your report.

- Ask the teacher if today's performance was typical.

- Include a time-on-task report.

Observable data may include the following:

- Statements about the way a student organizes her work. Did the student begin immediately or take time to make a preliminary draft? Did she look at what others were doing? Did she understand and follow the directions, or need one-on-one teacher assistance to begin? Was paper spatially organized or messy, as compared with those of others nearby?

- Statement regarding handedness and fine motor control.

- Statement about verbal fluency. Was the student able to communicate satisfactorily with peers and teacher?

FIGURE 6.1.

Sample Observation Summary.

Student __Shelley Anybody__   Grade __2__

Date __11-15-09__   Time __9:15__   Length of Observation __20 min.__

When I entered the room, the teacher was reading a story to the class. The students were supposed to follow along in their books using a book marker.

Shelley sits in the back of the room. When I walked by her, I noted she was not even on the right page. During the balance of the reading, Shelley looked around— not at the book. (As I circulated, 26 students were in the right place, 5 were not, including Shelley.)

The teacher told the students to pair up and "buddy read." They were to reread the section just read to them. Shelley's partner had to tell her at least 50% of the words. Shelley shut her book and said to her buddy, "You read it to me. It's too hard." The buddy read to her slowly, pointing at each word as she read it. Shelley looked at the book as her partner helped.

I asked Shelley to retell the story to me. She said, "Some elves made shoes." I asked, "What else happened?" Pointing at the picture of the shoemaker, she said, "They made clothes for the elves."

I asked her why she said the story was too hard. She said, "I don't read very good." I asked if she would read a bit to me. (See attached sheet for her miscues. She got 98 out of 153 words right—64%.) When Shelley comes to a word she doesn't know, she usually guesses something that begins with the same initial sound but that may not make sense. She goes ahead instead of trying to self-correct. She did seem to try harder when reading to me than when reading to her buddy.

The teacher reports this is typical of Shelley's daily performance and that her spelling is "atrocious." She showed me the paper and it was totally dysphonetic. (See spelling paper—see right-hand column for what words were dictated.) The teacher reports that the mother is a single working parent who works P.M.s (gone 2:00–11:30). The two children get themselves up and dressed for school. Shelley does not always comb her hair and sometimes looks totally disheveled. Shelley says the babysitter, who is 16, helps her with homework. Shelley reports that on days off, her "mom goes to see her boyfriend." Shelley and her brother are left home with a babysitter or at the grandmother's house. When asked if anyone reads to her, Shelley said, "No." The teacher is concerned about the poor quality of the homework that is returned. The classroom aide works with Shelley 1:1 for 15–20 minutes a day "because Shelley never understands the verbal directions and just sits until someone shows her what to do."

Questions to be answered:
—Does Shelley have an adequate grasp of receptive language?
—What can be done to increase time she spends reading to someone?
—What is parent's expectation of Shelley?
—Is Shelley adequately supervised? Can parent help at home?
—Why is Shelley so frail? Pale?

- Statement of activity level. Was the student in her seat, sitting appropriately? Did the student complete the task?

- What skills were demonstrated in the lesson? (If the observer sits between the observed student and another child and asks what they are getting out of the activity, he or she has a pretty good gauge of what the student comprehended, as compared with a peer's comprehension.)

- Clues about level of language functioning through quotes, knowledge of previously taught skills, and general information level.

- Perceptional speed. Does the student respond quickly or slowly? Are responses on target or off base?

- Statement concerning the status of grooming, allergies, and so on.

- Be careful to avoid exaggerated wording. Instead of saying, "The child's hands are filthy" or "She stinks," say "His hands and face were dirty" or "She had an odor." The latter statement, when shared with the parent, may lead to information, such as that the child wets the bed or that the child hates to bathe. If the problem is something that can be worked on, such as teeth brushing or hair brushing, ask the parent if it would be helpful for the school nurse to work with the child daily on grooming skills. Parents will sometimes say they aren't home when the child gets up, so they can't supervise the grooming.

Time-on-Task Assessment

Time-on-task is defined as time engaged (looking) at the task. One obvious pattern in Robert's sample observation summaries is that he had difficulty getting started and staying on task. A follow-up observation would find out how much this affects his work. **Research has shown that for regular education students, time-on-task ranges from 60 percent to 80 percent.** (Ideally this would be 100 percent, though no one is likely to be able to stay on task for an entire fifty-minute period.) **Research shows that time-on-task for LD students ranges from 30 percent to 60 percent.**

There is a simple way to assess time-on-task. Using two strips of paper marked off into ten slots, observe two students (the observee and another student [the control] whom the teacher reports as an average student). Look at the observee for ten seconds. If he is looking at the job, mark "+"; if not, make a note as to what he is doing. For the next ten seconds, watch the other student and mark her strip. Now, using slot 2, watch the observee again for ten seconds and mark his strip. Do the same for slot 2 of the control student's strip. Continue until you have marked ten slots for both

FIGURE 6.2.

Sample Time-on-Task Observation Sheets.

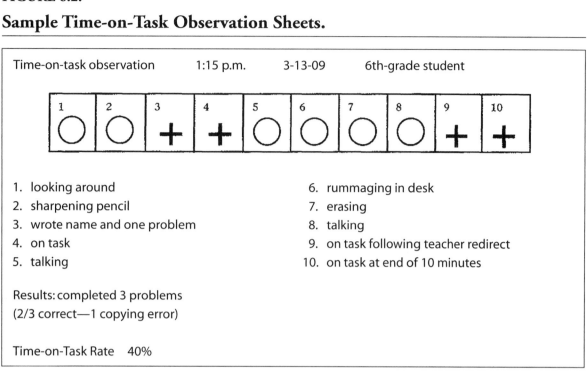

Time-on-task observation   1:15 p.m.   3-13-09   6th-grade student

1. looking around
2. sharpening pencil
3. wrote name and one problem
4. on task
5. talking

6. rummaging in desk
7. erasing
8. talking
9. on task following teacher redirect
10. on task at end of 10 minutes

Results: completed 3 problems
(2/3 correct—1 copying error)

Time-on-Task Rate   40%

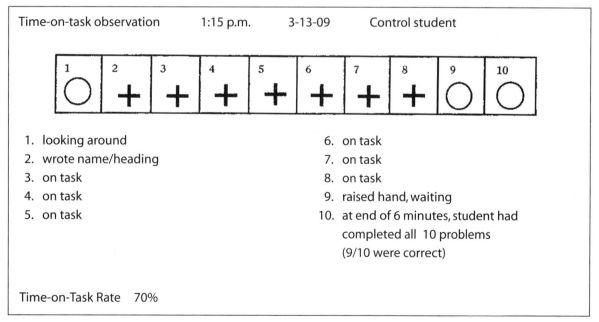

Time-on-task observation   1:15 p.m.   3-13-09   Control student

1. looking around
2. wrote name/heading
3. on task
4. on task
5. on task

6. on task
7. on task
8. on task
9. raised hand, waiting
10. at end of 6 minutes, student had
    completed all 10 problems
    (9/10 were correct)

Time-on-Task Rate   70%

students. If the student has 4 pluses, the time-on-task behavior for the sample observation is 40 percent (4 × 10). Figure 6.2 shows sample time-on-task observation sheets.

It is a good idea to do each observation on a different day and to vary the time of day, because student performance varies from day to day over the course of a day. For example, a child may be fine in the morning but inattentive after lunch.

Language Assessment

Speech and language are not the same thing.

- **Speech** involves the person's ability to make the sounds of our language.

- **Language** encompasses knowledge of word meaning, knowledge of how to put words together to form sentences, and ability to manipulate the words to convey meaning, as well as being able to produce speech.

A large percentage of LD children show language deficits. Many experience difficulty in receptive language (listening and following directions) and in expressive language (communicating their ideas and thoughts). Problems with receptive and expressive language are also signals that a child will most likely have problems with reading and writing.

There are a number of tests that can be used to assess language. The following are among those commonly used:

- The Peabody Picture Vocabulary Test–IV (PPVT-IV)
- The Test for Auditory Comprehension of Language–Revised (TACL-R)
- The Test of Adolescent and Adult Language–Fourth Edition (TOAL-4)
- Test of Early Language Development–Third Edition (TELD-3)
- Test of Language Development–Primary 3 (TOLD-P:3)
- Test of Language Development–Intermediate 3 (TOLD-I:3)

All the tests are individually administered, generally by the speech and language therapist. It is customary for this person to report the findings to the Multidisciplinary Team.

The referring teacher should observe the student's use of language by looking at

1. *Work samples.* What was the nature of the response: A word? A phrase? A complete and complex sentence? Run-on sentences?

2. *Spoken language.* How many words are used? Are utterances syntactically correct? Are tenses of verbs correct? Is vocabulary adequate to get meaning across to the listener?

3. *Listening.* Is the student able to follow conversation delivered at normal speed? Can the student remember and follow three clear, concise directions?

4. The student's *informal conversation* with peers, young children, and adults. Does the student alter interactions to fit listeners?

Health Assessment

All children who have trouble learning their school material should see a health care practitioner to rule out any physical issues that could affect school performance. For example, a child may have hearing problems due to repeated sinus or ear infections. This could affect the child's ability to follow instructions, understand assignments, and understand information during a movie or lecture. One child I knew had frequent headaches during the afternoons and late mornings, which his family physician found were caused by low blood sugar. When the student had two snacks during the day, the headaches ceased, and academic performance increased. In another case, teachers thought a student was "spacey," and perhaps had attention deficit disorder, because she also laughed at inappropriate times. Testing revealed that the girl was having frequent mild seizures and would laugh as she came out of them.

It's best to have a child evaluated for any medical conditions before jumping to conclusions about academic performance.

Behavioral Assessment

As part of any psychoeducational assessment, we need to address the individual's behavior. Behavior has an enormous impact on success, particularly on the person's ability to benefit from schooling. Assessing behavior is done through

- Multiple observations
- Interviews with parents and teachers
- Use of rating scales
- Use of personality inventories
- Use of projective tests

When assessing students, it is important to consider their adaptive behavior, including

- Ability to communicate

- Knowledge of their community
- Ability to be self-directing
- Awareness of health and safety issues
- Ability to care for themselves
- Social skills development
- Work habits and awareness of the world of work
- Use of leisure time

The school psychologist is the person who most often conducts behavioral and adaptive assessments. The psychologist chooses the testing devices most appropriate to the situation.

The classroom teacher's documentation logs can be a valuable resource in evaluating behavior. In documenting behavior, the teacher should keep a notebook that can be expanded to add further documentation as needed. When entering a notation about a child, include all playground and classroom observation summaries written about the student. Following is an example.

2-4-09   *11:35 AM*

Jon tore up his math paper and threw it on the floor. This behavior was ignored. He was quiet for the balance of the period. When asked later, he said, "I can't multiply when there are two numbers."

Summary

Following the receipt of a referral for formal assessment directly from a parent or from the Student Study Team, the Multidisciplinary Team, made up of representatives from several areas, conducts a thorough evaluation of the referred individual (see Figure 6.3 for a referral flowchart). Through the use of formal testing and informal interviews and scales, this team gathers as much information about the individual as it can within approximately two months. This information is organized into a report that will recommend possible ways to help the person referred (see Figure 6.4 for a sample formal assessment report). A meeting is then scheduled to share the results of the psychoeducational assessment with the parents (see Figure 6.5 for a sample psychoeducational assessment). In Chapter Seven, we look at the next steps in educational planning.

FIGURE 6.3.

Referral Flowchart.

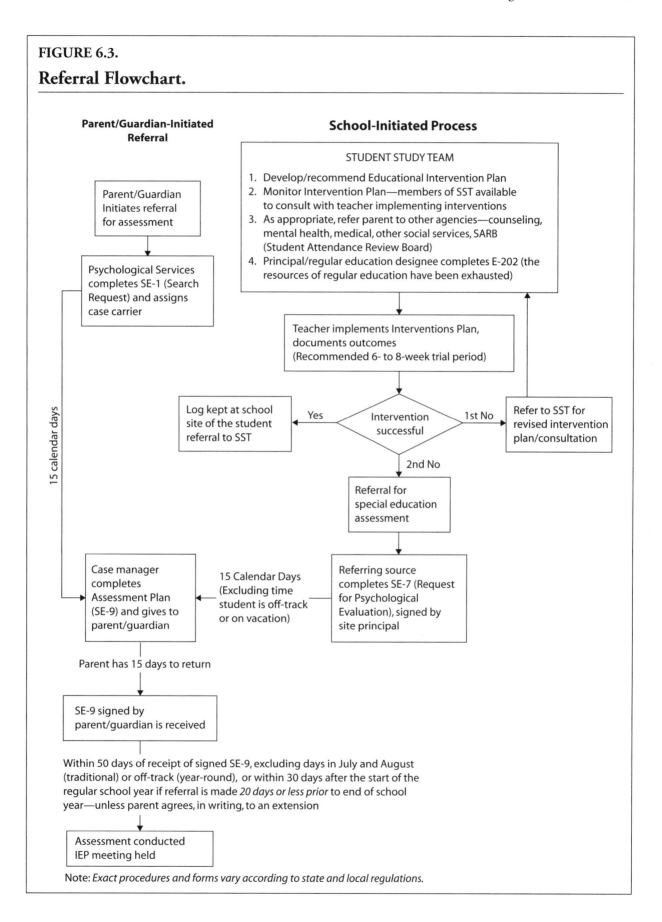

Parent/Guardian-Initiated Referral

Parent/Guardian Initiates referral for assessment

↓

Psychological Services completes SE-1 (Search Request) and assigns case carrier

School-Initiated Process

STUDENT STUDY TEAM

1. Develop/recommend Educational Intervention Plan
2. Monitor Intervention Plan—members of SST available to consult with teacher implementing interventions
3. As appropriate, refer parent to other agencies—counseling, mental health, medical, other social services, SARB (Student Attendance Review Board)
4. Principal/regular education designee completes E-202 (the resources of regular education have been exhausted)

↓

Teacher implements Interventions Plan, documents outcomes (Recommended 6- to 8-week trial period)

↓

Intervention successful

Yes → Log kept at school site of the student referral to SST

1st No → Refer to SST for revised intervention plan/consultation

2nd No ↓

Referral for special education assessment

↓

Referring source completes SE-7 (Request for Psychological Evaluation), signed by site principal

15 Calendar Days (Excluding time student is off-track or on vacation)

Case manager completes Assessment Plan (SE-9) and gives to parent/guardian

15 calendar days

Parent has 15 days to return

↓

SE-9 signed by parent/guardian is received

Within 50 days of receipt of signed SE-9, excluding days in July and August (traditional) or off-track (year-round), or within 30 days after the start of the regular school year if referral is made *20 days or less prior* to end of school year—unless parent agrees, in writing, to an extension

↓

Assessment conducted IEP meeting held

Note: *Exact procedures and forms vary according to state and local regulations.*

FIGURE 6.4.

Sample Formal Assessment Report.

Date: 1-5-2009

San Bernardino City Unified School District

MULTIDISCIPLINARY ASSESSMENT REPORT

For

Fictitious, Janet 7-9-2000
Student Name and DOB

000001
MIS Number

Liberty Elementary
School

The following individuals contributed to this report:

School Psychologist: B. Firth, PhD

School Nurse: I. Martinez

Special Education Teacher: C. Kelly

General Education Teacher: D. Langer

Language/Speech Specialist: T. Mahoney

Adapted P.E. Teacher: J. Carpo

Other:

copies: ☐ Special Education ☐ Specialist/Teacher ☐ Parent ☐ Cum

Note: *The names in this report are fictitious and in no way resemble actual persons.*

FIGURE 6.5.

Sample Psychoeducational Assessment.

SAN BERNARDINO CITY UNIFIED SCHOOL DISTRICT PSYCHOEDUCATIONAL ASSESSMENT

☒ INITIAL EVALUATION   SS # _____
☐ TRIENNIAL   ☐ OTHER _____   MIS # <u>000001</u>

I. STUDENT INFORMATION

PUPIL NAME: <u>FICTITIOUS, JANET</u>   D.O.B. <u>7-9-2000</u> AGE: <u>8-6</u> SEX: <u>F</u> GRADE: <u>3rd</u> ETHNICITY: <u>W</u>
ADDRESS: <u>011 Anystreet, Anywhere</u>   BUSINESS PHONE: <u>none</u>   HOME PHONE: <u>unlisted</u>
NAME OF PARENT/GUARDIAN ☒   SURROGATE PARENT ☐ FOSTER PARENT ☐ <u>Mr. and Mrs. Fictitious</u>
HOME LANG: <u>English</u> PUPIL PRIMARY LANG: <u>English</u> TESTING LANG: <u>English</u> LEP/NEP ☐ EO ☐ FEP ☐ U ☐
NEEDS INTERPRETER ☐   OTHER MODE OF COMMUNICATION ☐
RESIDENT SCHOOL: <u>Liberty Elementary</u> ATTENDING SCHOOL: <u>Liberty Elementary</u> TEACHER # <u>Staff</u>

II. REASON FOR REFERRAL

According to the Formal Referral, <u>Janet</u> was referred for a psychoeducational evaluation by the student study team at
<u>Liberty Elementary</u> school or his/her guardian, due to <u>X</u> school achievement; _____ school adjustment
_____ Re-evaluation of special education eligibility/placement

---

IIa. EDUCATIONAL HISTORY

Entered this district in grade <u>K</u> , date <u>9-04</u> , grades repeated <u>none</u>
Has received special education services including the following: <u>none to this date</u>

IIIb. THE RESOURCES OF THE REGULAR EDUCATION PROGRAM THAT HAVE BEEN CONSIDERED, AND, WHERE APPROPRIATE UTILIZED ARE (EC 56303):

<u>X</u>1 Individual time with the teacher and aide	___8 Adjusted seating arrangements	___14 Bilingual involvement
<u>X</u>2 Peer tutoring	___9 Behavioral interventions such as positive reinforcement, etc.	___15 Study carrels
___3 Cooperative learning groups	___10 Suspension	___16 Categorical programs
___4 Use of high interest low level materials	<u>X</u> 11 Extended time to complete assignments	___17 Consultation with counselor, principal, or other staff member
<u>X</u>5 Parent conferences	<u>X</u> 12 Use of alternative materials	___18 Site-based counseling
___6 Shortened assignments	___13 Use of concrete devices such as manipulatives	<u>X</u> 19 Student Study Team meetings
<u>X</u>7 Use of auditory and visual approaches to learning		___20 Family Support Team
		<u>X</u> 21 Other *helped as at risk*

IVa. THE RELEVANT BEHAVIORS NOTED DURING THE OBSERVATION OF THE PUPIL IN AN APPROPRIATE SETTING (EC 56327)(c). Setting <u>Janet was observed in her regular third-grade class on 12-15-07</u>

    Janet was observed, by this examiner, in her regular third-grade classroom. She sits to the left side of the room, in the middle of her row of desks. She scans the environment for clues as to the sequence of events in the class. She follows the actions of the other students to keep up with class activities. While she is quiet and shy, she is also isolated from the other students, in social communications and class activities. She appears to enjoy the class, and yet she does not appear to be happy. She is positive in her relations with the teacher and the volunteer teacher assistant in the class. While she is cooperative she is also apathetic as to school tasks, especially in written work products. Her general attitude in class could be described as insecure and unproductive.

IVb. THE RELATIONSHIP OF OBSERVED BEHAVIOR TO THE PUPIL'S ACADEMIC <u>AND</u> SOCIAL FUNCTIONING (EC 56327 (d))

    Observed behavior tended to depress student's academic functioning ☐ Yes ☒ No If yes, please specify below:
    Janet does not have behavior problems, other than her quiet, shy, withdrawn demeanor. She has good attendance and has not been referred to the office for behavior problems. She likes to take notes to the office for the teacher and enjoys helping with the children in the younger classes, especially kindergarten.

Page 1 of 3   Copies: ☐ Special Education   ☐ Specialist/Teacher   ☐ Parent   ☐ CUM
Note: *The names on this assessment form are fictitious and in no way resemble actual people.*

(continued)

107

V. ASSESSMENT (EC 56320 (a–g)), (EC 56324(a))

ABILITY/COGNITIVE TESTS MEASURE CAPABILITY FOR ACADEMIC LEARNING
____ WAIS-R, ____ WPPSI-R, ____ Slosson (SIT), ____ Stanford-Binet IV, ____ Leiter, __X__ TONI-III, __X__ WISC-III, __X__ DTLA-3, ____ McCarthy, ____ Other (Specify)_____

ACHIEVEMENT TESTS MEASURE ACTUAL ACADEMIC PERFORMANCE. MOST MEASURES DEAL WITH ACQUISITION OF BASIC SKILLS
__X__ WRAT-111, __X__ Woodcock-Johnson Achievement Test (R), ____ Brigance, __X__ Slosson (SORT), ___ Other (Specify)_____

ADAPTIVE BEHAVIOR TESTS MEASURE AN ABILITY TO COPE WITH ENVIRONMENT
__X__ Vineland, __X__ CABS, ____ Parent Interview, ____ Child Interview, ____ Other (Specify)_____

EMOTIONAL/SOCIAL TESTS MEASURE DEGREE OF ADAPTABILITY AND CONFORMITY TO SOCIAL NORMS AND EXPECTANCIES
__X__ Observation, ____ Check Lists, ____ Conners, __X__ Teacher's Report, ____ Sentence Completion, __X__ Drawings, ____ Piers Harris, ____ Other (Specify)_____

PERCEPTUAL TESTS MEASURE THE SENSES' ABILITY TO RECEIVE, PROCESS, AND EXPRESS IMPRESSIONS THROUGH AUDITORY, VISUAL, OR TACTILE CHANNELS
____ Bender, __X__ VMI, ____ VADS, ____ Motor Free Visual Perception Test, __X__ DTLA-3, ____ MAT, ____ TAPS, ____ WRAML, __X__ Other (Specify) *Test of Auditory Perception and Reasoning (TARPS)*

DEVELOPMENTAL TESTS MEASURE CONSECUTIVE GROWTH IN GROSS MOTOR, FINE MOTOR, SELF HELP, LANGUAGE, SOCIAL, INTEGRATION OF THE SENSES, ETC.
___ Denver, ___ Boyd, ___ Gesell, ___ Koontz, ___ Bayley, ___ Catell, ___ DASI-2, ___ Aopern, Boll, ___ Other (Specify) _____

VI. CURRENT ASSESSMENT BEHAVIORS

ATTENTION		X	VERBAL		X
absorbed		distracted	communicative		reticent
ACTTVITY	X		EFFORT	X	
normal		over/underactive	persistent		gives up
RESPONSE	X		INDEPENDENCE		X
quick		prompting needed	needs no praise		needs constant praise
ATTITUDE		X			
confident		distrust self			

OTHER BEHAVIORS Janet tries hard, but is easily discouraged especially with written tasks.

VII. EDUCATIONALLY RELEVANT HEALTH, DEVELOPMENTAL AND MEDICAL FINDINGS, IF ANY (EC 56327 (e))

Vision: Date 12-07   The last screenings were within normal limits (Title 5, 3027)   ☒ Yes   ☐ No
Hearing: Date 12-07   The last screenings were within normal limits (Title 5, 3027)   ☒ Yes   ☐ No
Comments: Health screening by the school nurse indicates that all areas are average, and she is not taking medication.

VIII. SUMMARY OF ASSESSMENT RESULTS (EC 56327)

Cognitive, academic, perception/processing/memory/communication

Test results will be reported as Standard Scores (average range = 85–115), or as Percentiles (average range = 16%'tile to 84%'tile). ASSESSMENT RESULTS: Chronological Age = 8 years and 6 months at the time of testing. Actual grade placement is grade 3.4 and her age is approximately three months younger than the average student in the third grade.

Test of Nonverbal Intelligence: SS = 98, 45%'tile, SEM = 5. There is 68% probability that her true intelligence score on this test is found in the range of 93–103. On the Weschler Intelligence Scale for Children—3rd. Ed.—Her Verbal IQ Index was 85, 16%'tile, Performance IQ Index was 99 (47%'tile) and the Full Scale IQ Index was 92 (31%'tile). Her general ability scores are in the average to low average range and a significant difference is present between verbal (lower) and performance skills. The difference between the two scores is close to one standard deviation of difference and may suggest learning difficulties in the verbal domain. Her overall Learning Quotient on the Detroit Test of Learning Aptitude-3, was 96, (39%'tile). On the Detroit Janet had difficulty with the Sentence Imitation, and Word Sequences subtests with the scale score for both being 6 (9%'tile). On the Developmental Test of Visual Motor Integration (VMI) she obtained a standard score of 97, (42%'tile), and this was in the average range. On the Test of Auditory Processing and Reasoning (TARPS), her standard score was 78, (7%'tile) and this score is in the borderline range. Academic skills were measured on the Wide Range Achievement Test-3: Reading = SS-75, (2%'tile), Spelling = SS-78 (7%'tile) and Arithmetic = SS 93, (33%'tile). On the Woodcock-Johnson Achievement Test-Revised she obtained the following scores—Broad Reading = 76, Broad Written Language = 83 and Broad Math = 98. Reading skills were also tested on the Slosson Oral Reading Test-Revised and her standard score for her age was 75, (5%'tile) and this score was at grade level 1.2.

Adaptive Behavior Prevocational/Vocational

Janet's teacher, Ms. D. Langer, administered the Classroom edition of the Vineland Adaptive Behavior Scale and she estimated that all domains were in the average range with the following scores: Communications Domain = 89, Daily Living Skills Domain = 9, and Socialization Domain = 102, Composite Adaptive Behavior Quotient = 94.

Social Emotional

No social or emotional problems are reported by any of the adults who serve Janet. Her parent also feels that there are no concerns in the area. Social skills on the Vineland were estimated to be in the average range with a score of 102. Projective personality drawings were not significant and were free of any emotional indicators. The drawings were age appropriate.

IX. STATEMENT OF ELIGIBILITY

The pupil may need special education and or related services EC 56327(a) and California Code of Regulations, Title 5, Section 3030(aj): Yes ☒ No ☐   If yes specify Section 3030 G, H, I, J   3030J _____

X. BASIS FOR MAKING THE DETERMINATION (EC 56327(b); 56337(a)). Check areas that apply.

 X   For pupils with learning disabilities, there is a discrepancy between achievement and ability that cannot be corrected without special education and related services ED 56327(f) _Basic Reading Skills_ EC 56337(a)

_____ No significant discrepancy exists between achievement and ability EC 56327(f)

 X   The discrepancy cannot be corrected through other regular or categorical services offered within the regular instructional program EC 56337(c)

 X   The discrepancy is due to a disorder in one or more of the basic psychological processes and is not primarily the result of environmental cultural, or economic factors EC 56337(b) _auditory processing—short term auditory memory_ (3030 j)(1)

 X   This discrepancy is not primarily the result of limited school experience, poor school attendance or multiple school changes

_____ Behavioral disruptions are not correlated with academic delays

 X   This pupil has needs that cannot be met with modification of the regular instructional program EC 56302

 X   The student's academic delays are not due to limited or non-English language status

 X   Test results are considered reliable and valid EC 56320 (a & b)

_____ Significant delays exist in cognitive and adaptive skills, which have been present since early development, and which adversely affect educational performance (3030 h)

_____ Because of a serious emotional disturbance, one or more of the following characteristics have been exhibited over a long period of time and to a marked degree, which adversely affect educational performance: an inability to learn which cannot be explained by intellectual, sensory, or health factors; an inability to build or maintain satisfactory interpersonal relationships with peers and teachers; inappropriate types of behavior or feelings under normal circumstances exhibited in several situations; a general pervasive mood of unhappiness or depression; a tendency to develop physical symptoms or fears associated with personal or school problems (3030~(I–5))

_____ The student exhibits a combination of behaviors, including: 1) the inability to use oral language for appropriate communication; 2) history of extreme withdrawal or relating to people inappropriately and continued impairment in social interaction from infancy through early childhood, 3) obsession to maintain sameness; 4) preoccupation with objects; 5) resistance to controls; 6) peculiar motoric mannerisms and motility patterns; 7) self stimulating, ritualistic behavior (3030 g)

_1-5-2009_
Date

_____
School Psychologist's Signature

Chapter 7

Planning for the Student with Learning Disabilities

Auguste Rodin (1840–1917)

French sculptor
Was believed to be learning disabled; was referred to by teacher as "uneducable" and "the worst boy in school"

Contributions:

Sculpture: *The Thinker*
              The Burghers of Calais
              Eve
              The Age of Bronze

In earlier chapters, we discussed the Student Study Team, the first level of support for struggling students, and often the most informal support group designed to monitor and increase student performance. In Chapter Six, we discussed the roles of the Multidisciplinary Team in evaluating and working with a student. After the Multidisciplinary Team meets and writes up a report, what happens next? This report and the team's findings are then shared with the parents or caregivers.

School district personnel will contact the parents or caregivers and request a meeting to discuss the findings of the Multidisciplinary Team and the test results. During this meeting, parents have a chance to hear the results of the evaluations and the feedback for the beginnings of an educational plan.

The meeting usually begins with team members presenting their observations and the results of their assessments. To parents this can sound as if everyone were speaking a foreign language, as team members may throw out such terms as "standard deviation," "percentile rank," and "age equivalency." Parents are often reluctant to ask for explanations; it is up to teachers as well as those using the unfamiliar terminology to explain what they are saying in everyday language. Parents may want to bring an advocate with them to this meeting or just another person to listen and take notes.

When the assessment process is completed, the members of the Multidisciplinary Team convene a meeting. The purpose of this meeting is twofold:

1. To share the information that has been gathered with the parents, the classroom teacher, and the principal

2. To look at the resources available to meet the student's needs

Eligibility Issues

When using a norm-referenced test, such as the Wide Range Achievement Test (WRAT) or the Peabody Individual Achievement Test (PIAT), we need to explain that the child's performance is being compared with that of other children of the same age who have taken the same test.

When giving scores in percentiles, we need to explain that a child whose score is close to the 50th percentile is making average progress for her age and grade. Percentile scores run along a bell curve.

For a child who scores below the 10th percentile in memory to gain facility in addition, subtraction, multiplication, and division facts, teachers are going to have to drill! drill! drill! This child may need to use a calculator to do math work. Some teachers feel it is unfair to allow one child to use a calculator when the other children aren't allowed to use one. The child with short-term memory scores below the 10th percentile has a disability. Just as we would not think of taking a hearing aid from a child who depends on it, we need to consider that this memory-challenged child also needs an assistive device—the calculator—in order to keep up with others in math class. *If a child needs a calculator or other assistive device, avoid any controversy by indicating so in the IEP; that way it does not become an issue of teacher discretion.*

How do you explain a score given as an age equivalency? If a child who is 9 years old earns an age-equivalent score of 5.6, this indicates that on the skill tested, the child is functioning at a level similar to what would be expected from a child age five years six months. Among children who qualify for special education, it is not uncommon to find discrepancies of several years in memory, language development, or visual perception. If the child has severe visual perceptual deficits, he can be expected to have great trouble copying from the board and from a book. His handwriting, spacing, and neatness will all be affected. We might decide to postpone teaching cursive handwriting. We want to allow a child to master reading and writing printed letters before going on to cursive writing. Learning word processing on the computer might be a boon for this child as a way to encourage neater assignments.

If expressed as a grade equivalent, a score of 2.3 would mean the child is functioning like an average child in the second grade, third month of school. Would this child be ready to tackle long division? Possibly, but most likely not. To expect her to read aloud would almost certainly be very embarrassing, frustrating, and defeating, and quite likely might result in "acting out." When this child reads aloud, she should be reading from a grade 2 text or a high-interest, low-vocabulary text so that she can experience success and be introduced to words she understands.

Not all scores of age or grade equivalency are completely accurate representations of what a student knows or understands. Curriculum standards may vary from state to state or even from school district to school district, and this can affect grade-equivalent scores. Age-equivalent scores may give an overall picture of where a student has knowledge deficits, but because of the wide variations among state regulations and in content among school districts, these are not necessarily more accurate in diagnosing learning disabilities. Age-based or grade-based scores can be used as a basic flag, but they should not be used as a determinative factor for assessing a student's functioning.

Stanine scores run from a low of 1 to a high of 9, with 5 being average. A score of 6 or 7 would be above average. A score of 4 would be below average.

Intelligence tests produce scores that are plotted along a bell curve (see Figures 7.1 and 7.2). The mean is obtained when the scores of a large group of participants of the same age are added together and then divided by the number of participants. The mean IQ is 100. Statistically, 68 percent of people will obtain scores that fall between –1 and +1 standard deviations (15 points) from the mean, or, in lay terms, between 85 and 115.

130+	Very superior	about 2% of the population
120–129	Superior	about 7% of the population
110–119	High average	about 16% of the population
90–109	Average	about 50% of the population
80–89	Low average	about 16% of the population
70–79	Borderline	about 7% of the population
Below 69	Mentally retarded	about 2% of the population

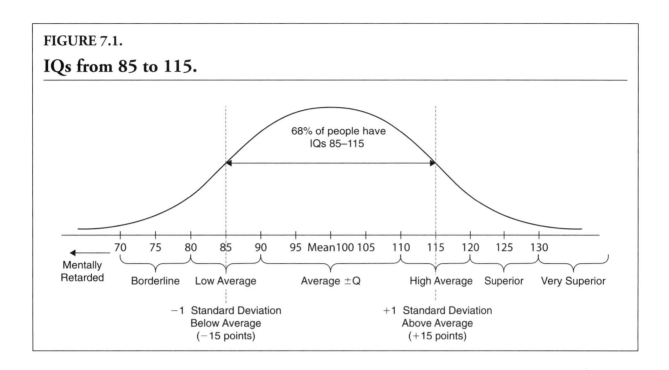

FIGURE 7.1.

IQs from 85 to 115.

68% of people have
IQs 85–115

70 75 80 85 90 95 Mean 100 105 110 115 120 125 130

Mentally
Retarded

Borderline   Low Average   Average ±Q   High Average   Superior   Very Superior

−1 Standard Deviation
Below Average
(−15 points)

+1 Standard Deviation
Above Average
(+15 points)

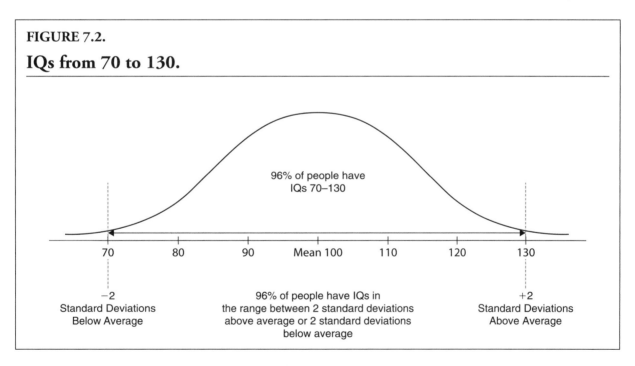

FIGURE 7.2.

IQs from 70 to 130.

96% of people have
IQs 70–130

70   80   90   Mean 100   110   120   130

−2
Standard Deviations
Below Average

96% of people have IQs in
the range between 2 standard deviations
above average or 2 standard deviations
below average

+2
Standard Deviations
Above Average

The Discrepancy Model

This model was previously used to award services for students with learning disabilities; it is no longer considered the only method for determining eligibility for services. In fact, many school districts assess students based on their test scores, schoolwork, and evaluation by a team of professionals (as discussed in Chapter Six). Originally the discrepancy model held that students must show a large "discrepancy" between their test scores in order to receive special education services. In other words, the student had to score very high in one area of the test and very low in another in order to prove that a learning problem existed.

The theory held that if students scored well in one area but not in another, another factor—like a learning problem—could cause the discrepancy between the test scores. Then, if the discrepancy was large enough, the student could be awarded services.

There are many problems with this model, one being that only a severe difference in test scores could cause a child to be labeled as having a learning problem. In reality, many children could score at an overall low, all the way across the board, but still not receive services. This system left a lot of low-functioning students out of the funding system because they never had one high test score to compare with a low one.

The discrepancy model just isn't a complete measure of a student's progress, and it shouldn't be used as the sole method of determining funding for students who are struggling.

Exclusionary Criteria

Question: Can a child who is mentally retarded be learning disabled?

Answer: Technically, no. Mental retardation is a handicapping condition in its own right. You will often find children who are having much difficulty in school; they are two or three years behind grade level, but they do not qualify for special education because their IQs fall between 75 and 84, which is too high to qualify for service under the mental retardation category. Their achievement is low, but it is not significantly below what would be expected based on their lower potential, and they may not qualify for services under IDEA. They may, however, fall under the umbrella of Section 504.

• • •

Question: Can a student who is mentally gifted be learning disabled?

Answer: A resounding yes. These students may qualify for assistance from special education if their achievement is not commensurate with their ability. Unfortunately, if they are able to meet minimum grade standards, they may never get referred, never get identified, and often remain underachievers for life.

• • •

Question: Can a student who is emotionally disturbed be learning disabled?

Answer: There are youngsters who are both LD and disturbed. But an emotional disturbance is completely different from a learning disability, and emotional disturbances are more likely to be associated with forms of criminal behavior.

• • •

Question: Can students with medical conditions be learning disabled?

Answer: There are students who have medical conditions and learning disabilities. In these cases, the IEP team must carefully analyze where and how the student needs to be served, and who will provide services.

• • •

Question: Can a student who is culturally deprived and who is a low achiever be served?

Answer: Yes. These students may show the severe discrepancy in test scores and may have low receptive and expressive language due to environmental influences. IEP teams must carefully look at each child's situation. The decision lies with the team and the policies of the school district, but parents may appeal the decision if they don't agree.

Assessment Scores and Their Implication for Learning

When younger, I put more stock in assessment scores than I do now. I have seen students with high IQs and mild disabilities, who should be expected to do well with extra help, make minimal progress, and I have seen kids who appeared to have every strike against them surprise all of us. Student motivation and parental involvement can work miracles.

Identified students usually continue to need assistance for the remainder of their school years. The research suggests that some LD students show less than a year's gain for each year of instruction, which results in a cumulative deficit (Deshler, Schumaker, and Lenz, 1984).

Profiles of two children are presented here. Both have problems learning. The profile in Figure 7.3 belongs to the kind of child typically placed in a resource specialist program. The child has average ability; his verbal scores are lower than his performance scores. The implication for learning is that this child will benefit from specific drills that help him gain general information. For example, "Jon will be asked twenty questions, three times

---

FIGURE 7.3.

Profile with Below-Average Verbal IQ Score.

Verbal		Performance	
Information	7	Picture completion	13
Similarities	10	Picture arrangement	10
Arithmetic	8	Block design	10
Vocabulary	8	Object assembly	10
Digit span	10	Coding	10
Verbal IQ = 94		**Performance IQ = 104**	
	Full Scale IQ = 98		

*Portion of scores taken from WISC-R

FIGURE 7.4.

Profile with Very Low Verbal IQ Score.

Verbal		Performance	
Information	6	Picture completion	12
Similarities	5	Picture arrangement	8
Arithmetic	6	Block design	11
Vocabulary	3	Object assembly	11
Digit span	4	Coding	13
Verbal IQ = 68		**Performance IQ = 106**	
	Full Scale IQ = 85		

---

a week, until he can answer all correctly three days in a row." The list of twenty facts for him to learn might include "How many inches in a yard?" "How many items make a dozen?" "How many minutes in an hour?" "Where is your cranium?" This type of child would also benefit from activities that help develop his vocabulary.

The second child's profile, shown in Figure 7.4, is that of a child who has a severe language disability. He has trouble expressing himself orally and on paper. He is in a special day class. He is miserable in school and, at the age of twelve, says he will quit school as soon as he can. He enjoys the computer. This student has very limited reading and math skills. He needs training in phonemic awareness and phonics and in basic math skills; he also needs texts for his grade level presented in a digital format to help him catch up on the content areas for his grade level.

If all scores are below 5, the child is in the range of mental retardation. If all scores are above 10 and some are above 14, the student may be gifted.

Eligible or Not Eligible? Developing the Individual Education Plan (IEP)

If the Multidisciplinary Team decides that a student qualifies for special education services and the family wants that kind of help, an Individual Education Plan (IEP) will be developed—usually during the meeting.

If the student meets the criteria for help under Section 504 of the Rehabilitation Act of 1973 (see Chapter Three, "Understanding the Laws"), then the Multidisciplinary Team will discuss and write a plan for the student that outlines what the school staff must do to help the child in the way of modifications and accommodations. A 504 document should be developed when it is clear that the student has a learning disability but does not meet the "severe discrepancy" requirement or other regulations for placement.

If the student does not meet the criterion set forth under IDEA or Section 504, the Multidisciplinary Team should refer the student back to the Student Study Team for further follow-up.

Choosing the Appropriate Educational Setting ("Least Restrictive Environment")

As noted earlier in the book, if the student is eligible for special education services, the law requires the student to be placed in the "least restrictive environment." We want students to be in the mainstream classroom as much as possible. Many factors are considered when determining what is the best situation for each individual child. In general, students who are fairly well adjusted and can perform some of the skills required in their regular classroom will remain in their classroom for the majority of the day, with resource assistance as needed or as determined by the IEP. Sometimes the Resource Specialist meets with the student in a resource room.

Most teams will almost automatically assign a student to regular education with resource support, with the thought that, until proven otherwise, that is the least restrictive environment.

When a student has severe deficits in most areas, needs modification of all assignments, and requires slower pacing of work, then a special day class may be recommended.

Most identified students will be served either in regular class with resource support or in a special day class. There are other environments where LD students are sometimes served, including classes for the severely emotionally disturbed, through home or hospital teaching, or in special schools if their needs require that.

The IEP team will consider the student's behavioral and disciplinary needs and, as needed, will develop plans for improvement. The team will consider whether the student requires special accommodations for assessment. Students with LD often do better when they are tested in small groups and (if possible) given additional time, and when distractions are minimized. Some students require assistive technology (calculator, spell-check program) during testing and are legally entitled to it.

Determining the Number of Hours

After deciding where a student will be served, the team must determine how many hours of assistance will be required. If the student is to be in regular class all day, with the Resource Specialist (RSP) coming into the room, this may involve minimal hours, perhaps one or two a week. For this assistance the student might leave the regular classroom to go to a resource room. The student can legally spend up to 49 percent of his school day there, but often that amount of time is not necessary. As a rule of thumb, each written goal requires approximately twenty minutes of instruction each day. Most RSP students work on three to four goals, so one to one-and-a-half hours a day is sufficient to achieve steady progress.

When writing goals for a special-day-class student, it is desirable to write goals in all deficit subject areas, such as reading, writing, and math, and in social studies and science as well. If a student is placed in a special day class, the IEP team may suggest that the student be mainstreamed into one or more regular classes if possible. The classes most often chosen are science, social studies, art, music, and physical education.

Writing Appropriate, Measurable Objectives

The type of objectives will be influenced by student placement. If the student is in regular class, the objectives will resemble the regular class curriculum. To illustrate, in a regular grade 4 class, there is an instructional range of about 3.0 to 4.9. The goal for an LD student reading at the 3.0 level might be that the child will improve in reading skills. The short-term objectives might be written as follows:

- Given twice-weekly practice sessions, using lists of twenty vc/cv words taken from the grade 4 text, Jeremy will orally decode the words. Requirement will be met when he can do this task at the 80 percent level on three consecutive days.

- Jeremy will learn to recognize twenty new vocabulary words from the grade 4 reader, matching them with their synonyms and using ten words correctly in oral sentences.

- Jeremy will read aloud to an adult for fifteen minutes a day from a reading book at his functional level, receiving immediate feedback of results.

The Purpose of Goals

The IEP is the teacher's road map for instruction. It takes training and experience to write goals that challenge students at just the right level of difficulty. Discussion and collaboration by the Resource Specialist and regular teacher on the writing of goals for the LD student in a regular class are not only desirable but required.

Goals that are too difficult may result in failure, and more failure is the last thing any student needs. Writing too few goals also can be a problem—lawsuits have been filed and damages collected over that issue. It is good policy to write goals in each academic area. When these are achieved, a special IEP review can be scheduled to write additional goals. There is psychological value in being able to report to parents that their child has met all her goals early and satisfactorily and is ready to move on.

An IEP must be "individualized," but that does not mean that every child's IEP will look different from all others. A goal is individualized when it meets the obvious needs of the student for whom it is written.

As goals are written, it is wise to consider how that goal, and that child, can be integrated with other students for instruction. This will allow small-group work rather than requiring time-consuming interaction with only one individual at a time.

Dissenting Opinions

Team members should not agree to do something if they have no intention of doing it. **The IEP is a legally binding contract between the school and the parent. If the IEP states that someone will work with the student four to five hours a week, this must occur. Failure to do so opens staff and the district to a possible lawsuit and payment of damages. If an IEP states, for example, that a student may use a calculator to do a test, you must furnish the calculator, regardless of whether or not that meshes with your philosophy of education.**

If a staff member does not agree with a recommendation, he should state so, and explain his objections. If, after discussion, the issue remains unresolved, a dissenting opinion may be written. Although dissenting opinions are rarely filed, the option is available.

Reviews of the IEP

There are three types of review processes.

The Annual Review

Once a year, parents and staff are required to sit down and review the student's progress. This is a time to share what the student has accomplished and write goals for the next year. The principal, special education teacher, and regular teacher meet with the parent for this annual review.

The Triennial Review

Every three years, the entire Multidisciplinary Team goes through the process of assessment to determine ongoing eligibility and need for services.

Special Reviews

A review can be called any time. If parents have a concern, they can request a review; if a student is not making progress, the teacher should ask for a review. If goals are met early, new ones should be written.

Due Process

There are times when issues between parents and a school district cannot be resolved. When this occurs, parents have a right to have the matter reviewed, mediated, and settled through due process. This process is called an *impartial hearing*. The impartial hearing is designed to hear both sides of an issue and to resolve it fairly through a third party. Either the school district or the parents can initiate this process. Most disagreements are resolved prior to an impartial hearing due to time and money concerns for both parties. A good description of this process is provided in *Parents' Complete Special Education Guide,* by Roger Pierangelo and Robert Jacoby (1996).

•   •   •

A portion of an IEP appears in Figure 7.5.

FIGURE 7.5.

Sample Individual Education Plan.

SAN BERNARDINO CITY UNIFIED SCHOOL DISTRICT SELPA
INDIVIDUALIZED EDUCATION PROGRAM

Purpose of Meeting
- ☐ Interim Placement
- ☐ Initial Meeting
- ☒ Annual Review
- ☐ 3 yr. Assessment
- ☐ Other _____

Data Change Only
- ☐ Return from Reg. Ed.
- ☐ Behavior Conference
- ☐ Change of Placement

Timeline Information (Dates)
12/8/98	Initial IEP
12/8/98	Entered/Returned to SELPA
12/8/98	Last Annual Review
12//00	Next Annual Review
/_/	Current 3 Yr. Review
12//01	Next 3 Yr. Review Due

Meeting Date: **2-15-00**

Student Name: **Justin Smith** DOB: **8-9-89** CA: **10-7**

Student #: **000 000** S.S.#: _____ Grade: **4** Track: **A**

Sex: ☒ M ☐ F Ethnicity: **Caucasian**

Parent/Guardian/Surrogate: **Ms. Reba**

Address: **635 Anywhere Lane, SB 92400**

Student's Address (if different): _____

Telephone (H): **none** (W): _____

Residency: ☐ Parent/Guardian ☐ LCI# _____ ☐ Foster #

Educational Rights held by: _____

Documentation: ☐ Parent Representative Form ☐ Court Minute Order

District of Residence: **SBCUSD** Home School: **Lovett**

School of Attendance: **Lovett** If not home school, rationale _____

Preschool Only: ☐ Home ☐ Classroom

ELIGIBILITY
- ☐ Not Eligible (199)
- ☒ Specific Learning Disability (090)
- ☐ Speech or Language Impaired (040)
- ☐ Hard of Hearing (020)
- ☐ Visually Impaired (050)
- ☐ Other Health Impaired (080)
- ☐ Mentally Retarded (010)
- ☐ Emotionally Disturbed (060)
- ☐ Traumatic Brain Injury (130)
- ☐ Deaf (030)
- ☐ Deaf/Blind (100)
- ☐ Orthopedically Impaired (070)
- ☐ Autistic (120)
- ☐ Multihandicapped (110)
- ☐ Non-categorical (190) (ages 0–2 only)
- ☐ RIS ☐ Non-RIS (Preschool 3–5 only)

Student's Language: **English** Home Lang.: **English**

Primary (First) Lang.: **English** Proficiency: ☐ LEP ☐ FEP ☐ EO

Determined by: **IPT** Date: **12-98**

English Level: _____ Primary Lang. Level: _____

Primary Language of Instruction: **Eng**

Linguistically appropriate Goals/Objectives needed: ☐ Yes ☒ No

Interpreter: ☐ Yes ☒ No Translation request: ☐ Yes ☒ No

Preschool Only: ☐ Home ☐ Classroom

SERVICES:

Transportation: ☐ Yes ☐ No Specify: 1 2 3 ④ 5 6 7 (circle one)

Justification: **district policy**

Extended School Year: ☐ Yes ☒ No

Justification: _____

Low Incidence: ☐ Yes ☒ No

Justification: _____

Special Education: **13** % of time

General Education: **87** % of time

PROGRAM/DESIGNATED INSTRUCTION AND SERVICES
(Provided only during the school term unless otherwise specified)

PROGRAM	AGENCY	SERVICE DELIVERY MODEL INCLUDING LOCATION (Lovitt)	TO/FROM (Dates)	FREQUENCY (Sessions per week)	TIME (Minutes per session)
☐ Regular Education Only					
☒ 420 Resource Specialist Program		Collaboration, Inclusion, pull out	2/00 to 12/00	4x	60
☐ 430 Special Day Class					
☐ 440 Non-Public School/Agency					
410 DIS Instruction	Begin/Cont.	Exit			
☐ (50) Speech	☐	☐			
☐ (51) Home/Hospital	☐	☐			
☐ (52) APE	☐	☐			
☐ (66) Vision Services	☐	☐			
☐ Other	☐	☐			

Special Education Exit Date _____

☐ 70 Return to Regular Education Class ☐ 71 Grad Requirements ☐ 73 Maximum Age ☐ 74 Dropped Out ☐ 78 Parent Withdrawal ☐ 79 Student Withdrawal (over 18) ☐ 80 Move

White—District Office   Yellow—Teacher   Green—Special Education Clerk   Pink—Parent   Goldenrod—Cum File

Note: The name used in this sample IEP is fictitious and in no way resembles an actual person.

FIGURE 7.5.

Sample Individual Education Plan (continued).

Student Name _Justin Anyone_

Individualized Education Program
Present Levels of Performance

Reading: _Currently reading at mid-3rd-grade level. Decoding skills are weak._

Writing Expression: _Writes 1-2 paragraph stories and is assisted with editing for spelling._

Math: _at grade level_

Communication: _age appropriate_

Fine/Gross Motor: _age appropriate_

Social/Emotional: _Cooperative and gets along well with adults._

Behavior: _Good self-control but needs encouragement; timid to attempt new tasks. Likes 1-on-1_

Regular District discipline procedures apply: ☒ Yes   ☐ No
☐ Behavior Interventions needed: IEP Goals _____ Positive Behavioral Plan _____
Behavioral Contract _____ Other _____

White—District Office   Yellow—Teacher

Date: _2-15-00_ _____

Vision: _20/20_   Hearing: _WNL_
Health: _no health concerns,_
had tested for ADD and did not qualify.

Daily Living Skills: _age appropriate_

Career/Vocational: _science field—maybe nursing or x-ray technician_

Community Participation: _soccer, Sunday school_

Student Learning Strengths/Preferences: _Auditory learner, loves math and excels in this area._

Parent priorities for enhancing the long-term education for the student:
To improve reading and spelling. Parent wants child to attend jr. college program.

Impact of disability: How does it affect the student's involvement & progress in general curriculum? _Reading and writing are well below grade level._

Green—Special Education Clerk   Pink—Parent   Goldenrod—Cum File

(continued)

FIGURE 7.5.

Sample Individual Education Plan (continued).

Student Name: _Justin Anyone_   Date: _2-15-00_

Comments/Summary:

- IEP team (Ms. Reba, Ms. Ferme, Mr. Perez, and Mr. Jones) met for Justin's annual review. Report card conference was held at the same time. Justin continues to do well in math but is below grade level in reading and writing skills. All goals written previously were met. New goals were written for areas of reading and writing. Parent reports they are doing reading practice daily and working on vocabulary development.

- Justin's behavior is good but he continues to require much teacher 1:1 attention in the form of keeping him on-task; and assurances that what he has done is correct several times within a 60 minute session with Rsp. In regular classroom he requires even more reassurance.

- Parent would like Justin to take standardized tests without modifications. Parent rights were given.

White—District Office   Yellow—Teacher   Green—Special Education Clerk   Pink—Parent   Goldenrod—Cum File

FIGURE 7.5.
Sample Individual Education Plan (continued).

Student Name: _Justin Anyone_   Date: _2/15/00_

San Bernardino City Unified School District
Program Options and Rationale

This provides written notice in a language that is understandable to the general public of actions proposed or refused and the placement options considered at this meeting; the reasons for the decisions made; each evaluation, test, record, or report that was relied upon by the IEP Team in making its recommendations; and a description of other relevant factors considered. That explanation is contained here:

OPTIONS CONSIDERED:

	Considered	Recommended
General Education	☒	☐
Designated Instruction and Services	☐	☐
Resource Specialist	☒	☒
Special Day Class (Non-severe)	☐	☐
Special Day Class (Severe)	☐	☐
County Referral	☐	☐
Non Public School	☐	☐
State Special School Referral	☐	☐
Home/Hospital	☐	☐
Instruction in non-classroom setting	☐	☐
Alternative Education	☐	☐
Other: _____	☐	☐

REGULAR PROGRAM PARTICIPATION

Physical Education	☒
Modified Physical Education	☐
Lunch, Recess, Passing Periods	☒
School Day Activities	☒
Bilingual Program/ESL	☐
Title 1	☐
Migrant	☐
Electives:	☐

Academic Areas:
- Language Arts: X
- Social Studies: X
- Math: X
- Science: X

_15%_ of time in Special Education

Reason for Decision: _Student continues to qualify and is in need of Special Educ services. Student unable to progress in general education without special education support._

Tests, Evaluation, and Information Relied Upon: _psychological report, class performance, running records, writing samples, observation by teacher and psychologist_

Other Relevant Factors: _____

Justification: What are the reasons for service delivery outside the general education classroom?: _Student has a visual processing deficit and requires Rsp services for this deficit._

For students with a specific learning disability: A severe discrepancy exists between ability and achievement as a result of a disorder in:

☐ Attention   ☒ Visual Processing   ☐ Auditory Processing   ☐ Sensory-Motor Skills   ☐ Cognitive Abilities

☒ Discrepancy cannot be corrected through general education even with interventions or categorical services.   ☒ Discrepancy is not a result of visual, hearing or motor impairment, mental retardation, environment, cultural or economic conditions.

White—District Office   Yellow—Teacher   Green—Special Education Clerk   Pink—Parent   Goldenrod—Cum File

Note: The name used in this sample IEP is fictitious and in no way resembles a real person.

(continued)

FIGURE 7.5.
Sample Individual Education Plan (continued).

Student Name: _Justin Anyone_   Date: _2/15/00_

San Bernardino City Unified School District
Supports and Services

Program modifications and support by school personnel to progress in general education
and/or activities: _modified (shortened) assignments_
at lower level; preferential seating near teacher
due to problems remaining on-task/need for
reassurance

Special Factors:

Blind/Visually Impaired: Braille Instruction/Use   ❑ Yes   ❑ No

Deaf/Hearing Impaired Communication Needs: _n/a_

Communication Mode: _____

Low Incidence Materials: _n/a_

Related to Goal(s): # _____

Assistive Technology Devices and Services: _not needed_
at this time

State and District Assessments:

☒ Without Modifications/Accommodations

❑ With Modifications/Accommodations

❑ Alternate Assessments—Justification: _____

Specify: _____

Physical Education:

☒ General Education

❑ Modified

❑ Specially Designed

❑ Adapted Physical Education

High School Proficiency Standards: _n/a_

❑ General Education Proficiency Standards

Date Met: Math _____ Reading _____ Writing _____

❑ Modified Proficiency Standards

Specify _____

❑ Differential Standards

❑ High School Credits to date _____

Methods of Reporting Progress Toward Goals:

☒ Quarterly   ❑ Trimester   ❑ Semester

❑ Other   By (means of reporting)
general education
parent–teacher conference

Mainstream activities to provide support for transition into general education:

• _peer tutor_

• _materials from resource room_
that mirror general ed curriculum

• _use of intermittent reminders & rewards_
to increase attention span while reading

• _self-evaluation form to internalize need for_
attention

Comments/Summary:

_____

_____

_____

_____

White—District Office   Yellow—Teacher   Green—Special Education Clerk   Pink—Parent   Goldenrod—Cum File

Chapter 8

Classroom Management for Teachers

Thomas Alva Edison (1847–1931)

American inventor
His teacher suggested that his mother take him out of school after only three months because he was so "addled." His father thought he was "stupid."

Contributions:

Science: Invented the incandescent electric light, the phonograph, the motion picture camera and projector, the alkaline storage battery, the multiplex telegraph, and the stock-ticker tape; patented over one thousand inventions

---

Creating an Attractive and Useful Classroom

One of the first tasks a teacher must undertake is to create a welcoming classroom—turning a jumble of furniture and blank walls into an environment where students will feel safe, comfortable, and accepted.

First, make sure the room is clean. Some students are willing to help clean in exchange for an ice cream or materials you no longer have use for. Sort, organize, dust, and put things you will use in places where you can access them quickly. Give away, recycle, or dispose of items you will not use.

Next, organize the furniture in a way that fits what you will be doing. Traditional rows facing the front make you and the board the focal point. For other kinds of arrangement, try the following:

- If you like to have students work in groups, put the furniture in clusters of four.

- If you like to have students perform, use an arrangement that allows all students an equal opportunity to see and hear. Create a "stage" by arranging desks in a horseshoe.

FIGURE 8.1.

The Writing Game.

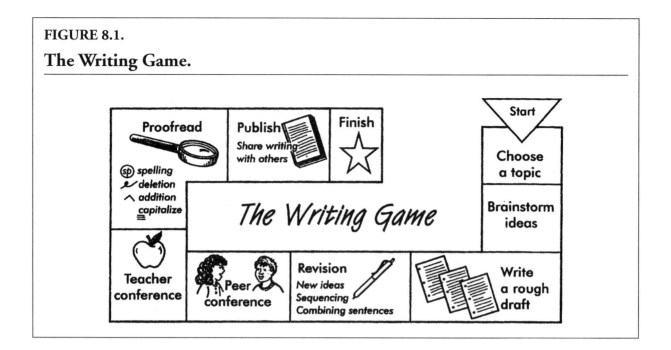

- If having children work in centers is your preference, think about placement that limits more active groups to one area of the room. Quiet areas, such as the library corner, writing center, or independent work spaces, should take place away from the more active areas.

Finally, add the decorative touches that make the room feel more cozy—an easy chair or two, a table lamp and pictures on your desk, and plants around the room. Pathos is a good indoor plant because it can live in a wide variety of conditions and requires only weekly watering. A mobile in a corner and a fish tank of colorful fish add interest. A globe is an essential item.

If the bulletin boards are dirty and in bad shape, cover them with new colored paper or cloth. Hang your classroom rules and a calendar. Use other boards to display student work in various subjects or information on strategies. Strategy boards are often left up all year and are referred to on a regular basis. Figure 8.1 shows an example of a strategy board.

Now you are ready to fill your classroom with the equipment needed, such as paper, pencils, overhead projector, and texts.

Planning the First Week's Activities

During the first week, you will need time to get acquainted with students. It is better to err in favor of too many activities than too few. While students are working, you want to be free to circulate among students, provide positive feedback, recognize talents, observe work habits, solve problems that arise, and teach classroom rules. It is wise to choose activities that

- Are simple to do
- Appeal to a variety of interests
- Involve reinforcement of previously learned material
- Build feelings of belonging to the group
- Allow students to be successful

These are some sample activities:

- Put a name tag on each child. Give each child an index card and ask all of them to go to a certain part of the room associated with the month they were born. On the card, have them write the names of classmates who share the same birth month. You can later use this information to make a list of birthdays.
- Instruct children to form groups according to their age.
- Pair students. Have them fill out a paper about their partner's favorite food and favorite activity at home and at school. Then ask partners to introduce each other to the group.
- Have children nominate and vote on a class name and mascot.

Behavioral Management Considerations

Positive Reinforcement

Positive behavioral reinforcement as a form of classroom management works better than negative disciplinary techniques; however, when discipline is necessary, it's important not to yell at or embarrass the student. Consistently providing rewards or incentives for positive behavior helps maintain a stable and happy classroom environment. When you think about it, all of us respond to motivating factors, both extrinsic (for example, money) and intrinsic (for pride in accomplishment or enjoyment of the activity).

By figuring out what elements can be used for positive reinforcement of good behavior, you have won half the battle of managing your class. Try to seek some immediate rewards, ones that will give instant gratification in the case of a hard job (such as stickers, a short break, time to work on a fun project, and so on) in order to reinforce the work habits you would like to see in the classroom.

A common mistake teachers make is assuming that students should come in and be ready to work in a classroom. We never know what the child has experienced at home before coming to school, whether or not someone has picked on her right upon entering the classroom, or if he has failed with the same material in the past. Start the children off with a simple activity when they come into the classroom for a positive start, and then introduce the methods behind the difficult lesson.

Children want to know why they are learning and how the subject applies to them and their interests. Sometimes there is nothing innately rewarding for the student in completing an activity of rote memorization (such as memorizing her multiplication tables), so a reward (motivator) helps direct her. An immediate outside reward for tackling tough subjects might be the most motivating factor for students to begin studying something they don't like.

I was working with preschool children who were told by an aide that they were to sit at the art table and cut out their project. One little boy did not want to cut out his shape. He had trouble with scissors and wanted to go to the computer. He kept stalling, dropping his material, and asking when he could be done. The aide repeatedly told the boy that he was not going to get computer time if he did not cut out his snowman. The little boy was frustrated and asked more times than was polite, all the while bouncing in his seat, arguing, and not cutting out his shape. The aide retaliated by taking away his computer time entirely for the day.

When the boy realized that his computer time was taken away for the entire day, he cried, and his behavior was intractably bad for the rest of the school day. The situation might have been changed if the aide had offered the computer time, or extra time, as a reward. By removing the only incentive she had to get the boy to work on a task that was hard for him, the aide removed all motivation and sentenced both herself and the young student to a day of frustration.

What motivates students may not be the subject matter, but perhaps the way they get to present it. Or perhaps the students need a reward such as an extra break, or maybe time to work on the computers when they are tackling a difficult subject. The first rule of classroom management is to use positive behavioral reinforcements in order to help keep your students motivated and willing to work.

Rules

The first week will be a period of familiarizing students with rules. Many districts provide a poster of rules for teachers to hang in their classrooms. If this is not available, you may make your own. Here is a sample list:

1. Do your work.

2. Be kind. Respect others and their property.

3. Let others work. Let your teacher teach.

You will also want to train students to respond to a signal. With younger ones, "One, two, three, eyes on me" seems to work. Looking at someone who continues to talk when you've requested quiet usually results in compliance. Using a rain-stick is a pleasant way to gain the attention of older students. You can request them to be quiet by the time you tilt the rain-stick three times. Another signal is to hold up a peace sign and count to five. Students can make a game of freezing and covering their mouth.

During the first week, be kind but firm about your expectations. "Jason, this is a quiet work period. You may not talk to Alex right now. Which rule are you violating?" (Wait for his answer, "Rule three.")

Before starting a quiet activity, let students know what they can do when they are finished. Students can

- Look at magazines or books in a library corner

- Draw, work a puzzle, listen to tapes, use the tape recorder

- Choose and work on activity papers that you keep on hand

- Work on homework or unfinished assignments

During the first week, incidents may occur in which you need to interrupt the class and replay what happened, having the students brainstorm better ways to handle the situation.

At the beginning of the year, when students raise their hands, try to recognize them as quickly as possible and thank the student for remaining quiet until recognized. Give lots of positive feedback. "Thank you for raising your hand, Ann." "I like the way you waited for your turn, Taylor."

From the start, hold students responsible for work production. By the end of the first week of observation, you will have a better idea of the amount and type of work a student can do.

After the first week, provide a logical consequence for failure to complete work, and come up with a way for the student to get tasks done—for example, as homework (with parent contact).

On-task behavior is usually synonymous with good behavior.

Here are suggestions to encourage effective work habits:

1. If students do not do an assignment, talk with each of them in private about why. If they did not understand how to do it, either teach the skill or substitute an easier skill assignment.

2. If the amount of work intimidates some students, agree to reduce their workload, provided they agree to get it done. Break a long assignment into smaller segments to help students and pace completion. You may want to use a timer to remind students to keep going.

3. Give lots of verbal praise for work completion.

Settling Students After a Recess

A warm-up activity is an excellent way to settle students as soon as they come in the room. When students enter the room, have work for them to do that takes five minutes. This allows you to take care of any problems that have arisen.

In elementary schools, after the first recess, try a half-sheet of review math to do before you start new teaching. After lunch, students might do silent reading. Little ones put their heads down and rest while you read to them. Following the afternoon recess, they might complete a spelling worksheet.

At the secondary level, the warm-up or follow-up activity usually concerns something taught earlier. For example, if students are studying the Revolutionary War period, you might write three questions and have them use their book's index to locate answers. Or you might post board notes regarding the previous day's discussion. This serves the purpose of settling students, and also refreshes their memory of important facts covered the previous day. It may be particularly valuable for the student who was absent.

Projecting a Positive Feeling

You want a classroom where both you and the students feel comfortable. Students report that they prefer teachers who "don't yell, who listen to us and care how we feel, who reward us for good work, who have a sense of humor, and who like us."

No matter what you may be feeling, **appear calm and relaxed. Speak in a soothing voice.** Move slowly. LD students do not handle stress well. A schedule on the board that shows the progression of activities is reassuring, but avoid listing specific time periods. Give yourself the option to extend or shorten the time depending on how the activity is going. When you see someone lagging, say, "I see that some of you are almost finished." This gets others moving. When you see that several students have finished, say, "We need to wind this down in five minutes."

Cross off activities as they are completed. This gives the student a feeling of accomplishment.

Use lots of positive feedback. "I like the way you are making your *w*'s." "I can see you have done that correctly." Reprimands should be delivered very quietly. If you need to speak with a student, try leaning down to the student's ear. Talk with her privately. Say, "What's going on between you and Ian?" or "I want you to . . ." Then walk away. Allow the student time to think about it.

Finding Better Ways to Talk to Students

When we talk to students we want to

1. Model respect

2. Make our expectations clear

3. Structure the situation so that students comply

Speak to students with the same courtesy you would show an adult. If a student speaks to you rudely, walk away. Generally the student will think about it and apologize. If he doesn't, find a time and a private place to gently tell him, "I will not speak to you rudely. I will try to be respectful of your feelings at all times. I expect you to treat me the same way."

In our rushed lives, many of us have forgotten the value of "Thank you," "Please," pats on the shoulder, and smiles. They do wonders!

Never use embarrassment as a control technique. Yelling at students, snapping your fingers at them, or threatening them with a failing grade may seem to work, but these approaches do not model respect. Youngsters want to save face in front of their community of peers. Embarrassing a student may result in worse behavior or may even aggravate him into hitting you.

Authority is granted, not seized. It is important to set clear, consistent, and fair expectations. The consequences for unmet expectations should be likewise reasonable and consistent.

Here are some representations of common challenges a teacher comes across, along with ineffective and successful ways to handle each:

Poor: "There's no name on this paper." The teacher wads it up and throws it in the trash.

Better: Grade the paper. When you return the papers, someone will probably claim it.

Poor: "Have you got gum in your mouth? Let me hear you moo."

Better: "Here is a tissue for you to put your gum in before you throw it out."

Poor: The teacher finds a note being passed. She reads its contents to the class.

Better: Just take the note, without looking at it, and put it on your desk. Return it to the owner at the end of the period. You really don't need to say anything.

Poor: "I'm sick and tired of watching you acting like kindergartners."

Better: "I think we need to review our class rules." Then do so.

Poor: "When you guys shut up, I'll begin."

Better: Go to the board and write "Open your books to page 56." Clap three times and point to the instruction.

Preventing Misbehavior

Keep the Environment Consistent and Structured

Students with learning disabilities are upset by changes in routine. When something out of the ordinary is going to happen, such as a fire drill or an assembly, you will need to prepare them for it. Let them know what will happen and how they are to behave. If possible, rehearse the expected procedures. Misbehavior can be prevented when students clearly know what is coming and what they are to do.

Likewise, when you are about to give free time, prepare students for it. Students need to clearly understand the parameters of activity, noise, and movement. Here is an example of such a preparation:

> *You have earned fifteen minutes of free time. The checkerboards are over here, the art materials are over here. If you just want to talk, you can do that in this corner. Please keep your voices down. Show me how loud you can talk* (pause, and wait for their demonstration). *What will you do if someone is talking too loud?* (Students signal the finger to lips and the shhh sound typically used in their classroom.) *Can you play tag?* (No) *Can you take other stuff out of the cabinet?* (No) *What do you do if someone else has something you want?* (Share) *Can you push and shove?* (No) *What will happen if you don't follow these rules?* (Free time will end)

Help Students Succeed

Students with learning disabilities often feel they cannot succeed. After many years of failure and frustration, they have given up. When students are not on task, they are likely to misbehave out of boredom. Conversely, when students feel they can achieve, they show a high degree of on-task behavior and are less likely to misbehave.

The teacher's job is to adjust the classroom conditions, assignments, and grading procedures so that students feel successful. Students thrive in the right classroom environment, and they respond to a teacher committed to helping students. You should not only consider the class members as a group but also come to them as individuals. Teach them to hone their talents and minimize or compensate for their deficits.

Use Rewards, Contracts, Tokens, and Reinforcers

Rewards

According to most students, "Rewards make learning more fun!" There is a hierarchy of rewards from edibles and small tangible items to privileges, to positive notes home or certificates, to good grades, and, foremost, to internal satisfaction. The most potent rewards are edibles and tangibles.

When giving rewards, it works best to reward only one or two students each period. You do not need or want to reward every student; if you do, the reward will lose its value.

You may begin with small edibles (if permission has been granted by parents), such as popcorn, crackers, or chips given for work production. As time progresses, the aim is to decrease how often you give the reward or gradually increase the amount of work necessary to get it.

The "I'm Sending You to the Principal" reward is very effective. When you have two to five students who have shown ongoing improvement in their work, arrange for them to "go to the principal." Write at the top of each student's paper why it shows improvement; for example, "improved handwriting," "better score," or "producing more work." The principal then reinforces your praise. This technique has several positive aspects:

1. Principals love it. They get tired of seeing only kids who are in trouble. The principal will admire your ingenuity.

2. Because being sent is based on "improvement," all students have a chance to be chosen. The students at the bottom of the class may benefit from this experience more than the top students.

3. This technique encourages students to want to improve.

Students like contests, such as for the best report, best project, or best drawing. Allow students to vote to choose the winner. Prizes do not have to be expensive—a ribbon is fine.

Contracts

When a student is having difficulty complying with classroom standards for behavior or work production, one of the tools teachers may try is the contingency contract. This written contract specifies what the student must do to receive a given reward. The contract is made in private, with the teacher and the student agreeing to its terms. Figure 8.2 shows a sample.

Lotteries

Another helpful technique is a lottery, whereby students are given tickets for good behavior or increased work production. This strategy seems particularly helpful in motivating students to return homework. Students deposit these tickets in a container; on Friday, the teacher draws names for three or four small prizes—a Popsicle, a notebook, a red pencil. Yard-sale items can go far in stretching a teacher's reward budget.

Token Economies

Token economies can be used to prevent misbehavior and ensure work production. Students can earn points that are traded for prizes or privileges. Figure 8.3 shows a sample card.

Reinforcers for Elementary Students

- Listen to radio or tapes, watch a TV program
- Talk to best friend
- Look at books, magazines
- Edible rewards (candy, cookies, ice cream, soda, popcorn)
- Extra time for art, to play with clay or use colored markers
- Extra computer time

FIGURE 8.2.

Contingency Contract.

I agree to complete my entire math assignment today. If I achieve an accuracy of 70% and complete it in 50 minutes, I will be allowed to have 15 extra minutes of computer time today.

_____   _____
Teacher signature   Student signature

FIGURE 8.3.

Points Card.

Week of _____   Name _____

	Period 1	Period 2	Period 3	Period 4	Period 5	Period 6
Monday						
Tuesday						
Wednesday						
Thursday						
Friday						
Comments:						Total

- Help out in a lower-grade-level classroom
- Help the teacher (carry out trash, pass out papers)
- Stickers
- School items, such as pencils, notebooks, erasers, rulers
- Write on the chalkboard
- See a movie
- Extra recess
- Extra time with the teacher (small group has a pizza party or goes with the teacher to a fast-food restaurant, field trip, or picnic)
- Work on puzzles or play checkers
- Visit the principal
- Receive an award in assembly
- Money reward given by the parent or guardian
- Note or phone call to parent or guardian

Reinforcers for Secondary Students

1. Free time
   - Watch TV or a movie on a VCR
   - Read books or magazines
   - Time on a computer

- Peer tutoring

- Listen to CDs

- Play a game

- Earn a model, then assemble it and bring it to class

- Draw, paint, create

2. Special privileges

- Help as a teacher assistant

- Help the principal

- Do clerical work in the building (answer phone, run copy machine)

- Help the coach

- Be a library assistant

- Work with the custodian

- Run errands

- Earn extra time in shop, art, PE

- Earn food coupons, movie ticket, or ticket to a game

3. Special time with the teacher (small groups)

- Field trips

- Watch a movie in class

- Picnic in the park

- Have a soda or go to a restaurant

- Note or phone call to parent or guardian

- Games

Handling Misbehavior

Preventing misbehavior is definitely preferable to *handling* it, but, alas, there are times when we must do so. When an offense is deliberate and recurring, it is a matter of weighing the total situation: Were the directions clearly given and understood? Did the behavior cause harm? What would be the logical consequence for this behavior? How much punishment is required? What kind? Should parents and principal be involved?

Let's look at some examples:

- Kanisha is continually one or two minutes late to class. The logical consequence is that Kanisha be given a short detention each time she is late. It is a good idea to inform parents of the problem and ask if your plan meets their approval. If they say no, then ask them how they want the matter handled. If they say they will take care of it, let them know that if the lateness continues, you will have to try the detention.

- Carl lives to play tetherball, but does not play by the rules. This results in pushing and shoving. The logical consequence is that each time this happens, Carl is removed from the tetherball court or the playground for that day.

- Mike trips others, says mean things, and hits. The logical consequence is referral to the office, with a parent conference to follow. Students must be made aware that they may not assault other students at school.

"Ball in Your Court" Technique

When a student is misbehaving, that student should be confronted. There is an easy and effective technique you can use. Let's say you ask Jaime to move and he complies, but shows his disgust by slamming his book down on the desk. Ask him, "Why did you slam your book down like that?" Use an inquisitive tone rather than a confrontational one. Jaime will either say "Sorry" or "I was mad." If Jaime says he is sorry, say "OK" and go on as though the incident did not occur. If Jaime says he was mad, say, "I didn't mean to make you angry. We need to talk about this." Set up a nonclass time to do that. When you meet, ask Jaime to explain what made him angry. Listen attentively and then ask, "How can we resolve this so that next time I ask you to move, you do not get angry at me?"

The "ball in your court" technique also works with irate parents. Say, "I can see you are upset. What is it you want to happen here? How can we work this out?" Listen attentively and try to honor as many of their wishes as you can. When you cannot, say, "I wish we could do that, but we can't. What else could we do?"

Timeout

Timeout involves removing a student for a period of time from whatever activity she was doing. For less serious offenses, you may say, "Roberta, take a timeout in the library corner. You may return to the group when you are ready to do what we are doing without being disruptive." If a serious situation exists where Roberta continues to be belligerent or uncooperative, you may want her to serve the timeout somewhere else (another classroom), and you may want to set a time frame (such as for the rest of the period). If the problem continues, then you may have to involve the principal's office. In general, an office referral should not be your first line of defense.

Crisis Management

There are times when we are not able to reach a student. There are children who do not respond to the efforts previously described. Sometimes a student will lose control and may bite, hit, or kick others. Sometimes they even produce a weapon. Here are some guidelines to follow if you are involved in such a situation:

1. Never grab or touch an acting-out or violent student unless he is causing harm to another person or himself.

2. Send for assistance. (If possible, always wait for help if you intend to become physically involved.)

3. If the student is threatening, keep a normal distance from him. Do not invade his space.

4. Keep your voice tone normal. Repeat any instructions until the student complies. (Try to remain calm.) If a student is violent or about to hurt another, yell "Stop" and the student's name, then lower your voice. Screaming many words or threatening only confuses or further elevates the student's activity level.

5. Immediately try to get the aggressive student into isolation where he can calm down. Talk to him in a low, calm voice or remain silent.

6. Do not leave the student alone until he visibly calms down. (You might have another adult stay with him if you cannot.)

7. Discuss his behavior and the consequences of his behavior only after he has become calm.

Source: From "Crisis Management Workshop," 1983. Permission granted by authors, Crane-Reynold, Inc., 9327A Katy Freeway, Suite 327, Houston, TX, 77024, 713-984-0688.

Four Types of Challenging Students

There are four types of students who present challenges to teachers. The chart in Figure 8.4 will help you identify the type of student by the behaviors exhibited. Use the chart to record each symptom the student displays—usually you'll find a cluster of marks under one category.

FIGURE 8.4.

Challenging Students.

1. **Attention seekers** operate from a faulty belief—for example,"I belong only when I am being noticed."

   ___quarrel with peers

   ___make excessive noise (tapping, moving chair, slamming books, rattling paper)

   ___tattle

   ___tell wild tales

   ___talk excessively

   ___frequently leave seat

   ___are frequently tardy, with loud arrival

   ___make mouth noises (whistling, humming, and so on)

   ___fretful; whine and pout

   ___use baby talk

   ___throw things, have tantrums

   ___clown around

2. **Dependent students** operate from the belief that they are helpless—for example,"Oh well, it's just my lot in life. I have no clout. I'm helpless and powerless."

   ___feel dumb

   ___withdraw

   ___frequently say,"I can't do it"

   ___won't try

   ___give up easily

   ___appear inept

   ___cry often

   ___are fearful or panicky

   ___frequently say that they're ill

   ___cling to adults

   ___act helpless

   ___are poor achievers

   ___do not work unless teacher is nearby

3. **Power seekers** operate from a faulty belief—for example,"I must be the boss. No one can boss me."

   ___are defiant

   ___must be right; argue

   ___act very aggressive (bossy/bullying)

   ___rebel

   ___manipulate peers

   ___manipulate adults

   ___put others down

   ___are perfectionistic

   ___lie

   ___are stubborn

   ___must be "first," get angry if they are not

   ___dawdle (passive aggression)

   ___talk back

   ___exhibit rigidity

   ___have few friends

   ___often are truant

4. **Revenge seekers** operate from the belief that the world is a hostile place; no one can be trusted; they cannot be loved.

   ___are physically aggressive (bite, fight, throw rocks)

   ___sarcastic, negative

   ___destroy property

   ___cheat, steal, ignore or put down others, name-call

   ___are loners

   ___are liked by few

   ___set fires

   ___start false rumors

   ___distrust others

Attention seekers. In private, try to find out whose attention they want, and let them know you will help them find appropriate ways to get it. For example, the class clown may be seeking the attention of his classmates, or you may find that he acts out when he feels he cannot do the class assignment. If he needs classmate approval or your approval, you may give him opportunities to help in class—by being a buddy or peer tutor or a team leader, or by helping in the office when his work is done. Before giving him these duties, you will want to let him know exactly what you want him to do, the kind of behavior that is expected while he is doing it, and that the privilege will be withdrawn if it is not going well for whatever reason. If the child is seeking parental approval, you may want to promise a positive note home on each day when all assigned work is satisfactorily completed. You can increase the amount of work as needed to keep him engaged. The use of a point system with rewards offered at various levels can be effective:

20 points = small edible, sticker, or fifteen minutes of free time

100 points = choice of a tangible reward from the "treasure box"

Dependent students. These students tend to cling and need inordinate amounts of your time. There are several possible solutions. Assign them a work buddy (preferably a student who works quickly and who can take time to encourage and keep the dependent child working). Make sure the independent tasks assigned to this kind of child are within her comfort level. Divide the assignment into smaller segments and ask the child to bring the segments to you by a given time. You might want to keep a time chart so you are reminded to check on her if she doesn't complete the assignment within the time frame. Put the child on a points-based reward system: let her know that she will get a point as she completes each segment on time. Give lots of positive feedback, pats, or handshakes for "good work."

Power seekers. Recognize that these students are feeling powerless and insecure. Offer them choices as to the type of assignment or the order in which they do assignments.

Avoid a confrontational situation if you can. If you must deal with an issue, do so where other students cannot hear (preferably with another adult present as a witness). Power seekers respond well to consistency, fairness, and contracts with payoffs. Sometimes you can get power seekers to change their orientation. Usually they need to deal with their true feelings of being victims. At first, they'll require a lot of help to take constructive action. Help them find opportunities to lead.

Revenge seekers. These students often rate high in the power-seeking column as well. They feel like victims. They are prone to getting angry easily, and they may let you know that they plan to "get even." They believe their difficulties are caused by others, and they do not see their behavior as part of the problem. They tend to come from dysfunctional families or from families where the adult models are character-disordered. They tend to be loners in primary grades because other students do not like them and may be fearful of them. The prognosis for these students is poor.

So what can we do?

- Set clear expectations for behavior. Make it very clear to the student that he may not hurt others.

- Seat the student near you or seat the potential "victim" near you.

- When the student is angry, try to position him so that he cannot see the person with whom he is angry.

- When he is angry, either do not send him to recess, or alert the yard duty person that he needs close and direct supervision.

- Once a student demonstrates that he is likely to "get even," he must be isolated for the safety of others. This could mean that he would not go to recess or would be kept away from other students for the balance of the day. (Prepare a signed Behavioral Improvement Plan, discussed in Chapter Three.)

- Doing physically exerting activities, such as using a punching bag or hitting objects with rubber bats, or writing out the details of what they perceived to have happened works with some students.

- Get the student into anger management therapy.

- If the student hurts someone, suspension is usually required.

- Reward the student with a privilege on those days when he behaves respectfully to all.

Record Keeping

Today's teachers are required to keep many kinds of records that show the student's progress—grade books, portfolios, running records, samples of work that prove an IEP goal has been met, report cards, intervention documentation logs, behavioral logs.

It is easy to become overwhelmed with all these requirements. But don't let record keeping slide—do some every day.

It is important to make entries to the intervention logs and behavioral logs as situations occur. If you don't record things promptly, you will forget to do it or won't remember accurately. A clipboard holding each child's discipline intervention log makes it easy for you to record details at the time the problem is handled.

As students meet IEP goals, write the child's full name, the full date, and the goal met on the IEP record. Let the student watch you check the goal off as accomplished. Comment, "One more down, three to go" or "Good job!" File the sample immediately in the folder. This way your records will be up-to-date at all times.

Start as early as you can on filling out report cards. It will make your life as a teacher less stressful.

Using the Classroom Aide Effectively

Most special educators have one or more paraprofessionals to help them. The best way to get the most from your aides is to encourage them to take responsibility for getting results in the classroom. To do this, you need to involve them in almost every aspect of the classroom—supervision, planning, grading, record keeping, and teaching. Allow them to use their abilities and talents; give them the chance to make and try suggestions. Let them see that you appreciate initiative. Make sure they realize that they are essential to the success of the students with whom they work. Treat your aides as "second teachers" in the classroom. Encourage them to look around, see what needs to be done, and do it. Make aides aware of the IEP goals for each student. Aides' personal growth will increase when you trust them and appreciate what they do. Writing short notes of thanks is a really good practice—for example, "I want to thank you for being so positive when talking to the students. I heard you when you spoke to Irwin today. Nice!"

First-year teachers seem very unsure of how to use their aide. If aides are idle, resources are being underutilized. Aides and teaching assistants perform numerous duties, including assisting with grading and duplicating worksheets. However, working with students, whether individually or in small groups, is their most important function. If problems arise with your classroom aide, you may want to discuss them with your principal to determine a way to resolve them. It is advisable to act promptly in these instances; the longer you wait to talk about a challenging situation, the more difficult it often becomes.

Twenty Tips for Successful Classroom Management

The most effective special education teacher is one who remains calm under all circumstances, is patient, and counsels students on better ways to handle life's frustrations. The following is a list of tips for successful classroom management:

1. Make no more than five rules and consistently enforce them.

2. Be sure students understand they are in school to learn. Insist on work production. Working students are less likely to misbehave. As students begin to feel successful, they make gains in self-esteem.

3. Watch for and intervene to prevent frustration and stress. Take stretch breaks to relax.

4. Before beginning an activity, set parameters for behavior. "You may . . .," "You may not . . .," "When you finish your work, you may . . .," "You may not . . ."

5. Reduce clatter and noise during working sessions. Have students practice whispering. Use white music or earphones to cover noise.

6. Use signals instead of yelling. Sometimes you can get students to reduce noise by lowering rather than raising your voice. If you yell, students may interpret it as a signal that you do not have things under control.

7. Move parts of the group instead of the entire group. "Table four may line up" (order) instead of "Everybody line up" (chaos).

8. Plan for transitions. When students enter the room, give a short five- to ten-minute activity or review worksheet so that students are occupied while you do essential things before starting class.

9. Keep directions short, clear, and supported by notes on the board and other visuals.

10. Make efficient use of your classroom aide. Enlist parent help.

11. When walking down a hallway with a group of students, put three trustworthy students in front to lead. Walk at the back of the line so that from there you can see what the students in front of you are doing. If a student is not doing what is expected, call that student to the end of the line to be near you.

12. When you are going to do a class activity, be sure you either have enough materials for everyone or explain how they are to share.

13. Vary the activities: rest and action, individualized and group, inside and outside.

14. Offer students some choice in the activities: where to work, with whom to work, what to do.

15. When you ask a question, tell students who put their hands up immediately that you are going to wait a minute so that everybody has time to "think" of an answer.

16. Be sure you call on all students. Students need equal opportunities to answer questions. Research has shown that LD students are called on less frequently. Sometimes it is necessary to keep a chart to ensure you are not overlooking anyone.

17. Classrooms need to be colorful and inviting, and to reflect what is going on. Display lots of student work.

18. Team-teach with another teacher at your grade level, and share ideas. Work together on academic preparations and disciplinary problems. Two heads are better than one!

19. If a student needs a reprimand, go to her, establish eye contact, and quietly deliver your message. One extremely effective message is to say, "Your behavior is inappropriate. Can you fix it?" (Wait for an answer.) Students almost always say they can, and almost always do. Return to that student later and thank her.

20. Do not allow grading and record-keeping chores to pile up. It is far better to occasionally risk that students may not grade their own paper accurately than to hold on to papers for several days. By that time the returned assignment is no longer meaningful to the student.

Sample Approaches to Handling Inappropriate Behaviors

"What do you do when students are talkative during work sessions?"

Say: "I like the way Jason is working so quietly."

"I really appreciate it when you whisper."

"Thank you for working so quietly."

"What are the rules for independent work sessions?" (Have students name them.)

"You have five minutes to complete your work."

Do: Use white music when students are to work independently. It becomes a signal that they may not make noise or talk while music is on. (Use music with a calming tempo, played low.)

Put your finger to your lips; make eye contact with the talker.

Give points or a reward ticket to the quietest or most on-task workers as gauged by the amount of work completed. ("Jerrie, you are almost finished.")

If you have a group of talkers, consider

- Standing near them to settle them
- Giving a short stretch break if they've been sitting a long time
- Changing seat assignments or placing talkers in a carrel
- Using a writing assignment to calm kids on days when they seem to be wound up
- Giving students "the look"
- Announcing timeout ("You may return when you can be quiet.")

"What do you do when a student is constantly out of his or her seat?"

Say: "You need to be in your seat," and repeat that message calmly until he returns to his seat. As soon as he complies, ask the class, "What do you do if you need something?" (They say, "Raise your hand.") Acknowledge student's hand quickly if he complies.

Do: Put your hand on the child's shoulder and gently lead her to her seat. It is wise to limit movement with special education students as much as you possibly can. The more movement you allow, the more likely you are to have to deal with students "messing with" each other.

"What do you do with ADHD students who tend to bother others?"

Do: Consider

- Preferential seating near you or the aide
- Having the student sit in a carrel or face the wall to limit interaction with others and minimize stimuli
- Being more vigilant
- Using verbal reminders, such as "Thank you for letting others work"
- Having student sit away from others

"What do you do if a student is doing something that is hurtful to others?"

Do: Use behavior modification.

1. Decide on the target behavior you want to change—for example, put-downs or negative comments toward others.

2. On a card, record the number and type of put-downs used on a given school day.

   Sample:

   > 8:00   Taylor cut in and said, "Out of my way, you miserable toad."
   >
   > 8:40   "You're reading a baby book."
   >
   > Results = 8 times on sample day

3. Privately counsel student, with parent present if possible.

   The first step to changing behavior is making the student aware of the problem behavior.

   Sample:

   > "Taylor, last week I recorded the number of times you put others down. There were twenty negative comments." Give some examples of the nature of the put-downs.
   >
   > "Let's work on changing this behavior. I'll reward you if you can reduce the number of put-downs to ten or less next week."

4. Write a reward contract. Have Taylor select a reward from a list.

   Sample:

   > "Taylor will be allowed to use the computer for ten minutes each day, if he is able to reduce the number of put-downs for the week to ten or less."

   If the student does not succeed the first week, write a new contract and give him another chance. If he has reduced the number but didn't reach the goal, be sure to tell him that you can see he is trying and that you believe he can do it. If he earns the reward, write a new contract, saying that the student gets the reward again if the behavior is cut to five times. Once this behavior is eliminated, you will want to replace it by teaching him to use positive statements to classmates and praising him when he does.

Counseling + Contracts + Rewards = Potent agents of change. Make factual statements (avoiding all accusatory and negative statements). If the student fails, you make eye contact and mark a tally on the student's card.

If a student reacts negatively, let it go for a day or two and then try again.

The goal is personalized to the student, and other students need not be aware of the details of your contract. The tally cards may become a part of the student's record if the IEP contains behavioral goals.

"What do you do when someone cheats?"

Do:
- Watch the student during the testing situation and make notes of the behaviors used to cheat.

- Counsel the student in private to try to learn why the cheating occurred. Tell the student that during future testing, you will watch even more diligently.

- File the test paper with your notes in a cumulative folder.

- Modify the next testing situation if possible and, to prevent cheating, sit nearby.

Summary

As a supervisor of student teachers and interns, I have become convinced that positive discipline as a form of classroom management works better than negative discipline. When I was a child, and early in my career, teachers used many aversive measures—phone calls to parents, referrals to the office, yelling at students and embarrassing them, and assigning detention. These techniques do not work with most children. Parents may tell teachers they don't know how to handle their own child, or worse, may be too punitive. They may believe their child's version of the situation and cause further challenges for the teacher. Sometimes similar challenges may crop up from the principal if a teacher makes a referral. Yelling at or embarrassing students only shows the teacher to be out of control, rude, and disrespectful. It also may result in escalation of a situation and in a student's possibly assaulting someone. A recess break is beneficial to both teachers and students; therefore, "taking it away" is not an effective punishment. The only positive value that can come from a detention is when the time is used to get to know the student on a personal level, develop awareness and contracts, or give the student extra help.

If you can remain positive, calm, and consistent, you will build trust with your students. You may even become a role model for them.

Chapter 9

Academic Management Considerations

Woodrow Wilson (1856–1924)

American statesman, professor and educator, president of the United States

Had a reading disability; did not learn the letters of the alphabet until he was nine; did not begin reading until he was eleven; refused to study subjects that he found "boring"

Contributions:

Education: Received a doctoral degree in government and history; was professor and president of Princeton University

Politics: Served as twenty-eighth president of the United States; successfully led the United States through World War I and guided the peace process

Business: Reorganized the U.S. banking system, establishing the Federal Reserve

---

The first month of a new school year is a busy time for teachers. For new special education teachers, it can be an extremely stressful time because they have so many questions that need answers:

- What am I supposed to teach?

- There is very little in my room. Where do I get materials?

- Which materials do I need for my students?

After the first few days, there are additional questions. When we have attached names to student faces—Jed, Gerrard, Tony, Lavonna—another pile of questions emerges:

- How can I help Jed? He can barely read or spell. He has almost given up. He's so embarrassed.

- And Gerrard . . . He clings to me all day. If I'm not right beside him, he does nothing.

- Tony seems to be one of my smarter students, but he has to be the center of attention.

- Lavonna just stares out in space. If I tell her to get to work, she writes anything—just to be done.

This chapter will give answers to many of these questions.

Curriculum, Setting, and Students' Needs

Students who have been identified and found to be eligible for special education services are significantly below grade level in one or more areas of achievement. For many years, these students were considered to be "remedial," and it was not uncommon for an upper-grade child to be using lower-grade texts. The current philosophy, however, is that we "expose" the student to grade-level curriculum, adapting assignments to the learning disabled student's needs. Each student will have the opportunity to access the content and absorb what she can.

The setting in which the child is served often determines the curriculum. For example, if the student remains in the regular classroom, he will be taught the curriculum of that classroom. A Resource Specialist and the classroom teacher may collaborate on how to adapt that curriculum for the student. A regular class with Resource Specialist consultation and monitoring is a good placement for a mildly learning disabled student.

Students placed in Resource Specialist pull-out programs tend to be farther behind and need more one-on-one assistance. The Resource Specialist may adapt the regular class assignment to the student's level of understanding or skill level. For example, a seventh-grade math skill requires that the student know such statistical terms as "range of scores," "mode," and "mean" and be able to apply them to a set of data. The examples in the regular class text involve larger numbers and require a knowledge of long division that our LD student doesn't have. The specialist teacher modifies the student's assignments so that the concepts are taught, but the student is able to work with the problems using lower numbers so she can solve them using short division.

Sometimes the needs of the lagging student require instructional methods not used by regular class teachers or require one-on-one time that the regular teacher isn't able to give. The Resource Specialist may have to teach skills that should have been mastered in a lower grade.

The IEP states the amount of time a student will be seen in the resource room. It cannot exceed 49 percent of the school day. The average student is seen about five hours a week.

Placement in a special day class usually signifies that a student has moderate to severe academic problems. The student may have behavioral issues as well. All curriculum in these classes has to be adapted to the student's functional level. The teacher must match the task to the learner to avoid emotional outbursts that are caused by frustration or anxiety. The pace is usually slower because some students in these classes have rare medical syndromes, autism, lower IQs, or sociopathic tendencies, and several will be ADHD.

Getting to Know Your Students' Academic Needs Quickly Through Informal Testing

During the first weeks of school, you will want to do some informal testing to get a clear picture of what skills your students lack. Give reading and spelling tests and a math quiz, and obtain a writing sample. Once you have a basic idea of where your students are, you need to adjust your lesson plans to address the gaps of knowledge among the entire class, and you also need to note those areas where particular students need individualized instruction. Following are some examples.

Class Areas of Remediation

- The entire class needs a review on the strategies used to solve long division problems.

- Half the class needs additional review on decimals and their placement.

- Only part of the class understands the elements of a good paragraph.

Single Areas of Remediation

- Sam's family has moved frequently, and he needs to brush up on U.S. geography and all the states and their capitals.

- Ana needs help with basic multiplication facts—she only knows through her 3s.

- David has trouble with test anxiety and multiple-choice tests.

Goal Setting and Effective Lesson Design

Most of us get more done when we have clear goals and a timeline for accomplishing them. You may want to look at the texts you will be using and develop a timeline of where you hope to be at a given time during the year. Studies have greater relevance if the information about Christopher Columbus in the social studies book, for example, falls somewhere in early October near Columbus Day, and if the story in the reader having to do with rain occurs during the rainy season. It is always possible to adjust timelines if you find that your students require a pace that is different from what you expected. Doing an overview of texts and courses of study also allows you to collect those materials ahead of time that you know will be relevant to what you will be doing later in the year. Check your state's recommended curricular guidelines for each year to be sure you address the relevant topics your students will need to pass on to the next grade.

Once you have established where you need to go in the long term, you will then want to establish goals for shorter periods of time. Some subjects are best taught in units or themes. Develop an outline for an entire unit. Consider your students and think of ways you can meet their individual needs. For instance, if your students need to learn about expository writing, provide opportunities in science or social studies for students to be exposed to well-constructed expository paragraphs to use as examples when you describe the elements of a good paragraph.

You will want to present the lesson in a way that reaches the entire class. The child with better auditory memory can benefit greatly from using verbal practice to spell words. The visual child will benefit from color-coding, configuration, missing letter, ladders, and other techniques described in Chapter Twelve. Keep in mind that each lesson should address the various ways that students learn the material and succeed in retaining it.

Finally, you want to write a limited goal for each daily lesson.

Many experienced teachers use an eight-step format for lesson planning. They have found that it improves the lessons they present, and procedures go more smoothly because they have thoroughly thought through what they want to do and accomplish. Teachers often file successful lesson plans for use in future years. You might also keep notes with suggestions for modifications that might lead to greater success. Here is that format and a brief explanation of the parts:

1. *Objective.* Once you decide what you need to teach, develop an objective to measure student learning. An objective may involve academic or behavioral performance. It covers the questions *when, who, what, how,* and *to what degree.* To illustrate, here are two sample objectives:

   By the end of September, my students will be able to pass a twenty-five-question multiple-choice test in American history for the period of 1600–1700 with a score of 75 percent or better. (*academic goal*)

   By the end of this week, working in pairs, students will complete an animal habitat diorama for our science unit. While working, they will share materials, give each other help and encouragement, and raise their hand if they need assistance. (*behavioral goal*)

2. *Materials needed.* In the case of the academic goal listed above, you would need to develop your twenty-five-question final test at the beginning of your unit so that you can be certain that you cover all items on the test.

   In the case of the behavioral goal, you will need to list all items to be shared—glue, sand, greenery, and so on. For both types of goals, it is important to clarify for students what is expected.

3. *Anticipatory set.* On the day you begin the lesson and on subsequent days, open the lesson by engaging student interest. One of the most common ways to do this is by asking students what they already know about a given subject. This may lead into some questions for the students. It will also help you assess what students already know so that you can build their understanding before developing new concepts. If students show no interest, you will need to give them a purpose or reason for learning the information.

   For the academic goal, you might explain that if they listen and complete every activity, they can expect to make a good grade on the test.

   For the behavioral goal, you can show them a couple of sample dioramas from previous years. You will also want to share with them your objectives so that they can encourage each other. You may want them to fill out a questionnaire at the end of each session, listing specific examples of the ways that they encouraged others.

4. *Input.* Your daily verbal input should be brief—ten minutes or less. For the balance of the period, engage students in locating, discussing, or writing about the subject. The more they do, the more they learn. Teaching students to use tables of contents, indexes, atlases, or other reference resources will prepare them to be lifelong learners. Support oral presentations with written notes. Use videos, illustrations or photographs, learning games, discussions, and question-and-answer sessions to help students retain information.

5. *Model the process.* When you give an assignment, model or demonstrate exactly what you want students to do.

6. *Check for understanding.* Have two students repeat the instructions. Or have students come to the board or overhead to demonstrate and explain what they did or have learned.

7. *Guided practice.* Once you are confident that a student understands what to do and understands the newly developed content, you can send her to work independently. You will continue to work with those who need supervision in a guided practice group.

8. *Independent practice.* Use independent practice until you are sure the skill has been mastered and, after that, give occasional reinforcement practice.

It is not necessary to complete all eight steps in a single lesson. It may take many lessons before some students reach the independent practice level.

Planning the School Day

Madeline Hunter, a famous educator, once said, "Teachers make hundreds of decisions a day." This is true. In the act of planning a school day, teachers make many decisions. Transitions, matching subjects and time of day, pacing, unforeseen events, providing variety in activities, grouping students, allowing students some choices, and using rewards are some of a classroom teacher's daily considerations.

As mentioned earlier, a class can begin more smoothly if you plan a five- to ten-minute warm-up activity each time students enter the room. This generally settles the students quickly. Special education students are often tardy, so it's a good idea to begin your instruction about twenty minutes after the first bell rings. A "warm-up" or "do now" plus opening activities will usually fill this time. Basic subjects—reading and math—are best taught as early in the day as possible.

For variety, alternate quiet work sessions with a chance to move around. Have substitute lesson plans to use if either you or the aide is absent. Use different kinds of activities so each child has maximum opportunity to assimilate instruction. Students with learning disabilities benefit especially from hands-on and firsthand experiences. These might include planning and developing a garden; collecting and labeling insects; or visiting a grocery store, where you talk about weights and use the scales to weigh things.

Afternoons pose additional considerations. Students with learning disabilities often tire as the day proceeds. Depending on the personality of the group, this will affect what you can do. You may want to plan stress-free activities like singing or using art materials. These activities can reinforce something learned earlier in an academic area.

Planning for Flexibility

Flexibility means the ability to bend, adjust, and adapt. Flexibility is critical for today's teacher. You must allow yourself flexibility in pacing, activities, and grouping of students for instruction. Allow your students some choice of assignments and rewards.

Scheduling and Pacing

To plan for flexibility in scheduling and pacing, put a schedule of activities on the board daily, but do not put time frames on each activity. If students finish faster, you can move on; if students indicate a particular interest in an activity, you can adjust. If the office holds an unscheduled fire drill, you can deal with the interruption and just move with the flow.

Using a Variety of Activities

Flexibility in activities often draws in reluctant students and can be achieved by using a variety of activities. Try educational games. Let students pair up and test each other in spelling, sing, or perform a play. Hold an art day. Invite a ballerina to give a demonstration or a violinist to play. Teach your students to play a recorder. Debate, discuss. Do science experiments. Cook. Have guest speakers. Make maps. Have students read silently, read orally to them, read chorally, have them read to you. Do some writing, some math. Go on walking trips. Write and publish a class newspaper.

Grouping Students

In order for students to get the most from their day, you will need to group them at times. Sometimes you may need to work on a skill with the whole class, sometimes with only two or three students. Pairs work well for seat-work activities. With small groups of three to five students, each student should have a clearly defined role.

Allowing Students Some Choice in Assignments and Rewards

There are times when a student will rebel against a particular assignment with an "I don't want to" or "I won't." At these times, it is good to have backup options, to be able to say, "Okay. Get out your own packet and work on it." This means each child has a packet containing a variety of alternative but educationally sound activities geared toward his own level that can be worked on independently.

When planning projects, offer students a choice, such as

- Make a map showing the location of all the Spanish missions in California.

- Make a model of a California mission.

- Answer questions about missions using your book and then write a report using what you learned.

Likewise, some students will not work for the standard rewards. If this is the case, interview the child to find out what would be appealing. Write a contract outlining specifically what the child must do to get the reward. Be careful not to agree to a reward of too substantial a cost; doing so would cause difficulty in motivating that child to work for lesser items in the future.

Transforming Passive Students into Participatory Students

Many students with learning disabilities are not active learners. They feel "disconnected" because they are not invested in the process of learning. They exhibit the symptoms of "failure syndrome." After years of academic failure, they give up. They would prefer being allowed to skip school; if parents insist, they attend, but do little work. Some daydream; some sleep in class. They may use the word "dumb" to describe themselves. Some are defensive and do not take reprimands well. Others are baby-ish, helpless, and immature. Some "act out"; others withdraw. They may complain of headaches or stomachaches because trips to the restroom or nurse's office allow escape when they are under pressure. Depression is common.

Getting students involved in their learning is one of the greatest challenges a special education teacher faces. You'll soon find that the cure to failure syndrome is replacing failure with regular success.

Overcoming Failure Syndrome

In the early days of your relationship with students, plan to spend some semiprivate time with each one. Invite the child to have lunch with you and your aide, and bring something children like to eat.

Ask the child how she likes school. Ask her if it is difficult and, if so, why. Ask what she likes best and least. Write down the answers. Let the student know you care how she feels and that you will try to make school a more pleasant place to be. Tell the child that you will try to give her work she can do successfully.

To ease the way:

1. Start at the student's level of understanding. For example, to accommodate his low reading level, at the beginning, use short lessons that require minimal writing.

2. Proceed at a pace that allows her to finish a lesson.

3. An aide, teacher, or parent volunteer can circulate to be sure the students are "on track" and to encourage.

4. When a student asks for help, try to get to him quickly and praise him for "being brave enough to ask."

5. When a student offers an incorrect response to a question, try to dignify the answer; for example, you might say, "That was a good try."

6. When a student gives a really good answer, ask her "to stand and say it so everyone can hear."

7. When you go over students' papers with them, be gentle and encouraging. Point out more of what's right with the paper than what's wrong: "I like the way you worked quietly," "I'm glad you were able to finish it," "You were very neat," and, best of all, "Wow, it is all correct! 100 percent." (This is said to the child, not to the whole class.) If you need to give instruction, say, "Let's look at this together." If you find several students are having trouble with a lesson, you may want to do a follow-up lesson the next day for a small group or with the whole class.

8. Let the student see you enter a grade in your grade book. Use a "+" for finished assignments. Circle the + if the student needs reteaching. If it is completely right, enter "100%." If the student is absent, enter a zero. Help students see that a partially completed assignment beats a zero.

9. Help students find as many good things about themselves as they can—for example, consider neatness, carefulness, a cheerful attitude, good manners, or their perseverance in completing a task.

Planning Cooperative Learning Tasks

It is tremendously important for teachers to teach students how to work cooperatively. The number one reason employers cite for releasing an employee from employment is that the person cannot get along with other people. Cooperative learning helps students learn to contribute their ideas to a group and work with that group to solve a problem or do a project. School districts usually offer in-service training to teachers on how to use cooperative learning techniques.

When you first begin to present cooperative learning experiences, it is easiest to begin with pairs. Students are given a task to do, and they work on it together, producing a single product. Before they begin, discuss how working cooperatively should look and sound. They need to listen to each other's ideas. They will compliment each other. They will not get mad at each other or be bossy.

With older students, pairs still work, but there may be activities you will want a group to do. Groups of four work well. Before you begin the activity, discuss the structure of a cooperative group. You may want to assign jobs within the group, or let students determine these. Typically there will be a leader, a scribe, a reporter, and a monitor, who watches the interaction, maintains order, and keeps members on task. If you have a student who is adamant about not wanting to work in a group, don't force it. Be flexible.

Suggestions for Maximizing Educational Results

In this section, we will look at ways to increase learning.

My first suggestion is to *involve parents in meaningful ways!*

Parents can be a real asset if they are assisting in achieving goals. Ask parents to help in the classroom. An extra pair of eyes is invaluable when the teacher and the aide are working with groups. Parent volunteers can circulate to keep children on task, answer questions, or sharpen a pencil. Some are born teachers and enjoy working one-on-one with students. They also can make copies or gather and help prepare materials for projects. To be sure that volunteers arrive when expected, it is important to explain what you will need done, work out a specific day and time you will be expecting them, and call the day before to remind them of their commitment.

Give homework assignments that engage parents in the teaching process in specific ways. For example, when you are teaching measurement, you can ask parents to support their child's understanding of this skill at home. Parents can work with their child to measure when following recipes, when sewing, or when figuring out dimensions of a room. When you are doing career exploration, parents can be invited to come to school to talk about what they do.

Money therapy is a reward system that is developed between parents and the school. The parent rewards the student with a reasonable amount of money for the child's age based on the teacher's reports. This system requires that the teacher explain the system thoroughly to the parent.

We used it with a first-grade child who refused to work. The teacher had tried several kinds of rewards, but nothing appealed to the student. When the parent came in, we asked if she rewarded the child for his work at school.

She said she did. We suggested that she withhold all rewards from him, even candy, unless he had earned the money to buy it. In spite of her protest that he would not work for a penny a paper, she followed through, and in less than two weeks, her child was not only working at school but also doing small chores at home so he would have "money when my mom takes me to the store."

Some parents may protest that this is bribery. You can point out that by making the child earn the money, the parent is teaching the child to be responsible. Money therapy can be used to teach children the value of money: the importance of saving for big items and the reality that you can't buy something if you don't have money to pay for it. Encourage parents to take the concept of saving further by labeling three containers—money for now, money for later, and money for much later—and requiring the child to contribute to each.

Improving Lesson Results Through Feedback

At the end of each lesson, it is wise to request feedback from students to check what was learned. Remember that feedback does not have to be written. Oral questioning can be used. Many teachers will follow a lesson with a series of true-false questions. Students signal that the answer is true with a thumb up; false is signaled with a thumb down. If you see students who are not sure—for example, looking around to see what others do or waffling with the position of the thumb—you may want to repeat the question, give the correct answer, and provide additional explanation.

Written individualized feedback allows us to see how a student is integrating new knowledge with prior knowledge.

The following humorous essay demonstrates that what we say is not always what a student hears. An upper-grade student wrote this paper:

> *The human body is composed of three parts: the Brainium, the Borax, and the Abominable Cavity.*
>
> *The Brainium contains the brain. The Borax contains the lungs and the liver. The Abominable Cavity contains the bowels. The bowels are a, e, i, o, and u.*

Many teachers have gotten the impression that it is not a good idea to have students correct their errors—that it will inhibit their willingness to write. When students make their first attempts at writing, this may be true. We want them to just let their ideas flow onto the paper.

It is not harmful to let students use invented spelling to get their ideas on paper, but by the time they are in upper grades, LD students need to know how to use the spell-check feature of the computer. Research shows that students benefit from making corrections. Although it is discouraging to get back a paper that has red marks all over it, if the teacher crosses out an occasional word and writes in the correct spelling in pencil, this should not result in undue trauma so long as it is balanced with positive comments, such as "This is a really clear sentence" or "Your transition from one paragraph to the next was excellent."

It is important for students to get immediate feedback of results. Teachers do not have time to grade every paper, and it is not even desirable that they do so. Students may be given an answer key to grade their own math papers. Students working on the same paper may compare notes and discuss what the correct answer should be. Students may proofread each other's writing before it is handed in. Parents should be encouraged to review student homework for mistakes and to provide positive feedback.

Improving Learning Through Specific Teaching Techniques

One of the major problems of students with LD is that they have deficits in short-term memory. They do not hold on to information for a sufficient period to transfer it to long-term memory. You can help students improve this skill by teaching them some study techniques. Among these are

1. Tests that teach

2. Story mapping, advanced organizers, and word and concept webs

3. Mnemonics

4. Use of higher-level thinking activities

5. Peer teaching

Tests That Teach

Use tests to teach those facts you consider important for students to know. Tests can be oral or written, and there are several kinds:

Matching: the easiest because there is minimal reading

Multiple choice: involves more thought and reading

Fill in the blanks: requires reading and spelling

Essay: most difficult because it requires total recall, organization, writing, and spelling skills

You might want to give students with learning disabilities several types of tests covering the same information as practice tests.

There is nothing unethical about giving students the actual test as a study guide several days before the test and reviewing the answers daily in class.

It also helps students understand the types of test questions better when they try to write them. You might have each student pick a section of text and try to write three test questions. You could supply answers (so that the students aren't grading each other) and then have the class talk through the tests and answers.

Story Mapping, Advanced Organizers, and Webs

Students with LD respond well to tools that help them organize information. Following are a sample story map (Figure 9.1) and a sample organizer (Figure 9.2). Both can help students identify, organize, and, ultimately, remember information that they read.

FIGURE 9.1.

Sample Story Map.

Name of story: _____

Author: _____

Setting (time, place): _____

Main characters:

_____

_____

_____

_____

The plot/the problem:

_____

_____

_____

_____

The outcome:

_____

_____

_____

What value did I gain from reading this story?

_____

_____

FIGURE 9.2.

Sample Organizer for a Social Studies Unit on the Transcontinental Railroad.

1. **Meaning of Terms**

    transportation _____

    _____

    communication _____

    _____

    survey _____

    _____

    construction _____

    _____

2. **Discuss the role played by Chinese workers in building the first transcontinental railroad, including the hardships involved.**

    _____

    _____

3. **Give the year and place where the Union Pacific and Central Pacific railroads were joined by a golden spike.**

    _____

    _____

4. **How did the transcontinental railroad affect**

    • **The Pony Express** _____

    _____

    _____

    • **The stagecoach companies** _____

    _____

    _____

Webs are common organizers used prior to doing a writing assignment. Students brainstorm ideas on a subject and prioritize them before writing. See Figure 9.3 for a sample web.

FIGURE 9.3.

Sample Web for Writing Assignment on Hummingbirds.

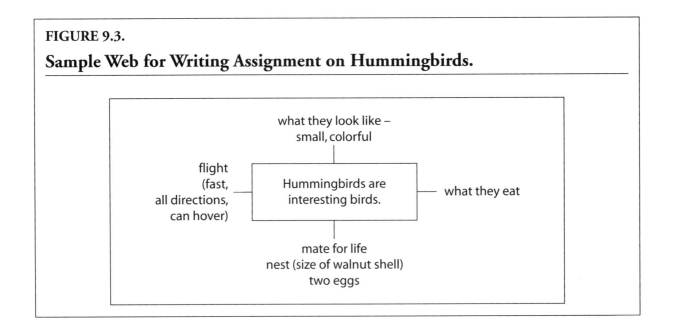

Mnemonics

Mnemonics are memory tricks that people use to hold on to information. An example is HOMES, a mnemonic that helps you remember the names of the Great Lakes: Huron, Ontario, Michigan, Erie, and Superior. LD students become very ingenious at making up their own tricks. For example, one student was trying to learn to spell *though*. He kept repeating "th.o.u. stupid gh."

Use of Higher-Level Thinking Activities

Some tasks involve merely repeating facts or paraphrasing information. Others involve higher-level thinking skills, which entail analyzing information and doing something new with it. Research shows that students retain more information when they use higher-level thinking skills. Examples of each type follow:

Lower level: What is 4 + 8?

Higher level: Make up a story problem to go with the fact that 4 + 8 = 12. Draw a picture that illustrates the problem you wrote.

Lower level: Summarize the story you read.

Higher level: The main character in the story you read is nearly your age but lived many years ago. How is your life the same as his? How is it different?

Lower level: Why is Abraham Lincoln famous?

Higher level: We celebrate two presidents' birthdays—George Washington and Abraham Lincoln. In your opinion, who was the better president? Justify your choice.

Lower level: What was the Boston Tea Party?

Higher level: Using the facts surrounding the Boston Tea Party, write a newspaper article titled "Tea in the Sea." Provide the who, where, what, when, how, and why.

Issues of Grading and Evaluation

One of the challenges we face in giving a grade to special education students—especially those who are mainstreamed—is how to grade them without discouraging them. If a special education student has made great strides, it would be wonderful to give him an A for excellent, yet if we compare his "excellent" work with the "excellent" work done by a regular education student, it more than likely won't match up. Some teachers have settled this by using pass-fail grading.

Another issue we need to be mindful of is that grades need to be based on objective standards. On a major assignment, it is helpful to outline for both students and parents the standards by which a project will be judged. Students need to be told that first impressions are very important. A "neat paper" tends to get a better grade even when content is about equal to one less neat.

Many issues arise from the fact that students with learning disabilities are often not good test takers. Some have retrieval issues and memory issues or don't know how to really study. A child who has demonstrated that he understands the processes of double-digit multiplication and long division may, unless provided with special accommodation, fail a test because of not having memorized the multiplication tables. Should this student be allowed to use a calculator to do math tests?

Is it all right to use a different format for testing the LD child while regular class students take an essay test on the same material? Can the student with LD take an oral test instead of a written test? The legal answer is that many kinds of modifications can be made in testing to ascertain a student's level of knowledge, but if you have ever had a faculty discussion on this subject, you know there are some teachers who are so rigid that they won't consider making modifications. It is important to note, however, that the teachers must follow the instructions in the IEP. The student who works slowly or reads slowly will most certainly need extra time to show what she knows. Test modifications, including time extensions or the use of calculators, word processors, and supportive devices, can be written into the student's IEP.

Evaluation needs to be a multifaceted process involving both informal and formal procedures. Among informal procedures are question-and-answer, discussion sessions, circulating and observing, projects, and portfolios of student work over a period of time. Among the more formal measures are ongoing records, quizzes, and tests.

Students gain additional learning when allowed to grade their own papers, particularly when you explain why a given answer is correct. Having students read their answers in small groups with a leader while you circulate among the groups and listen in and give feedback is another way to evaluate your students.

Tips for Academic Management

1. In planning classroom curriculum, follow your district's guidelines. Plan activities that maximize student participation. More learning occurs when you use carefully guided discussion, activities that require students to be participatory, and activities that engage students in firsthand experiences.

2. Help students feel that they are making progress and can be successful.

3. Plan the school day with basic subjects in the morning when students are less "fidgety." Use warm-up activities after each recess to settle students, check their understanding of previous learning, set the stage for the new lesson, or reinforce previously used skills. Make provisions for periods of rest, such as a time to stretch but not to talk.

4. Plan afternoon lessons that allow for more movement, more hands-on or firsthand doing or discovering activities. Novelty audio- or video-tapes can support learning. Displaying objects as props and using photographs, posters, and other images enhance the visual appeal of the classroom and are effective aids to learning.

5. Maintain a positive feeling in the room. Remain calm—no matter what. Teachers who move slowly and speak in slower, lower-decibel voices are better able to work with hyperactive students.

6. Rewards, grades, and privileges can make learning more interesting.

7. Set up a listening center where students can listen to stories you have recorded or to recordings you have purchased. It is sometimes possible to get recordings of textbooks.

8. Use computer games or lessons to reinforce information in class.

9. Use a wide variety of activities so that there is something of interest to everyone. Within a given lesson, include as many learning channels as you can (visual, auditory, and "doing" input).

10. Plan cooperative learning situations and teach social skills, such as saying "Please," "Thank you," and "Yes, sir."

11. Be consistent in enforcing rules.

12. Allow some choice in assignments whenever you can.

13. Get to know your students' parents or guardians. Take their wishes into consideration. Try to get them involved in school functions.

14. Use immediate feedback. Be specific about what you like. Use of a green pencil is less offensive than red.

15. Teach students to use organizers, daily note-taking, webs, and mnemonics to enhance learning.

Chapter 10

Interventions for Specific Problems

Sir Winston Churchill (1874–1965)

British author, orator, statesman

Had a writing disability; always functioned at the bottom of his class and had to repeat some early grades; once joked that "by being so long in the lowest grades, I got into my bones the structure of the ordinary English sentence—which is a noble thing"

Contributions:

Politics: Served as prime minister of Great Britain; inspirationally led the British to victory in World War II

The Arts: Wrote *The Second World War* (six volumes)

Working with learning disabled students is fascinating. Take the case of two students with LD who might appear to be very similar. They are both eight years old, in early third grade, with reading and writing skills that are just about the same according to achievement testing. Looking at their work samples, however, you will see marked differences.

Student A has visual processing deficits as well as poor fine motor skills. She finds it difficult to write on the line, spacing is a problem, and her work exhibits use of upper- and lowercase letters. Her visual memory is weak, but she spells phonetically:

> Wunday the little RED Hen
> PletiD CorN

Student B writes:

> me and my cat a ur taKinG
> a waLLK anD playInG

Student B appears to be less disabled. He isn't. When he writes, he chooses words he is sure he knows because he is dysphonetic when he attempts unknown words. Composing a sentence that makes sense is a real challenge for him.

Each student presents a unique profile of strengths and weaknesses. The job of the teacher is to maximize strengths and to remediate or help the student find ways to compensate for deficits.

The focus of this chapter is to give parents and teachers suggestions for ways to help students with their deficit areas.

Visual Perceptual Deficits

DEFICIT: reverses or inverts letters or numerals

Interventions

1. Make and attach a visual strip to the student's desk and notebook so that there is a model for those symbols that give trouble. Help the child build the habit of looking at the model each time she needs to write a letter or number.

2. Have the student work at a chalkboard for a few minutes each day. Take one troublesome symbol and draw it about a foot high. Have the student trace over it ten times with chalk and then erase it, or trace over it with his finger. Have him name the symbol each time he goes over it. Do this activity daily until he no longer reverses that letter, numeral, or symbol. Using the gross motor muscles seems to help the student internalize directionality and correct letter formation.

DEFICIT: loses place, skips lines, rereads lines, omits words

Interventions

1. Encourage the student to use a bookmark during reading. Set an example by using one yourself. Being engaged with moving a bookmark is helpful to inattentive and fidgety students as well as to those with perceptual problems. It also allows you to quickly and quietly monitor whether a child is following along. When you find that a child is out of

place, you are able to move the bookmark to the correct place without a verbal reprimand.

The best bookmarks are about six inches long and one inch wide, with a one-inch dark line in the center. This dark line is placed under the word the child is reading as she moves the marker left to right.

2. Reproduce material to be read. Have the student underline it with a pencil as he reads.

DEFICIT: yawns, has blurry vision, has itchy eyes during reading

Interventions

1. Suggest a professional eye examination to be sure that the student has normal acuity and that the eyes converge properly. Encourage students who need glasses to wear them.

2. Enlarge printed material if you can.

3. When the student begins to have trouble, tell the child to close her eyes and rest them for thirty seconds. A damp paper towel helps with itchy eyes. Some students find that they can solve these problems by reading with only one eye at a time.

4. Fluorescent lights on white paper produce a glare. Use reproduced copies, not dittoes, and print them on blue, tan, or green paper. If the student must read from white paper, reduce the amount of light by shutting off some of the lights, or allow the student to cover the paper with a piece of transparent nonglare plastic or even to wear lightly tinted sunglasses.

DEFICIT: cannot copy accurately

Interventions

1. Make sure the child has normal vision.

2. Seat the student near the board if he is copying from the board.

3. When copying from a book at her desk, show the student how to use the index finger of the free hand to hold the place on the material while copying.

4. Train the student to remember groups of letters so that he does not have to look back at the model after each letter. The ideal number of letters to train would be those in a syllable.

5. Eliminate copying tasks by using handouts.

DEFICIT: forms letters poorly

Interventions

1. Teach or reteach printing or cursive. Teach the student to place the paper at the proper slant, how to put the proper grip on the pencil, and how to form each letter. Working in a small group, teach letters by similarity of formation.

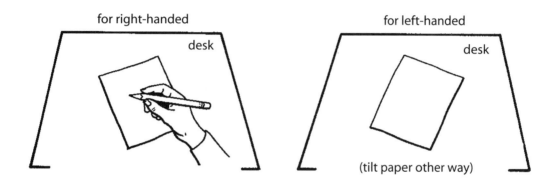

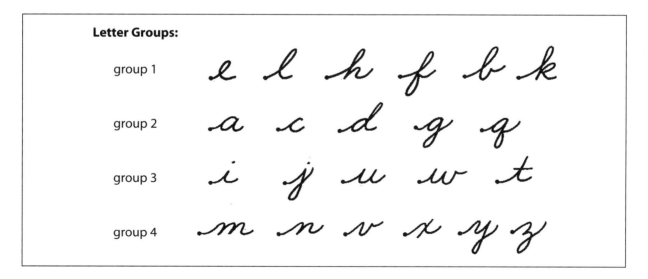

Note: The letters *o, p, r,* and *s* are taught separately.

2. Allow reluctant students to practice on the board. It can be motivating for them to use something other than pencil and paper.

DEFICIT: slow, laborious handwriting

Interventions

1. Allow student to take an oral test.

2. Shorten assignments.

3. Allow student to use a word processor.

4. Use a true-false, matching, or multiple-choice answer sheet whenever you can.

5. Let the student dictate answers into a tape recorder when taking recall tests.

DEFICIT: messy papers

Interventions

1. Talk with the student about neatness. Help her gain awareness by showing her several papers. Ask her which one she believes will get the better grade.

2. Create "sample" assignments in both messy and neat formats, and have the students grade them as a class; show the class how the neater work earns better grades overall.

3. Tell the student that he may not erase; if he cannot correct a mistake by writing over it, he is to cross it out using only one line and then to continue.

4. Allow the student to type her assignments.

Auditory Processing Deficits

DEFICIT: cannot understand conversation delivered at normal speed
(This may be evidenced by the student's "Huh?" or "What?")

Interventions

1. Have the student sit close to you and watch your lips.

2. Make sure he is paying attention before you speak.

3. Speak more slowly. Use short sentences. Repeat if necessary.

4. Tape-record lessons so that the student can stop the machine and relisten.

5. Assign a capable and patient student buddy to repeat directions and information.

6. Provide the student with written notes regarding major points covered in the lecture.

7. Encourage the student to give you some sign when she is not following what you are saying. Students are usually too self-conscious to raise their hand, but will agree to signal you with more subtle means.

8. Stop frequently to check for understanding and clarify.

9. Use lots of visuals and board notes to support aural input; notes should contain key words, definitions, and questions.

10. Use the digital visual programs that help provide a visual cue for basic commands, and post them next to the written directions on the board.

11. Refer the child to the speech therapist for evaluation of receptive language.

DEFICIT: unable to distinguish between spoken sounds

Interventions

1. Have hearing acuity checked. If it is normal, ask the speech therapist to check the child's auditory discrimination.

2. If the child is not hearing a given sound, exaggerate the sound you want her to hear; write the word, pointing out the sound you want the student to hear.

3. Show the student where to place the tongue and lips, and how much air is involved to make the sounds he does not hear.

DEFICIT: unable to filter out extraneous noises

Interventions

1. Have the student sit near you.

2. Be sure you have the child's attention before speaking.

3. Tell the student to watch your lips.

4. If the problem continues, suggest a professional hearing test.

5. Write important points on the board.

6. Try to keep the classroom as quiet as possible during instruction.

7. Tape the lesson in a noise-free setting. Let the student use earphones to listen.

8. During independent work periods, use white music to mask distracting noises.

DEFICIT: does not benefit from auditory input

Interventions

1. Give the student a copy of important information that is being presented auditorily; this way he can see the words while you are talking.

2. At the end of the lecture, have the student highlight important points and check for the student's understanding.

Spatial Awareness Deficits

DEFICIT: gets lost in ordinary surroundings

Interventions

1. Send a buddy with the student.

2. Take the student on jaunts around the area, asking her to observe stable visual data; for example, ask the student to count how many rooms she passes on the way to the bathroom.

3. Have the student draw maps of the school and neighborhood, noting distinguishing features of the area.

DEFICIT: cannot remember left-to-right sequencing

Interventions

1. Put an arrow on the student's desk that looks like the one shown in the illustration. The student lays his paper just below the arrow. Tell the student to begin on the side where the dot is and proceed in the direction of the arrow.

2. Put five rows of masking tape on the floor and play "typewriter." The student is guided to move as the typewriter does, stepping left to right on the tape; when she reaches the end of the row, the student doubles back to the beginning of the next line.

3. Teach left and right. For most students, you can say, "You *write* with your *right* hand."

DEFICIT: cannot write in a given amount of space, fails to place a space between words

Interventions

1. Ask the student what she wants to write. Student repeats the sentence three times. Have student make mental pictures of all the words. Say the sentence back to the student. (Meanwhile, you have drawn the correct number of spaces on the paper so that she can write one letter in each space.)

Example: *The boy went for a walk.*

— — — — — — — — — — — — —

— — — — —.

2. Allow the student to use a word processor.

3. Use graph paper that has squares in a size appropriate to the student's age. The student writes one letter in each space and leaves a square between words.

DEFICIT: disorganized

Interventions

1. Teach the student what to do as he changes tasks: first, to clear his desktop of all unneeded materials before beginning the new task; next, to take out only the items he will need for the new task. Some students need to be trained to talk themselves through these two steps.

2. Train the student to keep and use an assignment calendar so that assignments are done on time, or teach the student to use a personal planner by adding in all assignments and due dates.

3. Teach the student to organize her papers by indicating margins, writing headings, and remembering to indent.

4. In math, teach the student to fold paper into sections and to write only one problem in each section.

5. Enlist the parents to work on organization at home. Have them encourage "a place for everything and everything in its place": bed made upon rising; belongings labeled with student's name so that if found, they can be returned; and so on.

6. Consider the use of a laptop or digital personal organizer (PDA); adults use them frequently, and teaching a child how to organize his work with a computer or digital device will be a skill he will need in the working world. For some students, a pen and paper won't work.

Conceptual Deficits

DEFICIT: cannot read social situations or body language

Interventions

1. Role-play social situations in class. Have students act out scenes from a story they've just read or a movie they watched, or role-play some social situations. Stop frequently and discuss possible feelings.

Model ways to get through these situations and have students role-play what you modeled. Be sure to talk about people's need for personal space and the fact that when someone unfamiliar gets too close or invades the other's personal space, it makes the other person feel uncomfortable.

2. Whenever a situation arises naturally that calls for understanding of body language—such as a confrontation between two kids—begin to explain what a look or stance means and what a proper response is. Oddly, doing this can often diffuse the combatant's anger while serving as a lesson to others.

DEFICIT: cannot see relationships between similar objects, has poor inferential thinking

Interventions

1. Have students examine and describe two similar objects. After they describe them aloud and write ideas on the board, they then write a paragraph describing and comparing the two similar items for both similarity and difference. Use such objects as a cup and a mug, an avocado and a pear, or a briefcase and an overnight case; or have them look at pictures of a cradle and a crib or of a fork and a spoon.

2. When reading a story, stop students at appropriate places and ask them to make predictions as to what might happen next or what someone is feeling.

3. Make sets of cards that give some facts and ask students inferential-type questions. Examples:

The sky was filled with black clouds. The wind began to blow. Lightning flashed.

What will happen next?

The music was lively. Pretty soon, Sandy was keeping the beat with her fingers. She began to move her toes.

What will happen next?

DEFICIT: does not understand the concept of "hurry"

Intervention

Model the concept of "hurry." Have students watch and describe the difference in the rate of speed in walking, taking out materials, or putting materials away.

DEFICIT: reads words but does not convert them to mental images

Interventions

1. Have cooperative groups turn a story they have read into a play and act it out.

2. Demonstrate what it means to see something in your "mind's eye." For example:

    Mary built a snowman. Later she laughed because her cat was sitting on the snowman's head.

    Ask the kids, "What color was the cat?" They will go back to reread it. Say, "I pictured a gray striped cat like my cat at home. What do you see?" They will catch on and volunteer different colors of cats. Tell them it's okay for us to see cats of different colors in our minds unless the story specifies what color the cat is.

3. Use marginalia (see Chapter Eleven).

Memory Deficits

DEFICIT: cannot remember what was just seen

Interventions

1. Play memory games.

    Show the student ten objects in a box for thirty seconds. Close the lid and have the student name as many objects as he can. Vary the objects and repeat the game. Tell the student the tricks he can use to remember what's in there. *(What colors did I see? What is it used for? In what room is it found?)*

    Play games using a short vocabulary list, such as

    am   be   can   do   is

    are   been   could   did

    Have students study the words for a few minutes, then try to see how many they can remember. Teach students to use a formula: two *a* words, two *b* words, two *c* words, two *d* words, and one *i* word.

    "Concentration" is another game that stimulates memory. On one card, print a word. On the other, draw a corresponding picture. Make about ten of these pairs and arrange them so that pairs are not together. Have the child name each word and point to the picture. Then turn all the cards upside down. Time the child. As the child turns a card up, she should attempt to find its mate. Play often enough that the child can see she is showing improvement.

2. Teach older students to highlight, outline, and summarize information.

3. Teach note-taking skills and use advanced organizers.

4. Teach children to use resources (encyclopedias, dictionaries, indexes) to locate needed information and to locate the same information later.

5. Teach students to use verbal rehearsal when learning spelling. For example, in a word such as *satisfy*, the student's self-talk should go something like this: "I can hear the *s*, I can hear the *a*, I can hear the *t*—*s a t* spells *sat*. I see the word *is*. I can hear the *f*. The *y* sounds like an *i*, but it's spelled with a *y*. Hmmm . . . *sat is fy* spells *satisfy*." Model this activity daily with words until students internalize them. Self-talk done out loud will help them learn and retain spelling.

6. Teach kids to use mnemonic devices or associative clues to assist memory.

7. Allow students to take open-book tests.

8. Use art activities that involve observation coupled with verbal instruction.

DEFICIT: cannot remember what was just heard

Interventions

1. Write a list of questions to be answered as the lesson proceeds.

2. Tape-record the session.

3. Encourage note-taking.

4. Repeat as you proceed, or assign a peer buddy to repeat the information.

DEFICIT: cannot remember what was just seen or heard
(Severe memory deficits. Scores on the Visual Aural Digit Span test [VADS] fall at or below the 10th percentile.)

Interventions

1. Decide what information *must* be acquired. Weed out nonessential stuff.

2. Give the parent and student a list of what must be learned and show the parent how to work with the child.

3. Commit yourself to the task. Don't believe that "he just can't learn it." All students can learn—it just takes incredible amounts of time and effort to get the job done. This is why it is so essential to carefully

screen what must be learned—for example, survival words or phrases, such as "stop," "exit," or "keep out." You must commit yourself to the student, and it is crucial for you to work on the tasks *every day!* Start small. If you don't get results in a few weeks, do the drills twice a day. Once learned, this material will still need to be reinforced regularly.

4. Allow the use of calculators in math.

5. Allow students to take open-book tests (easiest), matching tests (easy), or multiple-choice tests (harder) rather than requiring tests involving pure recall (hardest). To test important knowledge, you may want to give all three kinds of tests on the material. As the child masters one kind of questioning, go on to the next.

6. Use concrete examples and experiences in teaching: the child sees it, hears it, does it.

DEFICIT: cannot remember to capitalize, punctuate, indent; has trouble spelling

Interventions

1. In the prewriting stage, help the child make a brief outline of what he wants to say. Have the child number his ideas in the sequence he will write them. Next, allow the child to write, not worrying at this point about mechanics. Help the student learn to edit.

2. Allow the student to use a word processing program that has an editing program built in.

DEFICIT: does not attend to directions

Interventions

1. Use a signal to indicate that directions will follow. At camp, for example, we used to sing "Announcements . . . announcements . . . announcements!" This signal got everyone quiet and ready to listen. You could substitute the word "Directions."

2. Have the students move to the front of the room during the input part of instruction. This is especially appropriate for primary grades.

3. If directions are given orally, hold them to no more than three. Hold up one finger, give the first direction, and have students repeat it. Hold up the second finger, give the second direction, and have students repeat it. Follow the same procedure for the third direction. Then ask at least two students to repeat all three directions.

4. Put directions on the board.

5. Teach students to read directions and underline or circle words that tell them what to do. For example:

<u>Look</u> at each set of words. On the blank line,

<u>write</u> the word that best fits the sentence.

6. Circulate early during independent work periods to see if students are proceeding according to the directions. Clear up any misunderstandings as quickly as you can.

Students with Poor Work Habits

DEFICIT: does not begin assignments

Intervention

Circulate early. Get stragglers working by having them sit near you or near a study buddy who will help them get started.

DEFICIT: difficulty sustaining attention

Interventions

1. When a youngster starts out listening but loses concentration midway, work her name into the lecture. "And as Anna knows, . . ."

2. Reduce distracting stimuli. For example, if you see the student begin to fiddle with an object, ask that it be put away. If it is taken out again, take it, but tell the student you will return it later.

3. Require students to take notes. They will get more out of a lecture and attend better.

4. Break an assignment into segments and provide a reward for each segment accomplished.

5. Use a peer buddy to remind a student to stay on task.

DEFICIT: distractibility

Interventions

1. Eliminate all possible distractions during independent work periods, including distracting objects. Use white music.

2. Assign a student to a carrel or a corner away from the area of movement.

3. Allow a student extra time on nonstandardized tests.

DEFICIT: low frustration tolerance, explosive tendencies

Interventions

1. Constantly monitor the stress levels of your students. Encourage parents and students to let you know when they are having a "real problem."

2. Make provisions for timeout. There are times when a student must escape. It is wise to have an ongoing arrangement with a colleague

whereby a student who needs timeout can go to the colleague's room for the balance of the period.

3. For a student who does okay in the room but gets in trouble at recess and lunch, arrange a supervised place for the student to go as soon as he has finished eating. Work with the child to develop strategies for self-control at recess. Call a conference with the parent, and explain this arrangement and the reason for it. Obtain the parent's agreement and write it as an IEP special review.

4. If a student regularly "explodes," parents should be advised to consult a physician.

DEFICIT: rushes through work, tries to "hurry up and do"

Interventions

1. LD kids who are ADHD often "hurry up and do" their work usually because as soon as they can hand it in, they can go to some other activity they find more enjoyable. They may even write all wrong answers just to be able to tell the teacher they are "through." If a student does this, talk to her before she begins the assignment about what standards you expect. Check the work before allowing the student to go to the more enjoyable activity. If you keep the assignment short, the student is more likely to try to meet your standards.

2. Arrange a daily two-way communication (notebook or phone call) system with the parent. Keep parents apprised of daily behavior, progress, and assignments with which they may need to give help.

3. Arrange for the parent to give a reward to the child when work is properly done the first time. This might involve money therapy. (See the section "Suggestions for Maximizing Educational Results" in Chapter Nine.)

4. Allow the child a choice of assignments whenever possible.

DEFICIT: incomplete assignments

Interventions

1. Shorten assignments or modify the way the child does the assignment. For example, it might be half written, half oral.

2. Allow extra time to complete the assignment.

DEFICIT: makes inappropriate noises, talks incessantly

Interventions

1. Many students make mouth noises, and many times they are not even aware of it. You must first make the student aware of the mouth noises, then motivate the student to want to try to eliminate them. You may

want to discuss this problem with the student in the presence of his parents; you will need their support to make any plan work.

2. Move the student to an area where his noises and talking are less disturbing to others.

3. Use a behavior modification chart and a parental reward system to eliminate unwanted behavior. On the chart, give a "smile" face for each period the child avoids making noises. The parent might pay the child a nickel per smile.

4. If the behavior appears to be deliberate and for the purpose of calling attention to herself, talk with the student and offer a positive way for her to receive attention if she abandons the inappropriate behavior.

DEFICIT: bothers others who are trying to work

Interventions

1. Place the child in a different grouping or seating arrangement to see where he functions best.

2. Talk to the child and explain she is not to touch others or their things or to talk to them when they are working.

3. Sometimes children behave like this when they are starved for a friend. Lacking the skills to make a friend, they prefer having others angry at them to being ignored. So you may have to help the child learn how to make friends.

4. During work periods, have the child work at a carrel or sit near you.

5. Use a behavior modification chart and a parental reward system to eliminate unwanted behavior. On the chart, give a "smile" face for each period the child behaves appropriately toward others. The parent might pay the child a nickel per smile.

Interventions for Other Common LD Classroom Problems

DEFICIT: excessive absence; child misses or is projected to miss more than twenty days of school this year for no obvious cause

Interventions

1. Send a letter to the parent pointing out that the child's absences are adversely affecting learning. Keep a copy in the folder.

2. If absences continue, talk with the student about the situation and explain why he needs to be in school every day. Ask what the student does when he stays home. If you find the student is being kept home

to babysit, you may need to involve your district's attendance review team. If the student tells you school is boring, inquire for more specific feedback of his likes and dislikes.

3. Select one or two people on the school staff who will agree to pay more attention to this child—making a point of being friendly, talking to the child about things that interest her. When the student is absent, let the child know she was missed.

4. Meet with the student's other teachers. Review and revise your expectations of the student. Modify curriculum so that the child can feel successful. Avoid embarrassing the student. If assignments are not done, find someone else who will help the student get the work done.

5. Children who miss many days of school often feel isolated, so you may need to help them make a friend. One of the easiest ways to do that is to invite two students to eat their lunches with you. Choose a child who is somewhat like the isolated child—one who also needs a friend. It is not a good idea to choose the most sociable or brightest child because that individual will have little in common with the isolated child. Such a pairing would tend to reinforce the loner's feelings that there is something wrong with him. After lunch, sit with the two students while they play checkers or work with some art materials. Be near at hand in case an awkward situation develops. At the end of the period, it is valid to confess why you wanted them to eat with you. "I noticed that both of you seemed to need a friend, and I hope that now you feel like you know each other somewhat." If this does not work, ask the isolated child to choose whom you will invite next, and then try again.

DEFICIT: student "cuts" the same class over and over

Interventions

1. Talk with the student to find out why.

2. If it is possible to change the student's program and give her another teacher, ask the student which teacher she wants; grant the wish if possible. If not, explain to the student why you can't change the schedule. Ask what it is that bothers her and then try to modify those factors.

DEFICIT: assignments not turned in

Interventions

1. Many students do not understand how teachers evaluate a student's progress. They may even be unaware that teachers keep an ongoing record of grades. Let students watch you enter a grade on several occasions. When a student who ordinarily does poorly has a good score,

grab your grade book and announce loudly, "It is a pleasure to record such a good job." This kind of remark dignifies the student receiving it, but also motivates others because they also want that kind of recognition. Likewise, you need to show students how a grade of zero adversely affects their overall average, whereas a 50 percent score may not be quite so devastating. Many students think they cannot hand in a paper that is not complete; some teachers will not accept incomplete work. The only way you can truly tell what a student has learned is to accept all papers, whether completed or unfinished.

2. Many LD students are reluctant to hand in their work, particularly if they feel it is not done well. If they ask to hand it in later, it is extremely unlikely you will ever get it. Unless you keep asking for the work, the student rarely completes it. If the student continues to miss assignments, you can then discuss your concern with her.

3. If homework is not returned, contact parents. Sometimes they will say, "I didn't know he had any. He said he did it at school." In this case, a parent conference with the student present should be followed with development of a plan for how to handle the problem. One suggestion is to make available a packet of alternative assignments that the parent can use if the child claims he has no homework.

DEFICIT: does not use time wisely

Interventions

1. Talk with the student regarding the problem. Many times the student is not aware he does this.

2. Let students know that their time is too valuable to waste just looking around. If the student is a fast worker, offer her a choice of things to do (pleasure reading, computer time, assignment as a helper with slower students, time to work on an ongoing project, or an art session) when she finishes the assignment. One art project that "keeps on giving" is mosaics. At the beginning of the year, have volunteers cut brightly colored construction paper into ½" × ½" pieces and place them in shoe boxes, one color to each box. Present one or two art lessons so that students understand how they can make stunning pictures with the pieces by gluing them to the paper. You can set up an ongoing display board for student projects. Mosaic activities are enjoyed by students ages seven to nineteen, are relatively mess free, and allow for quick clean-up.

3. Allow students to begin homework in class if time permits. If they finish it, make a big deal over "how they really used their time wisely

and can now do the things they want to do when they get home." It is wise to have them take home a note from you saying the homework is done.

DEFICIT: does not participate in classroom discussions

Interventions

1. LD students have met with failure so frequently that they often decide not to risk participating in class. To overcome this, you must ensure success on repeated occasions. (See the techniques for overcoming failure syndrome described in Chapter Nine.)

2. Verbally praise students who risk answering questions, even if they answer incorrectly. Say, "That wasn't the answer I was looking for, but I really appreciate your interest. The answer I was looking for was . . ."

3. Tell the student ahead of time that you plan to call on him, so you want him to listen carefully and be prepared to give an answer. You can even tell the student what you plan to ask him, giving him time to prepare an answer. When the answer is offered, be prepared to say, "Thank you for your contribution."

DEFICIT: does not stay seated, does not sit in the chair properly

Interventions

1. Talk with the child about your expectation that she will stay in her seat or sit properly in the chair.

2. Arrange a signal that you will give if the student forgets to stay in the seat or sit properly.

3. Consider using a sensory seat that students place on their chair.

Students with Poor Social Relationships or Behaviors

PROBLEM: poor peer relationships that lead to name calling or fighting

Interventions

1. Be alert. Always intervene, because name calling often leads to fights on the playground and parental complaints. Make reciprocal arrangements with a colleague so that if this occurs, you may send the student to the colleague's room with work to do. The student should stay there for the balance of the period and also give up the next recess.

2. Talk in private with the two students involved as soon after the incident as possible. Try to get to the bottom of the problem—why do they not get along? They may have been feuding for so long that they can't

remember, or they may find out that their disagreements began due to a misunderstanding.

3. Be sure the participants understand that there will be negative consequences for these behaviors. If the name calling happens a second time, tell the students that their parents will be asked to come in. A fight results in parents' being informed. If it is necessary to call the parents to the school, develop a Behavioral Improvement Plan.

4. Some students cannot handle unstructured time, such as on the playground. You may have to make special arrangements for them to spend their recesses under supervision that still allows them to be physically active.

5. Seat the student where he will be visible at all times.

PROBLEM: physically aggressive with teacher or staff

Interventions

1. Try to prevent frustration and anxiety-producing situations; if a situation develops that must be handled, have the principal summoned without letting the student know.

2. Never embarrass or tease the student.

3. Speak to the student calmly and respectfully at all times.

4. Talk with the student. Let the student know you want her to be successful. Develop a way the student can let you know if she is upset. Allow a timeout, when the student goes somewhere else until she feels she can return.

5. Take rumors about possession of a weapon seriously. Summon the appropriate authority to investigate.

6. If the student is threatening you, speak in a quiet, calm voice. Say, "I can see you are upset. I'm really sorry. What happened to cause this?" Do not threaten the student or make light of the circumstances.

PROBLEM: responds inappropriately to teasing

Interventions

1. Some students do not have the social skills to rebuff teasing. Students need to learn things they can say when they are being teased. For example, if someone says something about a student's mother and that person doesn't know the mother, the proper response might be, "That's ridiculous. You don't even know my mother." These are the kinds of situations that can be role-played during social skills training.

2. Intervene quickly. Send participants in opposite directions. Teasing can quickly escalate into fights.

3. If teasing occurs in your classroom, deal with the offender firmly. Remind the student that respecting others means that you do not tease or make unkind remarks. If the student says he was "just kidding," tell him teasing is not allowed, kidding or not, because it makes others feel bad.

PROBLEM: not accepted by other students

Interventions

1. Allow the student to be the leader in a group of your best-adjusted, kindest students.

2. Observe the student and try to learn why the others don't accept her. Don't be afraid to ask, "How do you feel about . . . ?" Listen carefully to their answers. They usually have merit. Then try to help the student alter those behaviors.

3. Sometimes these children get others in trouble. Be careful not to punish everyone in the group. Punish only those students you are certain are guilty.

4. If obnoxious behavior occurs under competitive circumstances, ask the student to leave the group.

5. Do not try to force interaction.

PROBLEM: blames other people, does not take responsibility for own acts

Interventions

1. In private, calmly confront the student with the facts. The child probably will go into his pattern of denial and projection. Calmly tell the student you are happy that he expressed himself, but the facts simply do not support his point of view. Levy punishment if it is a serious offense.

2. Try to get to know this child better and give her support. This behavior sometimes masks great insecurity. The parents may be harsh in punishment, so the child learns to use denial in order to avoid the punishment. Try to let this child know she does not have to be perfect to please you. It is sometimes helpful to relate stories in which you were not a perfect child either and got punished. For instance, "When I was little, my mom had this beautiful vase. I just loved it. She told me not to touch it, but I loved it so much I touched it anyway. It fell and broke. My mom was very upset and asked how it got broken. I said my little sister had broken it. Then I really got yelled at because

my little sister was only a year old, and there was no way she could have reached that vase. When my dad got home, my mom told him about my lie. From then on, even when my little sister was guilty, my parents often thought I was lying." In your social skills role playing, set up some scenarios and help the students practice the most palatable responses. Teach them to say, "I did it, but I'm really sorry. How can I make amends?"

3. In cases where you are less certain about what happened, try to uncover the truth. Say to the student or students involved, "We can solve this right here and now. But if you continue to deny responsibility, you will have to talk to the principal, which means you will miss recess and your parents will be called." Once the truth is out, ask the students to come up with at least three punishments they feel are appropriate. Choose one of these or, if none of them seem appropriate, come up with one of your own.

4. Counseling may be needed if denial and projection are frequently used by children under age ten. In older students, these mechanisms may be a sign of conduct disorder, in which case they are not likely to be extinguished.

PROBLEM: stealing

Interventions

1. Stealing among children under age nine is not as serious as it is with students over nine. Talk with younger students about why they should not steal. If a younger child steals, say, "That belongs to Jane. It's nice, and I can understand why you wanted it, but she wants it too, and it belongs to her, so we have to give it back." Tell the child that you will need to call his parent if the stealing happens again. If an older student steals, an office referral, parental involvement, and possibly counseling are in order.

2. If it happens again, inform parents and ask them to talk with the child about it while you are present.

3. In your social skills group, have the children give their views on this subject. Start by asking, "What is stealing?"

4. Keep a close eye on the student.

5. Store tempting and expensive items away from the child's reach.

PROBLEM: temper tantrums

Interventions

1. Excessive temper tantrums, even in preschoolers, may be a sign of mental health problems. Sometimes tantrums are attention-getting

behaviors—if you can eliminate the audience, the tantrum stops shortly. If the tantrums continue, you will want to refer the child for an evaluation through the proper channels.

2. When a student has repeated tantrums, talk with the class when the student is not present. Ask them to brainstorm things the class might do to help. Steer them to come up with such techniques as refraining from laughing, ignoring the behavior, or giving negative feedback, such as "You're acting like a small child."

3. If the tantrum seems to come because of frustration or anxiety, try to prevent future ones by neutralizing or avoiding situations that will cause the tantrums.

4. Temper tantrums are a power trip. The child feels helpless, so he has a tantrum to get out of the situation. Work that is commensurate with the child's level of knowledge helps. Testing the student one-to-one in a quiet setting may help. Giving the child a choice of activities also sometimes works.

5. If tantrums are a regular occurrence and are very long or violent, or include self-injurious behavior, counseling may be needed.

6. Removing the audience may shorten a tantrum.

PROBLEM: refuses to obey reasonable directives

Interventions

1. If your request was valid, evaluate how it was delivered. Sometimes under time pressure we are abrupt with students. If you decide you sounded like a drill sergeant, say, "I'm sorry, Jon. I think I barked that like an order. Please forgive me. Let me rephrase that. I would really appreciate it if you would . . ." Walk away at that point and give the student time to reconsider your request.

2. If the request was reasonable, delivered respectfully, but still ignored, wait until recess. Ask the student to remain and discuss why your request was disregarded.

PROBLEM: makes sexually inappropriate comments, displays sexually inappropriate behavior

Interventions

For a Younger Child

1. If a younger child talks a lot about sex, seems to have knowledge beyond others of the same age, or both, the child may have been molested. Take time to get to know the child better, and watch for other signs that may

indicate abuse. Do not be alone with the child, for your own legal protection. Check to see what your reporting obligation is.

2. It is not uncommon for younger children to engage in self-stimulation. If this happens, calmly take the child aside and explain that this kind of behavior is not appropriate at school and not to do it anymore.

For an Older Student

1. If an older pupil is sexually inappropriate, it may be an offense requiring referral to the principal. Sexual harassment is a serious issue and cannot be tolerated in school. Parents are filing lawsuits against schools that allow this to occur.

2. Do not allow the student out of class unless you are sure there is supervision wherever that student goes, including traveling to and from the classroom.

3. Seat the student near you and monitor any conversation.

4. Young adolescents are often "trying on" language and behavior they have observed in the media or elsewhere outside of school. Take the student aside and explain that his behavior is not acceptable at school. Identify the behavior specifically, whether it is a gesture, posture, or language. Agree on a signal you will use to remind the student to stop. If the behavior is not extreme or intimidating, allow the student a couple of days with your signal to eliminate the behavior, before writing a referral.

5. If the behavior does not stop, refer the student for counseling.

PROBLEM: cannot work cooperatively in a group

Interventions

1. Change the group the student is in.

2. Talk with the student about why she misbehaves at these times.

3. Allow the student to work alone; do not force her to participate in a group activity.

PROBLEM: does not respond to positive reinforcement

Interventions

1. Once in a while you will find a student who does not work for positive reward. Talk to the student about this observation. Ask him why. Older students may not want to be perceived as a teacher's pet; a "macho" image, for example, may be undermined by positive strokes from a woman teacher.

2. These students may work to avoid loss of privileges.

3. Have a conference with the student and the parent. Explain the problem and ask for guidance.

PROBLEM: cheating

Interventions

1. Guide a class discussion on the importance of honesty. With older students, introduce the word *credibility.*

2. Explain to students that teachers need to know what each student has learned or has not learned, so that they can plan lessons that help students make progress in all academic areas.

3. Provide an explanation of the severe consequences for cheating. With older students, guide the class in finding a grade average with a zero. Then use the same scores, replace the zero with a score of 40 percent, and find the average.

4. Reduce stress by preparing all students for tests. Let them know in advance about what day the test will take place. Provide study guides so that students will know which areas to study for their tests and won't spend time and energy studying something not covered on your test.

5. Many students, especially those with learning disabilities, do not employ effective study strategies and techniques when preparing for tests. Teach specific study skills and strategies appropriate for the subject, grade level, and the student's strengths. Practice these skills and techniques in class before assigning studying for a test as homework. These can increase a student's confidence in her ability to take tests and perhaps decrease her need or tendency to cheat.

Students with Dyslexia

All dyslexic individuals have trouble with reading tasks, but not every person who has a reading deficit is dyslexic. If a child reverses letters or numbers—that is, in writing turns them the wrong way or gets confused when reading words, such as reading the word *was* for *saw*—or sees the word *rabbit* and calls it *bunny*, it does not necessarily mean the child is dyslexic. Young children, below grade 3, may have a tendency to do this but will outgrow it usually by third grade.

Dyslexic individuals' problems in learning to read are evidenced by one or more of the following:

- Poor phonemic awareness (phonemic awareness is the ability to hear discrete sounds in words).

- Difficulty telling how many sounds are in a word.

- Inability to distinguish the order of sounds in a word.

- Inability to hear the similarity of rhyming words.

- Tendency not to hear subtle differences in sounds, such as short vowels *i* and *e* or consonant sounds *p* and *b.*

- Confusion of right and left.

- Slow acquisition of decoding skills.

- Lack of development in fine motor skills resulting in slow or poor handwriting (or both).

- Spatial deficits resulting in clumsiness or accident proneness.

- Slow recall of known sounds or words; they can appear confused when in the process of retrieval: "I know I know that . . . wait a second." Sometimes they may shake their head as though it will help.

- Tendency to experience problems in articulation of longer words, such as *spaghetti, particularly, chimney.*

- ADD or ADHD.

- Visual perceptual deficits.

- Social immaturity for their age.

- Organizational problems.

Although dyslexic individuals typically have issues in learning to read, they usually have average- to above-average intellectual ability, are intellectually curious, and are often hard workers. Dyslexic individuals are often very gifted. They may distinguish themselves in drawing, music, acting, math reasoning, physical education, use of imagination, or working with their hands. They respond very positively when parents and teachers encourage them to hone their talents.

What can we do to help these children make the most of their school experiences?

- Give the child extra time to complete assignments or focus on the most important points.

- Provide true-false or multiple-choice tests to help with recall; when appropriate, give oral tests.

- Help them with time management by breaking long assignments into manageable parts with a date for completion of each part.

- Teach and reteach phonetic elements.

- Allow students to read a section of text in advance before being asked to read it to you. After they have read it to you, read it back to them as they follow along word for word.

- Give frequent positive feedback.

- Teach them to use compensatory devices on the computer, and allow them to type any assignments they want to turn in.

- Students might create a PowerPoint presentation instead of a full report.

- Instead of assigning only writing projects, allow students a choice of projects so that they can use their talents and, as a result, feel successful. Students might want to act out a play rather than write one, or make a fort rather than do research about forts.

Following is an example of a history assignment that offers an array of options to suit different learning styles.

Sample History Assignment

Choose and complete two activities from the following list to demonstrate your understanding of the information in this unit on the period of the American Revolution.

1. Write a two-page report on the period.

2. Make a map of New England and place a star indicating the places of major battles. Include a key that tells what happened at each spot.

3. Make a diorama representing the American Revolution. Orally describe one of the following:

   - "The shot heard 'round the world" (Concord Bridge)
   - The Boston Tea Party (Boston Harbor)
   - The Boston Massacre
   - The Battle of Lexington Green (Lexington)

4. Perform a play of a conversation that might have occurred among the signers of the Declaration of Independence as they signed the document.

5. Name the ten rights we, as Americans, are guaranteed under the Bill of Rights.

6. Draw or find pictures of the houses of the times and write or tell about them.

7. Draw or find pictures of weapons of those times.

8. Draw or find pictures of the clothes of those times.

9. Draw or find pictures of the implements of the times, such as bellows, a bell with clapper, a primer, a musket, a spittoon, a chamber pot, or a wash bowl. Explain each item's function.

Students with ADD or ADHD

Attention Deficit Disorder (ADD) or Attention Deficit Hyperactivity Disorder (ADHD) occurs as a comorbid condition in a significant portion of the LD population. It is not a new condition, having been described as far back as ancient Greece.

Medical Treatment of ADD and ADHD

Treatment of these conditions has become a hot issue. Since the late 1930s, drug therapy has been used to treat them. Many people are alarmed by the rapidly increasing number of youngsters being given prescription drugs. They believe that some physicians dispense the drugs with little verification of the diagnosis and without adequate monitoring of the effectiveness of the medication. Both are legitimate concerns.

To medicate or not to medicate—that is only one of the questions that arise, and medication is only one of the treatment options. The symptoms being exhibited may spring from ADD or ADHD, from an anxiety disorder, depression, Conduct Disorder, Bipolar Disorder, Oppositional Disorder, or Obsessive-Compulsive Disorder. The symptoms that appear to be ADD may be side effects of certain drugs prescribed for other medical conditions, such as hyperthyroidism or movement disorders.

When a school becomes concerned about a youngster's behavior, the matter should be discussed with the parent. This is an appropriate task for the Student Study Team.

Who makes the decision to medicate? Even when a doctor prescribes stimulant medication, it is the parent who holds the final decision. Schools are not allowed to insist that a child be medicated. With parental permission and a doctor's order, school personnel do sometimes dispense medication to the student. The person who knows the child best needs to be diligent about monitoring the effectiveness of the drugs and reporting to parents any untoward side effects. Figure 10.1 provides useful pharmaceutical information to help you recognize the side effects associated with particular medications.

The side effects from medication vary widely between individuals. Serious side effects have been reported from medications used to treat ADHD,

FIGURE 10.1.

Medications Used to Treat ADHD.

DRUG	DOSING	COMMON SIDE EFFECTS	DURATION OF BEHAVIORAL EFFECTS	PROS	PRECAUTIONS
RITALIN® Methylphenidate Tablets 5 mg 10 mg 20 mg	Start with morning dose of 5 mg/day and increase up to 0.3–0.7 mg/kg of body weight. 2.5–60 mg/day*	Insomnia, decreased appetite, weight loss, headache, irritability, stomachache	3–4 hours	Works quickly (within 30–60 minutes); effective in about 50% of adult patients; good safety record	Use cautiously in patients with marked anxiety, motor tics or with family history of Tourette syndrome.
RITALIN-SR® Methylphenidate Tablet 20 mg	Start with morning dose of 20 mg and increase up to 0.3–0.7 mg/kg of body weight. Up to 60 mg/day*	Insomnia, decreased appetite, weight loss, headache, irritability, stomachache	About 7 hours	Particularly useful for adolescents and adults to avoid needing a noon time dose; good safety record	Use cautiously in patients with marked anxiety, motor tics or with family history of Tourette syndrome.
CONCERTA® Methylphenidate Tablet 18 mg 36 mg	Once a day dosing in morning. Start with 18 mg and increase up to 54 mg	Insomnia, decreased appetite, weight loss, headache, irritability, stomachache	About 12 hours	Works quickly (within 30–60 minutes); avoid needing a noon time or afternoon dose	Use cautiously in patients with marked anxiety, motor tics or with family history of Tourette syndrome.
DEXEDRINE® Dextroamphetamine Tablet Spansules 5 mg 5 mg 10 mg	Start with morning dose of 5 mg/day and increase up to 0.3–0.7 mg/kg of body weight. Give in divided doses 2–3 times per day. 2.5–40 mg/day*	Insomnia, decreased appetite, weight loss, headache, irritability, stomachache	3–4 hours (tablets) 8–10 hours (spansules)	Works quickly (within 30–60 minutes); may avoid noontime dose in spansule form; good safety record	Use cautiously in patients with marked anxiety, motor tics or with family history of Tourette syndrome.
ADDERALL® Mixed salts of a single-entity amphetamine Tablets 5 mg 10 mg 20 mg 30 mg	Start with a morning dose of 2.5 mg for 3–5 year olds. For 6 years and older start with 5 mg once or twice daily	Insomnia, decreased appetite, weight loss, headache, irritability, stomachache	4–6 hours	Works quickly (within 30–60 minutes); action may last somewhat longer than other standard stimulants	Use cautiously in patients with marked anxiety, motor tics or with family history of Tourette syndrome.
TOFRANIL® Imipramine Hydrochloride Tablets 10 mg 25 mg 50 mg	Start with dose of 25 mg in evening and increase 25 mg every 3–5 days as needed. Given in single or divided doses, morning and evening. 25–150 mg/day*	Dry mouth, decreased appetite, headache, stomachache, dizziness, constipation, mild tachycardia	12–24 hours	Helpful for ADD patients with co-morbid depression or anxiety; lasts throughout the day	May take 2–4 weeks for clinical response; to detect pre-existing cardiac defect a baseline ECG may be recommended. Discontinue gradually.
NORPRAMIN® Desipramine Hydrochloride 10 mg 75 mg 25 mg 100 mg 50 mg 150 mg	Start with dose of 25 mg in evening and increase 25 mg every 3–5 days as needed. Given in single or divided doses, morning and evening. 25–150 mg/day*	Dry mouth, decreased appetite, headache, stomachache, dizziness, constipation, mild tachycardia	12–24 hours	Helpful for ADD patients with co-morbid depression or anxiety; lasts throughout the day	May take 2–4 weeks for clinical response; to detect pre-existing cardiac defect a baseline ECG may be recommended. Discontinue gradually.
CLONIDINE® Catapres Tablets Patches .1 mg TTS-1 .2 mg TTS-2 .3 mg TTS-3	Start with dose of .025–.05 mg/day in evening and increase by similar dose every 3–7 days as needed. Given in divided doses 3–4 times per day. 0.15–3mg/day*	Sleepiness, hypotension, headache, dizziness, stomachache, nausea, dry mouth, localized skin reactions with patch	3–6 hours (oral form) 5 days (skin patch)	Helpful for ADHD patients with co-morbid tic disorder or severe hyperactivity and/or aggression	Sudden discontinuation could result in rebound hypertension; to avoid daytime tiredness starting dose given at bedtime and increased slowly

*Note: *Dosage varies from individual to individual. This list does not include all medications potentially prescribed for ADHD and is not intended to replace the advice of a physician.*

Source: *Harvey C. Parker, Problem-Solver Guide for Students with ADHD: Ready-to-Use Interventions for Elementary and Secondary Students. Plantation, FL: Specialty Press, 1999.*

Used with permission.

and deaths have been attributed to some stimulant drugs. To date, only one selective serotonin reuptake inhibitor antidepressant has been approved for use by children under the age of eighteen. The decision to use medication must always be made under a doctor's supervision, with frequent monitoring of the child.

Behavioral Considerations for Students with ADD or ADHD

Students with ADD or ADHD need close adult supervision at all times. Parents and teachers need to be trained in behavior modification techniques that can help the student with classroom performance. It is important to set expectations for each activity beforehand.

First, obtain eye contact with the student. Next, quietly and concisely explain what you want the student to do. Ask him to repeat the instruction. At first, you may need to give only one direction, and wait for the student to complete that step before giving a second direction.

Children with ADD or ADHD may respond poorly to loud or abrasive voices; they may misinterpret this as "being yelled at." A quiet, calm, slow-moving pace with positive verbal praise works best. Moving close to the student is sometimes an effective way to get the student to cease an undesirable behavior. If the child will be faced with a new situation or a change of schedule, prepare her for any such changes. Inform the student of acceptable and unacceptable behaviors. If appropriate, you may want to give the student a drawing pad and pencil should there be any "lag" time in the transition.

Behaviors that involve hurting others, destroying property, mocking or disrespecting adults, dangerous acts, or cursing are *never* acceptable and must be punished with some form of timeout. The place and length of timeout should be determined by the seriousness and frequency of the offense.

Having ADHD does predispose a child to some difficulties; however, there are benefits to having a mind that enjoys stimulation. Some people credit their ADHD with their ability to accomplish more tasks than those without ADHD. Others say their ADHD makes them better at handling a chaotic or noisy situation, because they really enjoy the stimulation. The caveats are that excessive stimulation, moving very quickly through something, and the tendency to forget or move on from something that just happened don't help a student in school.

Dealing with children with ADHD truly can be a balancing act, but in my experience, one thing that is always beneficial for children with ADHD is more movement and time for exercise. I worked with one little boy who couldn't sit still for a story until after recess; before that he could not focus his attention. Keep in mind that many children don't have a physical outlet for their energy if they watch television or spend excessive amounts of time indoors. I have found that using rewards, such as extra computer time or extra recess time, go a long way toward helping a student with ADHD.

If you can, incorporate movement into your lessons, or maybe just have time to dance to music when students show signs of slowing down. Sometimes giving an outlet to the energy can even be helpful to you: perhaps one particular student can run errands to the office, or maybe he can hand out papers, anything that involves extra walking. Experiment with different movement strategies, because other students benefit from extra exercise too.

Tips for Classroom Teachers

1. Be calm. Move slowly. Talk slowly. When you speak, keep your voice level so that it does not become strained. Students with ADD or ADHD interpret a stressed voice as a signal that things are out of control.

2. Consider the placement of the child in the class. Seat children with ADD or ADHD among quiet or calm children, at the front of the room, or near you.

3. For independent work, assign the student a carrel removed from heavy classroom traffic and free from distractions.

4. Divide each assignment into segments. Give the child one segment at a time and set a timer so that you remember to check on her progress. Organize these segments so that the child completes the most important portions first.

5. Make sure the student knows what to do, and supervise the child as he gets started.

6. Use verbal praise and positive approaches—for example, "Thank you for raising your hand and waiting" or "Your work is really good."

7. Ignore behaviors that don't disturb others.

8. Use a peer tutor to help the child stay on task.

9. Allow extra time for tests if possible.

10. Use a point system to encourage work production.

11. Use behavioral contracts to work on behavior.

12. Be very calm in giving reprimands.

13. Prepare the student for changes in daily routine. ADHD students adapt better to changes like substitute teachers and field trips when prepared ahead of time to expect them.

14. Give students time to move around when possible, and allow students to pick a work space for a quiet activity. They might prefer a beanbag chair or a spot toward the back of the room.

15. Offer to let students use headphones with classical or another soothing type of music, or with ocean or nature sounds, when they need to read quietly or are stressed. This often works well as a reward.

16. For students who become easily stressed, you may offer a "play table" as a reward, where there is play dough set out, paper to cut, building blocks, Legos, or possibly artwork that needs to be done on a bulletin board. All these activities require concentration, but they also require movement, and some students respond very well when the work they are doing brings them closer to a reward.

17. If a student is having trouble with a reading assignment, see if you can find a digital or audio text. Some students will use these texts all the way through college, as many textbooks have been published in a digital format. There are even free copies of digital texts available to those who are blind or have been diagnosed as dyslexic. This helps keep students from falling behind in other content areas while they are working on their reading skills.

Chapter 11

Reading and the Student with Learning Disabilities

George Patton (1885–1945)

American World War II general
Had trouble learning to read and write; had hallmark characteristics of dyslexia; was often tactless, but known for his persistence

Contribution:

The Military: Employed great military tactics that led to victory in World Wars I and II; was the major organizer and user of mechanized warfare—that is, tanks

---

Reading is the most important academic skill and the foundation for all academic learning. If a person cannot read efficiently, his opportunity for a productive and satisfying life is markedly reduced. Functionally illiterate adults, those who read below a fifth-grade level, generally find themselves limited to low-income jobs punctuated by frequent periods of layoff. Research shows the value of investing in education.

One in five students is likely to have trouble learning to read. Eighty percent of students who are identified for special education will have deficits in reading. Tools are available to diagnose these children at age five. If appropriate instruction is begun early and periodic follow-up remedial help given as needed, many children can be prevented from developing the emotional overlay of failure syndrome, which sometimes manifests itself in bad behavior and truancy. A higher percentage of students with LD can then graduate from high school, and their achievement levels will be higher.

Children from low-income homes are particularly at risk for educational failure. Providing quality preschools is beneficial for them.

Who Will Have Trouble Learning to Read?

Several indicators tend to appear among young children (kindergartners and first graders) who have trouble learning to read. Following are some early warning signs:

- The children talked late or had delayed speech at age two. This is one of the primary warning signs.

- These children have trouble communicating and show problematic speech patterns, such as dropping final consonants and mispronouncing common words.

- They have a limited vocabulary that does not match that of their peers.

- They are difficult to understand when they speak.

- They cannot rhyme.

- They have trouble singing songs or repeating simple nursery rhymes.

- They do not know the names for common objects or are slow to recall known information.

- They are inattentive and move from one activity to another more often than others.

- Their fine motor skills are below average; they have problems holding pencils and handling small blocks, letters, or other manipulatives.

- Their progress in learning symbols and letter sounds is clearly slower; they cannot "manipulate" sounds.

- When these children are asked to draw a picture of themselves, their drawings show fewer details and are markedly less "mature" than those of other kindergartners.

- When stories are read to them, such children show little interest; when asked to sequence events from a story read to them, they may make errors from their lack of understanding of story details.

Elements of a Balanced Literacy Program

A balanced reading program should include the following:

1. Reading to children

2. Shared book and writing experiences

3. Phonemic awareness training

4. Organized, explicit phonics decoding instruction and practice

5. Oral language development and listening experiences

6. Systematic vocabulary development

7. Guided reading, with attention to comprehension

8. Individualized reading lessons, with attention to the construction of meaning

9. Sustained silent reading

10. Modeling of writing skills and techniques

11. Opportunities for writing every day

12. Content-area reading and writing

13. Instruction and practice in editing

14. Ongoing diagnosis to ensure skills are acquired

To explore the research behind the elements of a strong reading program, you can download or order a free report called "Teaching Children to Read" (National Reading Panel, 2000; www.nationalreadingpanel. org). Further information on reading instruction is also available from the National Institute for Literacy (www.nifl.gov).

Phonemic Awareness

Phonemic awareness is the understanding that spoken words and syllables are made up of sequences of speech sounds and that it is possible to "tease out" or isolate these sounds in order to assist oneself in spelling and writing. Research has shown that phonemic awareness is a powerful predictor of success in learning to read. It is more highly correlated to the process of learning to read than intelligence, reading readiness, or listening comprehension (Stanovich, 1988, 1993).

When children cannot hear and manipulate the sounds in spoken words—a deficit commonly found in LD students—they have trouble reading. This inability is the most frequent cause of reading failure (Share and Stanovich, 1995). This is also one of the core issues for children with dyslexia. They cannot manipulate the sounds of words or process all the letter sounds.

Children with phonemic processing problems may have trouble with

- Counting the syllables in a word

- Sounding out words when reading aloud

- Spelling out loud and on paper

- Separating a word into its smallest sound parts: *bat = b + a + t*

- Learning to spell new words

- Reading passages for meaning; they tend to read slowly because they have trouble with processing words as single units, so they try to sound out each letter, and by the time they sound out new words, they have forgotten new subject matter

- Understanding the meanings behind parts of speech

- Writing complete sentences, because they don't understand fragments

Research shows that explicit training in phonemic awareness benefits all young readers. For at least one in five it makes the difference between success and failure in reading. According to Adams (1990), "the enabling importance of phonemic awareness is the single greatest breakthrough in reading pedagogy in this century."

In early childhood, developing phonemic awareness does not involve learning written symbols (*a, b, c,* and so on) or words. In homes, nursery schools, preschools, and kindergartens, there is a need for children to

1. Hear rhyme by singing rhyming songs, reading Mother Goose rhymes, and generating rhyme

2. Engage in alliterative language play by listening for and generating words that begin with the same initial sound (for example, "Peter Piper picked a peck of pickled peppers")

3. Identify ending phonemes that are the same

4. Break words into syllables (for example, by clapping out syllables)

5. Blend phonemes to make words (see sample lessons in next sections)

6. Segment words into phonemes

7. Make new words by substituting one phoneme for another

Sample Phonemic Awareness Lesson 1: Kindergarten–Grade 1

This sample lesson is appropriate for use early in the school year, as soon as children can sit on the floor around you and attend for a few minutes. A knowledge of letters is not necessary.

Objective: Given two separate sounds, children will be able to pull the sounds together or blend them to obtain a recognizable word.

Anticipatory Materials: Have a decorative party bag in your lap that contains a *map, pen,* baseball *cap,* bottle *top,* and paper *fan.* The bag usually focuses attention and curiosity.

Directions: *Say:* "We are going to play a game today. I have some things in this bag, and you are going to try to figure out what they are from listening to two sounds I will make. I will show you how we are going to do that on the first one. Watch closely."

Step 1: Put up your right fist (as shown in diagram below) and make the sound that the letter *m* makes while moving your fist up and down. Have the children repeat the sound. *Say:* "Can you remember how to make the sound that *m* makes?"

Step 2: Leaving your right fist up, raise your left fist and make the sounds of the phonogram *ap.* Wiggling the left fist up and down, have children repeat the *ap* sound.

Step 3: As you put your right hand up, make the *m* sound; put your left hand up, making the *ap* sound.

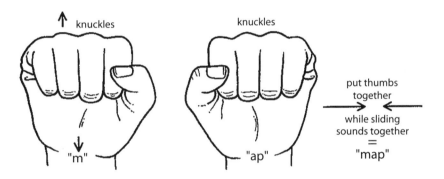

Step 4: Bring your fists together slowly while dragging and singing the sounds, "*m . . . ap.*" If no one hears the word *map,* model it again by speeding up a notch to "*m . . ap*" or "*m.ap.*" Once the children guess the word, pull the map out of the sack. *Say:* "Yes, the word is *map.* We used a map on our vacation, so we did not get lost."

Step 5: Use the same procedure to do other words. When working on this skill, on subsequent days, you can put a picture of the object in the sack. Do the blending exercise with about five words each day.

b + ed (bed), m + op (mop), n + et (net), n + est (nest)

Sample Phonemic Awareness Lesson 2: Kindergarten–Grade 1

This is an oral activity for young children. To heighten interest, construct a robot body from a large box. Cover the box with aluminum foil and add knobs and dials to the front.

This activity focuses on teasing out phonemes, which is an essential prerequisite to reading. During this type of practice, no letters are used, and nothing is done in writing.

Objective: Children will learn how to slow their voice flow so that they can "tease out" or isolate each sounded phoneme in a word and count the number of phonemes they heard.

Anticipatory Materials: Robot body with knobs and dials.

Directions: *Say:* "Today we will learn to talk like a robot so that we can get ready to learn to read. I call this game 'ROBOT.' Can you speak slowly so that you sound like a robot talking?"

Step 1: Demonstrate "slow talking" with the word *robot.* Have the children repeat the word one by one. You may suggest that they wear the robot body while they take turns speaking. Prompt them until they can say the word so slowly that you hear all five phonemes.

Step 2: Say: "This time, as I say *robot* we will count with our fingers how many sounds we can hear." As you make each sound, raise another finger. (Repeat twice.)

Step 3: Say: "I'm going to say a word very slowly like a robot, and each of you will listen and show me with your fingers how many sounds you can hear."

Suggested words: *a.t* (2), *b.u.g* (3), *u.p* (2)

By this point you will note that some children are catching on. You may want to have one of them go to the front and say the next word very slowly. Give the child the word he is to say—for example, *man.*

More words: *t.o.p* (3), *i.f* (2), *l.e.g* (3)

In subsequent lessons, follow this plan and gradually add four-letter words, such as *f.r.o.g* and *l.o.s.t.* You may give words that have silent letters, such as *m.o.r.e.,* but the children's answer will show three fingers, not four, because the *e* is not a voiced phoneme.

Extension Activities: These types of lessons need to go on daily for several weeks until each child can isolate the sounds in one-syllable words that have up to five voiced phonemes.

One-syllable words may be chosen from the word list that appears later in this chapter.

Sample Phonemic Awareness Lesson 3:
Grades 1–2 (Instructional Level)

Objective: Children will learn to substitute one initial phoneme for another; for example, *mop* becomes *top.*

Anticipatory Materials: For this lesson, have ready drawings or simple pictures to display on the board—a *mop,* a *purse,* a *cat.* Into a paper sack, place a toy *top,* a picture of a *nurse,* and a *hat* (not a cap).

Directions: Point to the picture of the mop. *Say:* "Who will tell me what this is? . . . That's right, it's a mop. We use it to clean the kitchen floor. The word *mop* begins with the *m* sound—*mmm.* If I take the *mmm* sound off and put a *t* in its place, I have a new word, *top.*" Take the top out of the bag and announce, "Here is a top." Do the same activity, changing *purse* to *nurse.* Then ask them to change *cat* to *hat.*

Step 1: Write the words:

> mop
> top

Ask: "How are these words the same?" You may have to point to the *op* portion of each word and say, "Yes, both words have an *op* sound in them, but the first letter is different."

Step 2: Write the words:

> purse
> nurse

Ask: "How are these words the same?" Help children hear that the words rhyme, and note that rhymes happen when the words sound alike except for the first sound.

Step 3: Write the words:

> cat
> hat

Ask: "How are these words the same?" Again, help the children hear the words rhyme and recognize that the first sound is different.

Step 4: Say: "I'm going to say a word. Then I'm going to tell you to change the first sound. You will try to make the new word. The word I'm going to say is *can.*"

"Change the *c* (make the /k/ sound) to *m.*"

The children should change *can* to *man*.

Using the same procedure, change *bed* to *red*

cap to *lap*

bat to *fat*

wet to *pet*

sit to *hit*

fun to *sun*

Extension Activity: Construct some *word family cards* as shown for a wall display:

can	pan		cot	not		fun
fan	ran		dot	pot		gun
Jan	Dan		hot	rot		sun
man	tan		lot			run

Sample Phonemic Awareness Lesson 4: Any Grade to High School

The format described here can be used with students with LD at many grades. For this exercise, the students are given a white board or piece of paper.

Say: "Today we'll work on a skill that will help you in reading and spelling. I will say a word, and we will repeat it three times, saying it more slowly each time. Each time we say the word, you will try to count the number of sounds you can hear. Let me show you what we will do. Watch what I do."

Say: "*lake*" Emphasize the first sound.
Write: ____ (one blank)

Say: "*l.a.k.e*" Emphasize the second sound.
Write: ____ ____ (two blanks)

Say: "*l.a.k.e*" Emphasize the *k* sound.
Write: ____ ____ ____ (three blanks)

Say: "That's right, you hear three sounds." Say the word slowly again and point to each sound as you work your way through the word.

In these lessons, you do not use letters. The purpose of the activity is just to model the process of teasing out sounds. This will be a critically important skill in teaching students sound combinations such as the *ough* that says *oo* in the next example.

Say: "This time do it with me. The word is *through*. Model the process described before—slow, slower, slowest—and ask children to listen for each sound they can hear. Students will hear three sounds: *th r ough*. On their white board or paper, they write "<u>th</u> <u>r</u> <u>ough</u>." (*Th* is one sound, *r* is one sound, and *ough* is the last sound.)

If you use this kind of activity three times a week, students will gain in their ability to hear sounds. Begin with words that have only two to four sounds. You can use a word such as "church," which only has three sounds, *ch, ur,* and *ch*. As students grow in proficiency, increase the difficulty to four to five sounds. Use words such as "joint"—*j oi n t* (four sounds), and "flower"—*f l ow er* (four sounds).

A Step-by-Step Guide for Teaching Reading to Students with Learning Disabilities

Step 1: Convince the child you can teach him to read. If another student gives testimony that you have helped him and the new student sees him reading, that is a powerful motivator.

Step 2: Discuss and note what kind of rewards the child prefers. The principle here is "just a little bit of sugar helps the medicine go down." A point system or edible reward can help a reluctant or frustrated student.

Step 3: Determine what the child does or does not know. Using alphabet cards, ask the child to give you the name and sound for each letter you present in a random presentation. (See the reproducible alphabet cards at the end of this chapter.) Using a list of the alphabet letters (as shown in Figure 11.1), mark a "+" if he identifies the correct sound, a zero (0) for an incorrect one. (Also note whether it takes a long time for the child to recall the sound.) In the case of vowels or letters with more than one sound, record which specific sound(s) the child gives. For example, he may make the *s* sound for the *c* sound. If this happens, ask if he knows another sound for the *c*. If he knows only the *s* sound, record a plus; if he doesn't name the *k* sound, record a zero (as shown in Figure 11.2).

Step 4: Using the Wide Range Achievement Test; a similar word test, such as the running record; or the word test from the Peabody Individual Achievement Test, *determine the level of word recognition.* When the child miscalls a word, recording what he said may help you pinpoint some areas of needed instruction.

FIGURE 11.1.

Letter-Sound Assessment.

_____ **A** sounds like the beginning of *apple*. If the student gives you the long sound (*a* as in *ape*), say, "Yes, it does sound like that sometimes. Do you know any other sound for *a*?"

_____ **B** is a little poof of air that you hear at the beginning of words such as *ball*. If the student says "buh," you will need to reteach the sound until the student no longer adds the short *u* to the *b*.

_____ **C** is the sound you hear at the beginning of *cat*. If the student gives you the soft *c* as in *city*, say, "It is true that *c* always makes an *s* sound, but *c* has another sound. Do you know what it is?"

_____ **D** sounds like it does in the word *door*. Again we want to be sure the student makes a pure *d*, not "duh."

_____ **E** sounds like it does in the word *edge*. Remember, the *e* can have the long sound as it does in *eel*.

_____ **F** sounds like it does in the word *fish*.

_____ **G** sounds like it does in the word *goat*. If the student gives you the soft *g* sound as in *gym*, acknowledge that it can sound like a *j*, but ask if the student knows another sound.

_____ **H** sounds like it does in the word *house*.

_____ **I** sounds like it does in the word *itch*. Remember that *i* can have the long sound also, as it does in the word *ice*.

_____ **J** sounds like it does in the word *jar*.

_____ **K** sounds like it does in the word *kite*.

_____ **L** sounds like it does in the word *light* or *lamp*.

_____ **M** sounds like it does in *moon*.

_____ **N** sounds like it does in *nose*.

_____ **O** sounds like it does in the word *octopus*. As with the other vowels, it has a long sound also, like in *Ohio*.

_____ **P** sounds like it does in the word *pan*.

_____ **Q** sounds like it does in *queen* (*kw*).

_____ **R** sounds like it does in the word *red* or *her*. Be sure the student is not saying "ruh."

_____ **S** sounds like it does in *sun* or *snake* (a hissing sound).

_____ **T** sounds like it does in *tack*.

_____ **U** sounds like it does in *up*. It also can sound like a long *u* as it does in *use*.

_____ **V** sounds like it does in *vase*.

_____ **W** sounds like it does in *water*.

_____ **X** says *x*.

_____ **Y** has three sounds. It can sound like it does in *you* or *yes*. It can sound like an *e* as it does in *happy* or *baby*. Finally, in some words such as *my*, it sounds like the long *i*.

_____ **Z** sounds like it does in the word *zipper* or *zoo*.

Step 5: Using nonsense words, determine whether the child can blend sounds into words he has never seen before:

lub (think of *tub*)   *fot* (think of *got*)   *maft* (think of *raft*)

If a student does not attempt the first word, model it slowly, robot-fashion.

FIGURE 11.2.

Scoring Letter-Sound Assessments.

Nonreader	Emergent Reader

Nonreader

Student's name ___ Jan Lin ___

Date of test ___ 8-11-09 ___

a	0		i	0	q	0
b	"buh"		j	+	r	"ruh"
c	k	s	k	+	s	+
	0	+				
d	+		l	+	t	+
e	0		m	+	u	+
f	+		n	+	v	+
g	g	j			w	+
	+	0	o	0	x	0
h	+		p	+	y	knows y—as in you
					z	+

(slow to respond)

Total right ___ 17 ___

Words recognized ___ 6 ___

a̶n̶d	b̶o̶y̶	can	d̶o̶	go
like	not	p̶l̶a̶y̶	see	to

Cannot decode nonsense words.

Emergent Reader

Student's name ___ Jason Mack ___

Date of test ___ 8-11-09 ___

___ Recognizes all letters by name.

___ Can give correct sound for all but q, c (k sound known), g (says j), vowel e.

___ Recognizes all words on list of 50 sight words.

___ Does not know two-vowel rule or does not apply consistently.

___ See running record. Begin at level 15 (gr 1.9).

If he cannot do the second word, model it. Failure to get the third on his own would tell you he needs practice daily to learn this skill.

Step 6: Listen to the child read at his independent reading level, which has been determined in step 4. Check his fluency and how he approaches unknown words. Does he try to sound them out? How many letters does he sound out before either guessing correctly or figuring out the word? Does he give up early and look to you for help? Does he use context clues? Does he self-correct when he makes an error, or is he oblivious of the fact that he made an error? Can he tell you, in some detail, what he read about?

Step 7: Analyze your data. Refer to the discussion that follows.

Step 8: Make a plan. Set goals and strategies for developing the child's phonics skills based on his particular deficits.

Letter Recognition and Sound Knowledge

Typically, you will find that students can identify the letter names and most consonant sounds. It is the letters with multiple sounds that students often miss—*c, g, q, x,* and all vowels. You will also sometimes encounter an error in a sound for *b*; they may say "buh," or *r* may be spoken as "ruh" instead of "er." If either happens, mark it as a sound to reteach.

If a student has trouble recognizing or providing a sound for half the letters of the alphabet; recognizes only a handful of simple sight words; cannot sound out a simple nonsense word, such as *lub, fot,* or *maft*; or reads below grade 1.5, then refer to the section "Working with the Nonreader" in the next section. See Figure 11.2 for a profile of a nonreader.

The student is an emergent reader if he is able to

- Recognize the letters of the alphabet (though may show *b/d* reversal)

- Give the correct sound for nineteen letters

- Blend the nonsense words

- Read at grade 1.5 to 1.9

See the section "Working with the Emergent Reader" later in this chapter for tips on filling any gaps you may discover as the child progresses. See Figure 11.2 for a profile of an emergent reader.

If the student is able to read at or above the grade 2.0 level, his program will consist of reading orally for thirty minutes daily. He will read fifteen to twenty minutes with you or the aide and ten to fifteen minutes daily with a parent or peer tutor from texts at his independent reading level. The person who reads with him should document all errors made, so that you can follow his progress. See the section "Working with the Guided Reader" later in this chapter.

Keep a binder containing the teacher's resource lists that appear at the end of this chapter in a place that is easily accessible. As students work on a particular sound, the teacher's resource lists will be helpful to you in finding words that have that sound.

Working with the Nonreader

There are few experiences more rewarding than that of being able to teach a nonreader to read. Parents, paraprofessionals, or teachers can accomplish this if they are patient, encouraging, kind, and persistent.

The nonreader will need to learn several skills.

• • •

Skill 1. This activity focuses on teaching accurate attentive tracking and is best taught by using memorized materials. With young children it works well to use specific Mother Goose nursery rhymes, such as "Humpty Dumpty," "Little Boy Blue," "Hickory, Dickory, Dock," and "Wee Willie Winkie." These choices have rhyming words with similarities in their spelling, such as the *wall, fall, all* in "Humpty Dumpty."

When working with an older group, look to literature texts to find rhyming poems at the appropriate age and reading level.

Grouping: Four or fewer is best.

Method: Write the rhyme on the board and read it for fun several times, using a pointer stick to touch each word.

The next day, read the rhyme in unison again. Tell the children to watch the way you move the pointer left to right, top line to bottom line. On the next reading, assist one reader, then another, in moving the pointer correctly.

On a subsequent day, give them large-print handouts of the rhyme to use in following along with their finger as a pointer. While you say the rhyme, scan to see if each child's finger is moving in the right direction. In the beginning, they may move too quickly or too slowly. After you are sure they understand the directionality concept, teach them to observe that there is a space between each word. Have each demonstrate to you that she can find each word by drawing a block in each space on the handout. Ask them to go back and read slowly, pointing to each word.

Next, begin working on visual perceptual discrimination skills. Write the word *all* on your white board and ask the children to scan the entire poem on their handout and to circle every word that has the same letters in it (*wall, fall, all, All*). Repeat the exercise with other words. Vary directions and ask students to put a rectangle around *the*. Begin to have pupils chant "*t.h.e* spells *the*," as this will be on an early word list.

By the time you have worked your way through four poems in this manner, ask students to follow left to right as you read. When you stop, check to see if each has her finger in the right place, and if so, give praise.

If not, start rereading and guide any laggard fingers as you read. Make it fun! Use an occasional "Gotcha," but always with a smile so that no one feels embarrassed.

• • •

Skill 2. Simultaneously do lots of phonemic awareness activities. Many of these are described earlier in this chapter.

• • •

Skill 3. Simultaneously with skills 1 and 2, begin teaching the pupil *a single sound for each letter* of the alphabet. At this point, teach only the short vowel sounds; teach *c* as the *k*; teach *g* as the hard *g* in "go."

• • •

Skill 4. As soon as students have mastered four letters, it is wise to begin *blending practice.* For example, if you teach the sound of the vowel *a* and the consonants *b, c,* and *t,* students are ready to begin learning such words as

Use your letter cards with their picture referents.

Gradually add the *s, k, p,* and *m*—this will allow the children to decode such words as *ask, pat, sad, sat, map, cap, camp,* and *past.*

When you have the child decode a word, it is a good idea to write a sentence containing the word on the board. Ensure that the child recognizes the word by having her find and circle it.

Word Walls

This is a great time to put up a word wall, which might look like this:

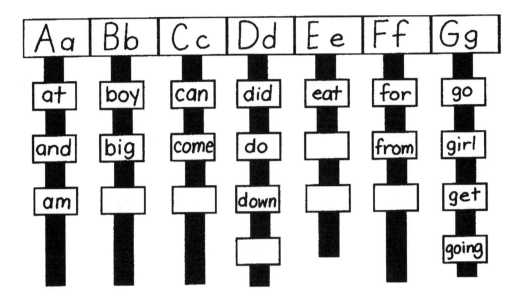

In the wall above, words are attached to streamers with staples.

The word wall serves as a visual index and as a motivator. Add words as they are taught in both spelling and decoding. Continue to add words as the year progresses. Do daily review of the word wall to remind students of all the words they have studied.

At first you may want to count the words on the word wall and change the number as you add more. This "word inventory" is exciting and motivating to many students.

When you are absolutely sure the students have mastered words with the short sound of the vowel *a*, begin to introduce words with the short vowel *o*. Show the child how *pat* becomes *pot* if you change the vowel sound, *cat* becomes *cot*, and *map* becomes *mop*.

You may be ready to introduce *f, g, h,* and *j* words, such as *job, fan, got, hop, flag, cost, cast,* and *hop*.

Word Families and Word Clumps

Introduce the concept that when we spell, not every word is a new word, and that we can look within the word for "clumps" we already know. Hang charts with rhyming words, such as:

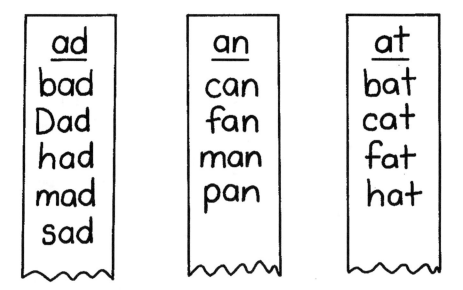

After you teach *l*, *n*, *r*, and *v* and you are certain *o* has been mastered, the next vowel to introduce is *u*. Spend additional time in blending practice to solidify your students' decoding skills involving most of the consonants—*b*, *c*, *d*, *f*, *g*, *h*, *j*, *l*, *m*, *n*, *p*, *r*, *s*, *t*, *v*—and three vowels, *a*, *o*, and *u*.

Next, introduce the vowels *e* and *i*. These are difficult for some students because they cannot hear the difference between them. Teaching them side by side seems to help.

Teach children hand motions to use for the short vowel sounds. This will assist them in holding on to the sounds. For *a*, ask them to pretend they are biting an apple and their mouth is wide open. For *e*, have them pull their finger off the edge of their desk as they listen for the *e* sound in the word "edge." For *i*, teach students to say "itch," and they scratch their noses. For *o*, instruct them to hold the hand palm down so that the fingers remind them of the legs of an octopus. For *u*, they can point upward with the index finger.

At some point, you want to show children that the order of letters is important within a word. Words that illustrate this concept include *top* and *pot*, *ten* and *net*, and many more that will come later.

You may be wondering what happened to *w*, *x*, *y*, *z*, and *q*. These letters are introduced as students begin to encounter them in reading or spelling words.

• • •

Skill 5. Simultaneously with skill 4, begin teaching some sight words. Students need to be able to recognize these words, but they also need to learn to spell them. At the end of this chapter, you will find a list called The First 100 Most-Used Words. Start with five or six of these words. In the beginning, choose words that begin with different letters—for example, *boy, can, read, the,* and *go.* Students should practice writing these words daily, and look at them on flash cards. When you feel fairly confident that all students can spell these words, students may begin making and illustrating their own reading book.

At the bottom of the first page of this book, ask the child to print:

> *The boy can read.*

At the bottom of page 2, tell the child to print:

> *The boy can go.*

When the first words are mastered, add the words *play* and *help* so that the next book pages can read:

> *The boy can play.*
> *The boy can help.*

When the first seven words are mastered, you can introduce the words *jump, eat,* and *work,* and have the child create the related pages.

The following are other words that need to be taught early:

Nouns	Verbs	Common Words
mother	is*	At*
girl	are	To
man*	like	and*
father	go*, going	work

Some words are what I call "Ear" words because all the sounds in them can be heard. In the examples here, Ear words have an asterisk by them. The others are "Eye" words, which require the child to do a little memorization, such as the *ing* in *going,* the *e* in *like,* and the *o* in *work.*

As each child finishes a book—and you are certain the child can read it—it is bound and covered and sent home. Unfortunately, many students come from homes where there are no books, newspapers, or other reading materials; the children never see their parents reading.

Send a letter home to parents to encourage them to ask their child to read their books to them once a week. That way, the words will be reinforced, which is important for children with memory problems. Encourage parents to read with their children. One effective way to do this is to ask parents to use the documentation log in Chapter Five (see Figure 5.9 and Worksheet 5.2) to document words they had to help the child decode.

Parents are pleasantly surprised and excited when they realize that their child can read and spell the words. Make a copy of the children's early books for your classroom library.

Working with the Emergent Reader

I'm a sevn year olb boy.
I Like to pLay whit my frNds.
I Like skol. I caN reab.

The student who wrote these sentences has had approximately seven months of phonics and spelling instruction. Although he uses some inventive spelling, you will note that you can understand what he is trying to tell you. He has learned to spell *play* and *read* correctly in spelling. What do we need to do for him now? Here are some tips:

1. To become a proficient reader, one must read every day. At the emergent stage, the child still needs to read to an adult. The daily practice time needs to be about thirty minutes, broken into three ten-minute sessions. If you are a teacher, you may want to have your assistant listen to two children read chorally from a selection and discuss what it is about for a period of ten minutes. Following that reading, the children might go to their desks and work as a pair to answer simple questions about what they read. Later the same day, you could follow up by listening to one child, then the other reread the same material for about ten minutes. Ask the parent to listen to the child read the same material for ten minutes that evening. This procedure increases fluency.

2. Introduce the concept of the silent *e* that makes the preceding vowel give the long sound.

   Explain it to the children by telling them that "the *e* is a bully." He reaches over and tells the preceding vowel that it has to say its name or get hit on the head. So the other vowel complies. Blend the sounds together slowly, deliberately overemphasizing the long vowel sound. As you make the long sound of the vowel, use your finger to point to the long vowel and write a long mark over it. Students will later find that the pronunciation key in the dictionary uses the same mark to signify that the vowel "says" its name. Thus,

can	becomes	*c͞ane*		*hop*	becomes	*h͞ope*
us	becomes	*͞use*		*cap*	becomes	*c͞ape*
fed	becomes	*f͞eed*		*kit*	becomes	*k͞ite*
slid	becomes	*sl͞ide*		*hat*	becomes	*h͞ate*
cut	becomes	*c͞ute*		*pin*	becomes	*p͞ine*

In their daily decoding practice sessions, ask students to say, "The vowels are *a, e, i, o, u,* and sometimes *y* and *w.*" Prior to decoding a word, they should mark each vowel in the word. This is a seatwork activity that can be done independently before the decoding session. Their papers will look like this:

Word Patterns

Using red and blue papers taped to the board, begin to teach the students the following word patterns:

vc pattern (a word such as *up, on, it*)
1 vowel = short vowel sound
Words such as *at, as, us, on, it, is, if*

cvc pattern (words such as *dog, man*)
1 vowel = short vowel sound
Words such as *dog, job, cup, hat*

cvcv pattern (words such as *here, came*)

Review the concept of the "bully." The first vowel is long; the second vowel is silent. Words such as *came, home, use, late, wake*

cvvc pattern (words such as *rain, team*)

Again, the "bully" takes over: the first vowel is long; the second vowel is silent. Words such as *team, boat, mail, suit*

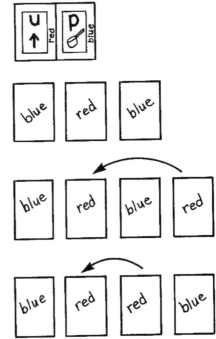

3. As the sounds come up, teach *sh, th, ch, wh,* and *ph.* When talking to children, you may refer to these as "peanut butter" sounds. Why? Remind them that if you put peanut butter on bread, it becomes stuck to the bread; you can't pull it off. When the *s* is next to the *h,* they become stuck. They have a whole new sound: *sh.*

Likewise, the *c + h* becomes *ch,* which sounds like the *ch* in *chair* or like the sound you make when you are sneezing.

When you make a *th* sound, your tongue comes out of your mouth; your teeth rest in the middle of the tongue, and you blow air. Say "with" or "then" and look at yourself in the mirror.

The *ph* makes the same sound as an *f* as in *phone.*

4. By this time, students will have begun to encounter other special combinations, such as *ou.* If they are able to spell the word *out,* they have already taken the first step.

Additional words for decoding practice with the *ou* can be found in the teacher's resource lists at the end of this chapter.

5. Make copies of and distribute the Student's Reminder for Decoding (Figure 11.3).

Materials for Beginning and Emergent Readers

Some districts may already have chosen materials to use with beginning readers. If you are assigned to select the materials for teaching your students, here are some sources:

- Scholastic, Inc. (555 Broadway, New York, NY 10012) offers leveled beginning readers under the name *Scholastic Phonics.* www.scholastic.com

- The Wright Group (19201 120th Ave. NE, Bothell, WA 98011) provides the *Sunshine Fiction* series and *The Story Box.* www.sunshine.co.nz

- Reading Rockets offers information on reading programs online. This is an excellent resource that offers videos for teachers and parents, information on reading programs, and information on reading problems. *I highly recommend that you visit the site, even if you have nothing you need to order.* www.readingrockets.org

FIGURE 11.3.

Student's Reminder for Decoding.

Rule 1: Count the vowels.

If there is one, say the short vowel sound.

a = as in ant   e = as in elephant   i = as in iguana

o = as in octopus   u = as in umberella

Rule 2: Watch for vc/cv and vc/ccv.

If this occurs, the word breaks into syllables. Example: <u>bet/ter</u>
                                                           vccv

Otherwise, be̅ came

Rule 3: Watch for combinations.

sh =   as in: wr = w̸r

ch = or k   h<u>er</u>   kn = k̸n

th =   er   gh = ghost
                                 ir   g<u>ir</u>l
ph = f   ur   b<u>ur</u>n   nig̸ht

                                 or = as in f<u>or</u>   laugh (f)

                                 ar = as in c<u>ar</u>

oo = as in t<u>oo</u>   al = all   c = k
ing = thi<u>ng</u>   oi/oy = as in   ce
ou = <u>ou</u>t   <u>oi</u>l or b<u>oy</u>   ci } says
                                                                 cy }   s

ow { as in n<u>ow</u>   au/aw = s<u>aw</u>   g = go
     or sn<u>o̅</u>w

<u>tion</u>/<u>sion</u> = shun   y = <u>y</u>es   ge } may
                                 my (i̅)   gi } say
wa   happy (e)   gy } j

- For older students, the SRA Division of the McGraw-Hill School Publishing Company has an excellent series of leveled readers titled *Multiple Skills*. You may find these books already in your school. They do not look babyish, yet the vocabulary is introduced and reinforced on a regular basis. The books ask questions that require students to think critically. Picture Level–C is appropriate for most classes.

Working with the Guided Reader

Students with LD who are reading above a grade level of 2.0 still need to read aloud and practice decoding.

1. Students should read aloud for thirty minutes each day, but they can read with volunteers. Approach local service clubs such as the Masons, Elks, Rotary, or senior citizens organizations to ask for three helpers who can volunteer for two hours, three times a week to listen to children read aloud.

   I have found that these adults are more likely to continue to help when they come in small groups rather than when they come alone.

2. Students should continue to work on decoding practice. Teach the sounds and the decoding rules they have missed.

Common Deficits

Several common deficits are seen in students with LD:

1. They are still confused about when to use the long and short vowel sounds.

2. They do not know the vc/cv rule. Review with them that many longer words syllabicate according to this rule. For example:

   a (th) | lete (the *th* is one sound)
   vc | cv

3. They do not generalize from one word to another as regular children do. For example, the child with LD may thoroughly know what *and* spells, but be thrown by the word *stand*.

   Children with LD need to be trained to look at the entire word for clumps or elements they recognize. This is best done in daily decoding practice sessions, for example,

   in | *ter* | *ro*   G (ate)   is   *in*
   vc | cvc | cv   *ter* as in *terrible*
                                                 ro as in *robot*
                                                 gate with an *ate*

Refer to the List of Bigger Words (among the teacher's resource lists at the end of the chapter) for decoding.

4. When the student encounters an unknown word, she may glance at the first letter and name any word that begins with that letter. Or she may just stop in her tracks and look to you to provide the answer. If it is a fairly decodable word, the solution is to encourage her to blend the first four sounds before guessing. If students will do this, nine out of ten times they will guess the word correctly. For example:

dinosaur

5. Some students do not recognize punctuation. Prior to beginning to read, have them draw a stop sign or slash wherever they see a period. Teach them to pause appropriately.

6. Students often make sequencing errors on words that resemble each other, such as *being, begin, bring.* On a separate paper, put the words in a vertical line and have them compare one letter at a time.

Organizers

Students usually benefit from using an organizer that requires them to answer the following questions:

Who is the story about?

What is the problem?

Where does the story take place?

When does the story take place?

Why does the main character do what he or she does?

How is the problem solved?

List of Questions

To improve comprehension of longer selections, give students a list of questions to answer as they read. An example follows.

On page 1, you learn that the shoemaker and his wife have a problem. Describe their problem.

On page 2, the elves help the shoemaker and his wife by _____.

On page 3, how did the shoemaker and his wife reward the elves for their help?

On page 4, you read "the shoemaker and his wife never saw the elves again." Why do you think the elves never came back?

Think of a different ending for the story.

Students aren't always tuned in to prefixes, roots, and suffixes. As they encounter these, teach them thoroughly. For example, early on they will come across the prefix *un,* meaning "not." For several days, review words with this prefix by using such words as *unhappy,* meaning "not happy," *untied, undo, unsightly, unused,* and so on.

As students grow in competency, you can teach word parts, such as

pre	*scrip*	*tion*
"before"	"write"	(indicates the word is a noun)

Turning Words into Mental Images

Students must be "taught" to see things in their "mind's eye." Help students develop the ability to form visual images in their mind. There are several ways to improve comprehension and imaging. Early on, provide students with sentences to convert to drawings (see the activity Visual Imaging of Single Sentences). Later you can have them relate to longer passages with drawings and feelings using *marginalia* techniques; see Figure 11.4 for samples.

If you carefully examine the two examples of marginalia, you will see that Student A has greater understanding. He learned such concepts as "shocks of corn" by looking them up in the dictionary. Note also that he interacts with the text from his own experience, whereas Student B relates in much more limited ways, through the use of single words.

Visualization and Verbalization

Use visualization and verbalization techniques along with a twenty-question format to help students learn to see mental images of words. Have them ask questions about a picture you are holding faced away from them (see Figure 11.5 for an example). Have one student stand with you to answer the questions. You can teach such concepts as foreground, background, upper left corner, and so on. After playing this game for many days, the students will become better at asking useful questions. Write the questions and answers on the board or overhead for them to use later.

1. What is happening in the picture? "It's raining."

2. Is there a person in the picture? "Yes." (Later they will learn to say, "How many people are in the picture?")

3. Are there animals in the picture? "Yes."

Name _____ **Date** _____

Visual Imaging of Single Sentences

Draw a picture that goes with each sentence.

The man stepped on the skate and fell.	My mom got a new hat.
I went to sleep on the couch.	The little boy pushed his toy off the table.

224

FIGURE 11.4.

Visual Imaging of a Short Story: Marginalia Samples.

Student A

I love Halloween. It is my favorite holiday. I like it better than Christmas

It was late in the evening—a cool evening at the end of October. In the field beside the house, the corn stood in shocks and a variety of pumpkins sat in a pile. You could tell they were pumpkins because there was a full moon that night. On the fence a big black cat *mouse in tummy* lazily washed her paws after having just devoured a mouse who hadn't seen her in time. Suddenly out of the corner of her eye, she saw a witch, a ghost and a pirate coming toward her.

I think these are children who are playing trick or treat. They will get some candy at the house.

Student B

10 P.M It was late in the evening—a cool evening at the end of October. In the field beside the house, the corn stood in shocks and a variety of pumpkins sat in a pile. You could tell they were pumpkins because there was a full moon that night. On the fence a big black cat *meow* lazily washed her paws after having just *paw* devoured a mouse who hadn't seen her in time. Suddenly, out of the corner of her eye she saw a witch, a ghost and a pirate coming toward her.

FIGURE 11.5.

Picture for Visualization and Verbalization Activity.

4. Is there an object in the picture? "Yes." (Later they will begin to ask how many objects are in the picture. They will ask what the objects are and where they are located.)

5. Is there an umbrella? "Yes."

6. What color is it? "Red."

When the last question has been answered, each person draws what she thinks the picture looks like. Then the students compare their drawings with the actual picture and begin to discuss what other questions they might have asked to elicit more detailed information. Hang all the drawings; put a blue ribbon on one or two of the "closest" ones. On subsequent days, let a student choose who gets the blue ribbon and explain why he picked that drawing.

To plan more experiences with visualization and verbalization, use additional images from coloring books and magazines.

Choral Reading, Reader's Theater, and Singing

There are many ways to get students to use reading in their lives other than by using textbooks.

For the emergent reader, use choral reading and reading from a teacher-made songbook as ways to help students develop fluency while participating in a comfortable environment. Older students enjoy Reader's Theater.

Students usually like to perform at a tea for their parents or for classes of younger children. They can read in unison or in a combination of choral and solo parts.

In Reader's Theater, students work with prepared reading scripts, taking solo parts. One of the most dramatic I have seen was a history lesson about the events leading up to and through the Civil War. Opening with a recording of the "Battle Hymn of the Republic," solos included a female slave who lost her husband and son because the owner had to sell them, a participant in the Underground Railroad, a plantation owner, President Lincoln, and General Sherman. It was an effective way to make history come alive and to use reading in a core subject. The multiple performances fixed the facts in students' minds.

Singing is another way to incorporate multiple readings into your curriculum. Make songbooks appropriate to students' grade level. Music time is an informal time. Teachers of young students may have them gather around on the floor. If you do not play an instrument or sing well, use tapes. If you don't want to make songbooks, put the words on the overhead and use a pointer to track them.

Students who profess to hate to read will often find themselves caught up in the joy of learning songs. Sing the same song daily for several days until you can see your students showing signs of having the words memorized. At that point, add a new song to their repertory.

Younger children take to music as ducks do to water. Older children are more self-conscious, so you may want to begin by having them listen to the song on the tape and follow the words in the book. Invite students to sing along, but do not force older students to sing. Let the activity develop naturally. Young children like "Old MacDonald Had a Farm," "The Wheels on the Bus," "Are You Sleeping? (Frère Jacques)," "The Grand Old Duke of York," "Row, Row, Row Your Boat," "Twinkle, Twinkle, Little Star," "Bingo," "Skip to My Lou," and "She'll Be Coming 'round the Mountain." For older students, incorporate songs into the study of history. Use such songs as "Yankee Doodle" (1770), "Battle Hymn of the Republic" (1861), and "I've Been Working on the Railroad" (1866).

Vocabulary Development Suggestions
Students with learning disabilities have limited vocabulary development due to such factors as limited experiences, poor socioeconomic backgrounds, and limited memory.

Vocabulary development requires multiple exposures during a limited time frame. Having students look up words in a dictionary is not only tedious for them but also without value for their vocabulary development. I have seen students copy definitions without reading them. Teaching students to identify prefixes, suffixes, and root words is a better way to help them approach new vocabulary.

As discussed earlier, teach students to master the fact that the prefix *un* attached to the root word (for example, *happy*) alters its meaning to the opposite ("not happy"). Have them confirm their understanding with such words as *pack* and *unpack; lock* and *unlock; tie* and *untie;* and *do* and *undo.*

When using your district's reading materials, watch for the introduction of suffixes. Generally, *un* and *ful* are among the first to be introduced. Students will encounter the words *care* and *careful.* Adding the suffix *ful* means "full of"; thus *careful* means "full of care."

As your students grow in their reading skills, you can talk about word roots. Each part of the word *prescription,* for example, tells something about the word: *pre* denotes that it is done beforehand, *scrip* refers in some way to the act of writing (scribe/script), and *tion* indicates that the word is a noun.

A list of prefixes, suffixes, and root words appears in the teacher's resource lists. It is not an exhaustive list, but includes many of the more common ones.

21 Tips for Teaching Reading

1. Start low, go slow. When you discover a gap in an LD child's knowledge, try to fill it.

2. Do phonemic awareness lessons and phonics activities with students at all levels. This is a major area of weakness for them. Teach them that when attempting to spell, they will need to repeat the desired word very slowly. Remind them to "say it like a robot" and to say it over and over in order to tease out (hear) each individual sound. Continue to remind them of this until the students establish the habit and do it every time without being reminded.

3. Teach reading, writing, and spelling hand in hand. A spelling lesson is a particularly good time to present the phonetic elements they will need to master.

4. When teaching decoding skills, use both real and nonsense words. To decode nonsense words correctly, students must use such rules as the vc/cv rule.

5. Although you may be required to "expose" students to texts at their grade level, when you ask a student to read aloud, be sure to use materials at his functional level. For independent reading, have him read from materials at his "easy" level so that he can experience the joy of reading.

6. Help students realize that using a bookmark (described in Chapter Ten) will make reading easier for them. Bookmarks help students stay on task and eliminate the distracting influence of some of the print.

7. Provide enlarged versions of the printed page to LD students.

8. When a student makes an error, reread what she said, stopping just before her mistake. This will help her self-correct.

9. LD students tend to look at the first letter of a word and guess. We can significantly improve their reading skills if we can train them to sound out three or four letters.

10. Train students to demand "sense" from what they read. When it doesn't make sense, they should pause and say, "What? I didn't understand that."

11. Use a point or other reward system to encourage reluctant readers to continue reading.

12. Words that are spelled similarly are particularly confusing. When the student makes a mistake, write both words and help the child see the difference and find a way to remember it.

13. Develop vocabulary by teaching synonyms.

14. Teach prefixes, roots, and suffixes.

15. Teach students to recognize clumps of letters. This will help them with longer words.

    By exposing students in a single lesson to such words as

    sup per   *sup pose*   *sup ply*
    pa per   *com pose*   *re ply*

    you can help them realize that within words we can find common elements that will help us decode.

16. Do not call on a struggling student to read to the group. Find time to listen to these students one-on-one.

17. Find ways to help students monitor their own progress so that they can see they are improving.

18. Multiple readings of the same material increase fluency: you read, students read chorally with you, students read to each other in pairs, students read individually. Students write summaries of what they read and make lists of words they were not sure of.

19. Give lots of positive feedback—"Good," "Super," or "Right." If the student misses, say, "Look at that one again." When reading with the group, do not allow one student to correct another's error or to supply a word. Insist that she "wait," and if help is to be given, you will decide how and when. This practice will prevent much frustration and ill will. If one of the students cannot "wait," ask her to put her hand over her mouth so that she won't blurt. If it happens again, have her remove herself from the group "until she thinks she can return to the group without blurting."

20. To become a good baseball player, one must practice. To become a good reader, one must practice. *Students need to read at least thirty minutes a day.*

21. An adequate classroom library usually requires about fifteen hundred books and covers a range of abilities and interests.

WORKSHEET 11.1. WORD LIST FOR NONREADERS.

Words with short vowel

a		o		u	
am	and	on	lot	up	but
cat	ask	off	dog	us	bud
fan	has	rob	doll	cup	gum
can	ham	top	plot	bus	sun
hat	nap	mob	lost	run	bug
cap	jam	pot	cost	hug	bus
at	past	hot	spot	fun	bulb
bag	last	hop	stop	gun	plug
pal	map	box	soft	cut	jump
pat	plan	dot	fond	pup	full
pan	scan	log	soft	nut	tuck
fat	task	pond	mop	mud	rug
sad	lamp	fox	long	rub	drum
dad	camp	job		jug	hunt
man	raft			put	snug
slap	fast			lump	tub
trap	snap				
flat	brag				
hand	back				
flag	slam				
ran					

Words with short vowel

e			i		
fed	pen	sell	big	him	slip
red	ten	left	is	tip	will
let	yes	belt	in	gift	hill
pet	web	felt	it	list	lift
wet	tell	tell	if	grin	hid
neck	when	help	lip	lick	Sit
men	ten		hit	drip	milk
bed	get		his	did	
			lift	wind	

WORKSHEET 11.2. WORD LIST FOR READERS AT GRADE LEVEL 2.0.

sh (easy)

shut	she	ship	shop	shed
shall	shell	shock	dish	wish
splash	rush	fish	fresh	rash
crush	gush	brush	push	trash
cash	mash	sash	crash	flash
dash	hash	hush	shelf	shift
shot				

sh *(harder—long vowel)*

shape	sheet	shade	shame	shake
shine	sheep	shore	shone	leash

sh *(with two or more combinations)*

sh ar p	sh ir t	sh oo t	sh ou t	sh ow
wa sh	sh or t	sh ow er	sh ut ter	

th (easy)

this	that	them	then	thick
thumb	think	thank	thus	than
thin	tenth	path	with	bath
cloth	ninth	moth	fifth	math

th *(harder—long vowel)*

these	those	faith	both	teeth

th *(with two or more combinations)*

th un der	th ir d	s ou th	th ing	w or th
th or n	th ir ty	th r ow	th ir st	th r ew

ch *(easy)*

chin	chip	chop	chest	check
catch	much	such	stretch	chick
lunch	inch	chat		

ch *(harder—long vowel)*

chair	chain	chase	cheek	chose
cheap	cheese	cheer	chill	choke
chunk	bench	which	branch	each
teach	reach	beach	beach	bunch
peach	cheat	chime	lunch	

ch *(with two or more combinations)*

ch ie f	ch an ce	ch ar ge	ch ur ch	p er ch
wa t ch	ch an ge	p or ch	ch al k	ch art
ch an t	ch ap ter	ch oi ce	ch oo se	ch ub by

(continued)

WORKSHEET 11.2. (*Continued*)

wa (*as in "water"*)

was	wash	walk	want	watch

oo (*as in "too"*)

soon	tool	loose	pool	cool
food	goose	stool	school	smooth
boot	roof	hoof	room	spoon
scoop	broom	zoo	troop	booth
tooth	noon	tattoo	balloon	shoot

ing

sing	bring	swing	sting	ring
spring	string	thing	wing	finger

ow (*as in "now"*)

how	cow	plow	brown	down
crowd	town	drown	crown	powder
power	scowl	allow	flower	towel

ow (*with **w** acting as a vowel to make **o** say "o"*)

show	slow	owe	grow	Flow
follow	bowl	low	below	Own
borrow	window	yellow	glow	Sown

ew (***oo** sound as in "new"*)

few	flew	blew	chew	crew
threw	stew	grew		

ou (*as in "out"*)

loud	cloud	count	about	round
sound	hound	proud	around	mouse
house	pound	found	scout	doubt
oust	ground	amount	our	south
mouth	ouch			

ar (*as in "are"*)

car	bar	dark	far	farm
card	jar	hard	mark	bark
part	March	star	smart	carve
arch	art	arm	scar	scarf
start	party	park	yard	sharp
army	shark	charm	chart	large

kn (***k** is silent*)

knee	knit	knot	knife	knew
know	knuckle	knock		

WORKSHEET 11.2. (*Continued*)

er (*as in "her"*)

later	after	water	offer	enter
sister	ever	mother	other	winter
better	operate			

ir (*as in "girl"*)

bird	stir	firm	first	dirt
shirt	birth	circle	circus	swirl

ur (*as in "turn"*)

burn	purple	turkey	urge	hurt
surf	during	purse	nurse	curve
curl	occur	hurry	further	curb

or (*as in "for"*)

form	north	orbit	born	order
storm	horse	porch	orchard	cord
fork				

aw (*as in "saw"*)

jaw	claw	paw	hawk	raw
draw	thaw	crawl	law	awful
awning	lawn	yawn	flaw	straw

au (*as in "because"*)

haul	August	auto	faucet	fault
daughter	sauce	caught	sausage	author
audience	laundry	dinosaur	launch	

oi (*as in "oil"*)

boil	soil	broil	point	foil
join	coin	moist	joint	void
hoist	spoil	poison	avoid	

oy (*as in "boy"*)

toy	joy	enjoy	royal	oyster
annoy	decoy	employ		

wr (***w** is always silent*)

wrong	wrist	wreath	wreck	wrench

234

WORKSHEET 11.3. THE FIRST 100 MOST-USED WORDS.

List 1	List 2	List 3	List 4
1. and	1. are	1. all	1. away
2. boy	2. at	2. am	2. blue
3. can	3. but	3. ask	3. every
4. come	4. could	4. do	4. father
5. did	5. doing	5. down	5. from
6. girl	6. eat	6. for	6. green
7. go	7. get	7. good	7. had
8. help	8. going	8. has	8. house
9. like	9. he	9. have	9. how
10. man	10. here	10. him	10. in
11. mother	11. it	11. is	11. just
12. not	12. look	12. keep	12. little
13. out	13. make	13. let	13. much
14. play	14. new	14. me	14. need
15. read	15. now	15. must	15. old
16. see	16. one	16. my	16. put
17. the	17. said	17. of	17. ran
18. this	18. she	18. over	18. red
19. to	19. they	19. so	19. ride
20. us	20. two	20. some	20. run
21. want	21. use	21. that	21. there
22. will	22. we	22. them	22. walk
23. with	23. were	23. thing	23. was
24. work	24. would	24. what	24. went
25. you	25. your	25. why	25. yellow

WORKSHEET 11.4. SECOND 100 MOST-USED WORDS.

List 1	List 2	List 3	List 4
1. big	1. after	1. about	1. again
2. black	2. be	2. around	2. because
3. came	3. been	3. baby	3. began
4. day	4. does	4. before	4. brother
5. find	5. done	5. best	5. car
6. five	6. friend	6. don't	6. children
7. found	7. garden	7. eight	7. close
8. four	8. give	8. live	8. first
9. gave	9. long	9. more	9. hard
10. grow	10. may	10. never	10. if
11. her	11. morning	11. night	11. kind
12. his	12. next	12. nine	12. left
13. home	13. no	13. once	13. love
14. know	14. on	14. our	14. made
15. many	15. saw	15. school	15. most
16. other	16. seven	16. should	16. name
17. sleep	17. six	17. show	17. open
18. three	18. soon	18. store	18. or
19. under	19. stop	19. talk	19. people
20. up	20. think	20. tell	20. pick
21. very	21. too	21. ten	21. sister
22. when	22. try	22. these	22. then
23. where	23. water	23. those	23. thought
24. white	24. which	24. woman	24. together
25. who	25. yes	25. write	25. upon

WORKSHEET 11.5. TOP 500 MOST-USED WORDS.

A	B	bring
able	baby	brother
about	back	brought
above	bad	brown
across	ball	build
afraid	be	built
after	beautiful	busy
again	because	but
against	bed	buy
air	been	by
all	before	
almost	began	C
also	begin	call
always	being	came
am	believe	can
and	below	car
angry	best	carry
animal	better	cat
another	between	catch
answer	big	caught
any	bird	cent
are	black	change
around	blue	chase
as	book	child
ask	both	children
at	box	city
ate	boy	clean
away	bread	climb

WORKSHEET 11.5. (*Continued*)

close

clothes

cold

color

come

cook

corner

could

country

cow

cried

cry

cut

D

daddy

dance

dark

day

deep

did

didn't

different

dig

dinner

dirty

do

does

dog

doing

done

don't

door

down

draw

dress

drink

drive

drop

during

E

each

early

easy

eat

eight

enough

even

ever

every

eye

F

face

fall

family

far

farm

fast

father

feed

feel

feet

felt

few

finally

find

finish

fire

first

fish

five

flew

fly

follow

food

for

found

four

friend

from

Friday

front

(*continued*)

WORKSHEET 11.5. (*Continued*)

fruit	happen	hunt
full	happy	hurry
fun	has	hurt
funny	hat	
	have	**I**
G	he	ice
game	head	idea
garden	hear	if
gave	heard	important
get	help	in
girl	her	is
give	here	it
glad	herself	
go	hide	**J**
goes	high	join
going	hill	jump
good	him	just
got	himself	
grass	his	**K**
great	hold	keep
green	home	kept
grew	hope	kick
ground	hot	kind
grow	hour	kitchen
guess	house	kitten
	how	knew
	huge	know
H	hundred	
had	hungry	
hand		

WORKSHEET 11.5. (*Continued*)

L

land

large

last

late

laugh

learn

leave

left

let

letter

life

light

like

listen

little

live

long

look

lose

loud

love

lunch

M

made

make

man

many

may

me

mean

men

met

might

mile

milk

mine

Monday

money

more

morning

most

mother

mountain

Mr.

Mrs.

music

must

my

N

name

near

neck

need

neighbor

never

new

next

nice

night

nine

no

noise

north

not

nothing

now

number

O

ocean

of

off

office

often

old

on

once

one

only

open

or

(*continued*)

WORKSHEET 11.5. (*Continued*)

orange	print	room
other	prize	round
our	problem	run
out	proud	
over	pull	**S**
own	puppy	sad
	push	said
	put	same
P		sat
page		Saturday
paint	**Q**	saw
paper	question	school
park	quick	second
part	quiet	see
party	quit	seem
pass	quite	send
penny		sentence
people	**R**	seven
pick	rabbit	several
picnic	rain	she
picture	ran	short
piece	reach	should
place	read	show
plant	real	side
play	red	since
please	remember	sing
point	ride	sister
pony	right	six
pretty	river	

WORKSHEET 11.5. (*Continued*)

sleep	that	travel
slowly	the	tree
small	their	tried
snow	them	truck
so	then	true
some	there	Tuesday
soon	these	turn
south	they	two
space	thing	
stand	think	**U**
start	third	under
stay	this	until
stop	those	up
store	thought	upon
story	three	us
street	through	use
such	Thursday	usually
suddenly	time	
swim	to	**V**
	today	very
T	together	visit
take	told	voice
talk	tomorrow	
teach	too	**W**
tell	took	wait
ten	toward	walk
than	town	want
thank	toy	was

(*continued*)

WORKSHEET 11.5. (*Continued*)

wash	which	write
watch	while	
water	white	**Y**
we	who	yard
Wednesday	why	year
week	will	yellow
well	with	yes
went	woman	yesterday
were	word	you
west	work	young
what	world	your
when	would	

WORKSHEET 11.6. LIST OF BIGGER WORDS.

Use this list to train students to apply the vc/cv rule and to look for known "clumps" or families of letters. The list is geared toward LD students whose functional reading is at 2.9 or better.

Write a word on the board. Have them copy it, syllabicate it, and circle clumps they recognize.

The purpose of these lessons is not vocabulary development. There is no reason, however, that you could not use the words as a spelling list or for vocabulary development once they have served their original purpose of teaching students to watch for clumps.

Lesson 1 (Point out the common elements: *sup, pose, ply, in, ter, com, pro*)

interfere	suppose	compose	interact	propose
intercom	supply	reply	interlock	complete

Lesson 2 (Review elements *com, ply, in, ter, pro*)

internal	comply	interpret	command	provoke
interest	protect	complain	provide	comply

Lesson 3 (New elements *sion, mis;* review elements *in, mis, com, pose*)

intrusion	mission	mistake	compression	misplace
mishap	compulsion	repose	interpose	compromise

Lesson 4 (New element *dis;* review elements *ply, com, pose, pro*)

computer	imply	compare	display	intervene
misfire	dispose	propel	remain	dissatisfied

Lesson 5 (New elements *ex, re;* review elements *dis, imp, in, com*)

distinguish	impose	dispel	exit	interplay
exercise	compel	exert	repel	expel

Lesson 6 (New elements *ary, de;* review elements *ex, pro, dis, re, mis, sion, sup*)

expansion	exist	propulsion	dissension	relate
deplete	deport	missionary	import	support

Lesson 7 (New element *trans;* review elements *de, pro*)

misprint	depend	transfer	delete	transmit
retain	protest	detain	entertain	deter

Lesson 8 (New element *im;* review elements *trans, re, ment, en*)

devout	translate	receive	immersion	impale
entwine	international	compliment	department	entrap

(*continued*)

WORKSHEET 11.6. (*Continued*)

Lesson 9 (New element *ple;* review elements *dis, con, ex, in, re, mis*)

enlist	contain	discover	misfit	recent
supple	example	distend	extraordinary	infant

Lesson 10 (New elements *ture, per;* review elements *in, tion, ex*)

infer	terminal	future	sensitive	picture
mixture	explain	composition	sensation	permit

Lesson 11 (New elements *al, ive;* review elements *per, im, ture, re, de*)

fixture	permission	impersonal	nature	pertain
recline	incline	furniture	expensive	decline

Lesson 12 (New element *con;* review elements *ex, re, in, de*)

deplorable	explore	release	increase	contemplate
confuse	extension	confer	decrease	confession

Lesson 13 (Review all elements)

extinguish	relinquish	remarkable	staple	sample
encompass	fantasize	misconceive	trample	disdain

Lesson 14 (New element *ment;* review elements *re, tion, ex, de, ate*)

reaction	nation	implement	quotation	exaggerate
inflate	deflate	mentor	mention	separate

WORKSHEET 11.7. LIST OF NONSENSE WORDS.

Some assessment documents ask students to decode unknown words. LD students need daily decoding practice using both real and nonsense words. Decoding nonsense words can be a lighthearted activity. Laugh. Be silly when decoding from the list below. Students will then be more willing to take a risk with unknown real words.

Functional Level Grade 1.5

nos	guk	zep	nig	sal	mull	tim	mek
ris	vam	wif	han	nad	saft	les	flud
wot	blon	rep	gan	mil	sut	dus	pem
klaf	wev	rop	pij	gosk	lud	fot	cuz
bim	len	neb	cun	nisp			

Functional Level Grade 1.9
Mix words from 1.5 level with these:

coam	shan	peet	mait	sete	ram	wike	flate
neek	hede	frim	chot	gream	cay	nay	oach
kine	jigh	pash	raim	rite	thise	koap	bight
neer	fie	chape	boal	basp	thum	nule	gome
laik	pime	ril	sabe	naip	feec	kight	tay

Functional Level Grade 2.5
Mix with words from previous levels:

sool	poil	ker	wert	tady	yoot	ceit	shile
lout	goid	reeg	knos	sowt	frough	woos	noid
atoil	wres	bry	cheal	wrok	sody	tice	geome
tweep	aij	boud	knibe	dought	siphe	owsh	chaim
poog	whime	knyle	snaw	auth	gely	cept	lipy
hice	gife	broot	teft	mees	foop	wois	knobe

Functional Level Grade 3.0
Combine with words from all of the preceding lists:

septig	unfob	kneeble	famgibtum	sheetle	qued
orfant	palmy	raimshy	wiftaimby	chaiply	fets
untag	reaky	polygub	libetoge	belfit	aglib
hoy	crade	linning	conwasion	polykud	exnal

WORKSHEET 11.8. PREFIXES.

Student Handout

ab—away from

acro—high

ad—to

an—not

anti—against

ast—star

auto—self

bene—good

bi—two

circu—around

co—together/with

col—together/with

com—together/with

con—together/with

contra—against

counter—against

de—down

dia—across

dis—bad/lack of

en—in

ex—out

extra—outside

hyper—too much

hypo—under/too little

il—not

im—into/not

in—into/not

inter—between

intro—inside

micro—small

mis—bad

mono—one

multi—many

omni—all

peri—around

poly—many

post—after

pre—before

pro—forward

quadri—four

re—again

retro—back

sub—under

sym—together

syn—together

tele—distant

trans—across

tri—three

un—not

WORKSHEET 11.9. ROOTS.

Student Handout

act—do

aero—air

anthr—man

aqua—water

arch—chief

audi—hear

belli—war

bio—life

cede—go

ceed—go

cert—sure

chron—time

cide—kill

cise—cut

claim—shout

cline—lean

clude—shut

cogn—know

cur—care

cycl—ring/circle

derm—skin

dict—speak

donat—give

duct—lead

fac—make

flect—bend

flex—bend

fract—break

frag—break

geo—land

gnos—know

gon—angle

grad—step

gram—letter

graph—write

gress—step

here—stick

hom—man

ject—throw

lab—work

lat—side

liber—free

lit—read

lith—stone

loc—place

log—word

lum—light

man—hand

mand—order

marine—water

mater—mother

max—greatest

merge—dive

meter—measure

min—small

mob—move

mot—move

nat—born

neo—new

opt—eye

pater—father

ped—foot

philo—love

phono—sound

pod—foot

poli—city

port—carry

quer—ask

ques—ask

rupt—break

scend—climb

scribe—write

script—written

sect—cut

spect—look

strict—tight

tain—hold

terr—land

therm—heat

tract—pull/drag

urb—city

vac—empty

vag—wander

ver—truth

vid—see

vis—see

volv—turn

vor—eat

WORKSHEET 11.10. SUFFIXES.

Student Handout

study of—**nom**

nomy

ology

full of—**ful**

ous

without—**less**

one who/person who—**ant**

arian

ent

er

ist

act of/state of—**ism**

ive

tion

ure

place for—**arium**

orium

able to—**able**

ible

to make—**ate**

en

ize

fear of—**phobia**

WORKSHEET 11.11. ALPHABET ANIMAL FLASHCARDS.

To make a set of alphabet flashcards, you'll need to cut white bristol board or white cardboard into twenty-six rectangular pieces approximately 3½" × 6" in size, as shown in Figure 11.6. Cut apart the following flashcards and glue them to the white cardboard.

FIGURE 11.6.

Alphabet Animal Flashcards.

(continued)

c

d

e

f

WORKSHEET 11.11. (*Continued*)

(continued)

k

l

m

n

WORKSHEET 11.11. *(Continued)*

o

p

q

r

(continued)

WORKSHEET 11.11. (*Continued*)

s

t

u

v

WORSHEET 11.11. (*Continued*)

w

"x"

y

z

Chapter 12

Writing, Spelling, and Speaking

Albert Einstein (1879–1955)

German mathematician and physicist

Was believed to be learning disabled; did not learn to speak until he was three years old; had difficulty recalling known words and forming sentences; experienced difficulty in all school subjects. His teacher predicted that "Nothing good would become of him."

Contributions:

Science: Formulated the theory of relativity

Developed new ways of thinking about space, matter, time, energy, and gravity

Was awarded the Nobel Prize for physics (1921) for his work in photoelectric law and theoretical physics

---

The previous chapter emphasized how essential writing and spelling experiences are for students with LD; those skills go hand in hand with reading. These students need daily lessons in writing and spelling. This chapter will suggest ways to improve students' skills in these areas.

Writing, spelling, and speaking are often discussed interchangeably among educators, and yet they refer to distinctly different processes of learning and development. Assessing speech and the ability to create verbal language is often a teacher's first step toward evaluating spelling and writing, because problems with producing speech correlate highly with problems with spelling and writing. Spelling simply refers to a student's ability to create words that are grammatically correct, but it is often used to judge a student's writing ability. Spelling and expressing one's ideas in print are often two different processes. A child with severe dyslexia may never learn to spell from memory, always relying on spell-check or digital reminders, and yet that child may grow into a person who writes a book.

The complexities of spelling are taught after handwriting and penmanship, and after that teachers may try to address speech or speaking abilities in students. Often a child will also meet with a speech pathologist for intensive speech remediation if necessary. A physical therapist may assist in intensive remediation of motor issues related to handwriting. In cases of reading and spelling difficulties, if the student doesn't respond, a reading specialist or educational psychologist may be called in.

Since the first part of the early school years involves teaching handwriting skills, this is often the first area in which teachers may notice a problem with motor skills. And since many young children are graded on their "writing/expressive language" by the neatness of their penmanship, this is often the area that gets the most attention. In the early schooling years, the broad definition of "literacy" encompasses a child's ability to create and write out the alphabet, so this is another reason that penmanship often gets more attention in school.

When children enter kindergarten, teachers may note a wide range of "literacy levels" in writing development. It is not uncommon to find youngsters who are at the scribbling stage of development. If this is noted, it is important to allow children the opportunity to continue experiencing this stage. In this stage, the child is learning to control the writing implement so that she can make it do what she wants it to.  She is also learning about pressure. This child will benefit from a pencil with a grip attached and instruction in the proper way to hold it. Once a child has learned to hold a pencil in an awkward way, it is very hard to get her to want to change, because the new way feels odd to her. Unfortunately, those children who hold their pencils in an alternate manner may find that their hand tires quickly when the volume of written work increases in the upper grades. Correct placement of the paper on the desk is another issue teachers need to teach. (See Chapter Ten.)

The child whose motor control is below normal needs daily tracing opportunities. To provide these, just draw simple pictures like the one shown. Instruct the child to "Go slowly and try to stay on the road" (the dashes). During his first two or three attempts, it is good to have an adult sit with him to remind him to go slowly and to stay on the line.

Designed by an occupational therapist, the Handwriting Without Tears program has been successfully used to teach printing to students, beginning with lessons copying shapes. The classroom kit also includes manipulatives for students to begin creating letters by using basic shapes of curves and straight lines. (See Figures 12.1 and 12.2.)

FIGURE 12.1.

Sample Shape Copying Lesson.

Source: Get Set for School *workbook. Copyright © Handwriting Without Tears (www.hwtears.com).*

Once students have the idea of writing lines and know the direction of letters and numbers, they can move on to other forms of formal printing instruction.

Printing

The teacher or parent of a young LD child should provide the child with daily experiences in practicing handwriting. Begin by demonstrating how to make the letters. As you demonstrate, point out to the child where to begin each letter. In the beginning, model each letter stroke by stroke. Student papers should include several traced examples before they are instructed to trace the letter freehand. Watch as the child forms each letter.

FIGURE 12.2.

Sample Letter Formation Lesson.

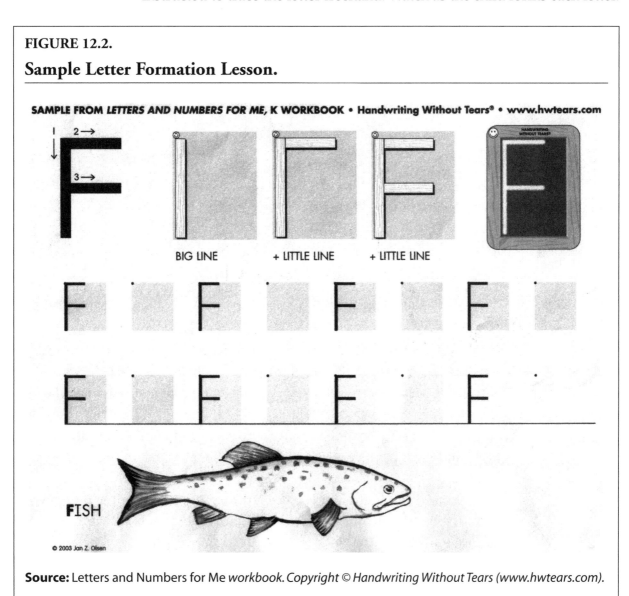

Source: Letters and Numbers for Me *workbook. Copyright © Handwriting Without Tears (www.hwtears.com).*

For preschoolers, sample letters with the elements of letter formation broken down into stages is helpful. Each school or school district tends to have a preference for a handwriting program. I have used Handwriting Without Tears as an example in this book because I have seen it used successfully with students with LD. In the schools I have worked in, the Handwriting Without Tears program was used in the early grades, pre-K through kindergarten or grade 1, and then teachers created a program from other sources that emphasized block print. Some studies point out that using D'Nealian forms of handwriting instruction may cause more letter identification errors (Kuhl and Dewitz, 1994). This is something to keep in mind when choosing a handwriting program.

For students struggling with letter identification, block print may be the easiest to teach and read. That said, because children will be exposed to many fonts, scripts, and letter shapes, it makes sense to introduce a variety of fonts and letter shapes after children begin recognizing the basic shapes of letters.

Teaching the Mechanics of Writing

Most children entering school will be writing their names. Some will be able to make all the letters of the alphabet. A few children will enter school with little or no writing experience. They demonstrate this in many ways, such as by not knowing how to hold a pencil or how to move it in a purposeful way. It may take the child several months to get control of his crayon or pencil. As noted earlier, this process of scribbling can't be rushed.

For children who are at the scribbling stage, small group instruction works best for learning how to hold writing implements and turn their papers when writing. These children also need additional letter-tracing activities. More advanced children will benefit from instruction on the size of letters, spacing between words, continuing words to the next line, and so forth. You can use different markers, pens, and pencils as motivators to get children to practice writing. Children like using a variety of paper sizes and colors.

To motivate children to practice writing, set up a writing center in your classroom, a small table with a little light, and a wide variety of writing utensils and papers. Provide letter models nearby, and keep stencils or other letter formation manipulatives nearby. Posting some regularly used words and names—*I, like, love, Mom, Dad, the, mine, she,* and any other words students routinely request help in spelling—on a nearby board helps students begin writing messages independently. Alternatively, you can supply a daily writing message that students must work on during the day; have it printed above your "writing table."

It is important to engage children in daily writing lessons. You can begin by using word boxes with pictures to support the words. Ask students to tell you their favorite foods, then write the word and draw the pictures on the board. It might look like this:

Using an overhead transparency, model the lesson:

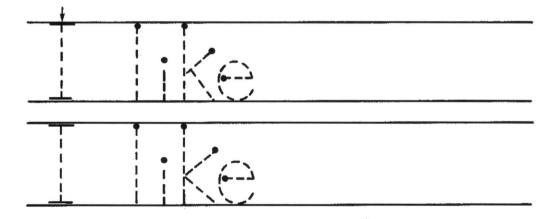

Give them their papers (the same as the one you put on the overhead) and circulate to be certain students are tracing over the words and adding a word or words to complete each sentence. Leave the overhead on. Have extra papers on hand in case someone makes a mistake and must start over. In this lesson, you have concentrated on the words *I* and *like*.

On the second day, you can do the same sort of activity using the words *I see* . . . On the third day, try *I like* . . . (list choice of toy). On the fourth day, go outside and use *I see* . . . (trees, grass, slide, swings, and so on). On the fifth day, use *I like* . . . (kind of house pet).

I have a . . . (could be a pet or toy)

I play with . . . (can be a friend's name or toy)

I can . . . (things they can do—jump, play, and so on)

At this point, introduce them to the idea of having another person as the subject:

Mom likes . . . (food, pet).

We like to . . .

Dogs like to . . . (run, play with a ball, eat).

Each day, introduce one or two words and post the new words on a word wall. Teach students to put a period at the end of their sentences. You can also give examples of good sentences and bad sentences for children to choose from when writing a story. Talk about what makes a good sentence and what makes a bad sentence. Introduce scrambled sentences for children to straighten out and write:

mom. I my like

Sample Interactive Writing Lesson (Instructional Level 1.3)

Objective: Children will write a group story about their field trip to the zoo.

Materials: Large paper chart on easel; several colored pens

Directions

1. Gather students around the chart so all can see.

2. Ask them if they liked going to the zoo.

3. Say, "We're going to write a story about our trip. I'll write on this chart."

4. Set behavioral expectations. This type of interaction works well with young children:

    Let me see pretzel legs and pancake hands. *(wait)*

    Can you touch someone else? *(No)*

    Do you wiggle and squirm? *(No)*

Do I want you to look up here? *(Yes)*

Can you blurt out? *(No)*

Show me what you'll do if you want to say something. *(raise hand)*

5. Write, in black: *Yesterday we went to the [St. Louis] Zoo.* Read it chorally twice, then give the pointer to a student and ask him to point to two or three random words.

6. Say, "Think about something you saw at the zoo that you really enjoyed seeing." Allow wait time for children to think and raise hands.

7. Let three contribute answers, then ask, "How many of you saw the . . .?"

8. Write, in red: *We saw little monkeys playing in trees.* (This will be what the child says with a little prompting. The child says, "We saw monkeys." Ask, "What were they doing?" Choose one of the children's responses to write.)

9. Have children read back the sentence chorally. Say, "What word is this?"

10. Write, in green: *We saw a big gorilla eating fruit.*

11. Have children read chorally.

12. Write, in purple: *We saw big elephants swinging their trunks around.* (The response is sometimes obtained only after some prompting.)

13. Read the written group story again.

Have students write what is on the chart into their journal or start a book, writing one sentence to a page.

On the second day, use the same procedure.

Reread what they wrote in the previous activity. Ask them to find and point to some of the smallest words, such as *big* and *saw*. Then turn to a new chart page and record three more entries. At the end of the activity, have them copy these entries into their books.

Teacher Tips

- Using different colors helps children keep their place.

- In subsequent activities, you can use interactive writing to describe other experiences and retell familiar stories.

- When students have achieved greater fluency, have them create their own stories. Do a class activity where each person contributes only one line.

- You can take a turn too, if the story needs to be redirected.

SAMPLE WORKSHEET 12.1. USING PICTURES TO MAKE SENTENCES.

Name _____ **Date** _____

Using Pictures to Make Sentences

Directions for Teacher: Use four to five pictures cut from old workbooks to make worksheets. Early in the year you may want to use a word box (see below). This helps if students are not proficient in spelling the words needed.

For example:

The man	like walking	to work
The boy and girl	is going	with a ball
The cat	is playing	in the rain

Later you can use the worksheet without the word box.

Directions: Write a sentence for each picture.

_____

_____

_____

_____

_____

_____

_____

Sample Writing Lesson (Instructional Level 2.5)

Objective: Children will learn how phrases help sentences make more sense and give us important information.

Materials: Overhead projector

Directions

1. Write the objective on the board: "Phrases help sentences make more sense."

2. Read the objective to the students.

3. Say, "Can anyone tell me what a phrase is?" (Most likely they can't.) "You will learn about phrases today."

4. Write this one on an overhead: *We went.*

   Ask: "Is this a good sentence?" (They will say no.)

   Ask: "Why not?" (Answers will vary, but someone will say it doesn't make sense.) At that point, review the lesson's objective.

   Ask: "Can someone suggest how I could change this sentence so that it does make sense?"

5. You will need to evaluate the sentence to see what they add. Does it say *where, when, with whom, why, what, which one?*

6. Write: *The girls are planning . . .*

   Let someone suggest what to add to the sentence.

   Ask: "What question does the phrase answer?"

7. Write: *She shivered . . .*

   Follow steps described in 6.

8. Here is a list of sentences that require phrases to complete them:

   - I am going to . . .
   - She could see the . . .
   - My dad is . . .
   - The dog has . . .
   - The teacher wants me to . . .
   - I put on my . . .
   - You can go out to play after . . .
   - Mom said she put my homework . . .
   - The teacher gave me . . .
   - My little brother hit . . .

- Can you open . . .
- I am careful when . . .
- My dad likes to . . .
- At 4 o'clock, I have baseball practice but I will be . . .
- It is really hot, so I'm . . .
- I really like . . .
- The rabbit hopped to . . .
- This story makes me feel . . .

Have children write phrases to finish a few of these sentences each day.

Spelling for Young Students with Learning Disabilities

Spelling activities need to be a daily focus at school if students with LD are to be successful. This is particularly true if the child has short-term memory deficits.

It is useful for students to have their own word dictionaries. These can be made using a separate page for most letters. One page can serve for *d-e*, *j-k*, and *u-v*. W will need a full page; *x, y,* and *z* can be together on a single page. When making each booklet, enter the letters in the top right-hand corner of each page.

Each week, after you thoroughly introduce the spelling words, the students will enter each word on the proper page.

Spelling activities can be introduced as soon as children can recognize fifteen letters of the alphabet. The most important letters to know are *b, c, d, f, g, h, l, m, n, p, r, s, t, w,* and the vowels *a, o,* and *u.*

Some students find that a digital reader helps them greatly in their writing, because it allows them to hear their written work read back to them, thereby enabling them to find the mistakes they miss when reading their work. If a student can't spell the word she would like to use, she often doesn't recognize a misspelling of the word when she reads it to herself. A digital reader can be an invaluable teaching tool. You can check out the Center for Applied Special Technology (CAST) Web site for more information on digital readers: www.CAST.org.

Materials

Your district may specify and provide the materials you are to use. If not, you may choose five or six words from the first column of the First 100 Most-Used Words list at the end of Chapter Eleven. The words *the, boy, can, go, play,* and *read* work well for the activity. Note that each of these words starts with a different letter, which will allow you to use them later as your first lesson in alphabetizing by the first letter. This also makes learning the words easier. When the children have learned these words, they will be able to write three sentences:

The boy can go.   *The boy can read.*   *The boy can play.*

Methods

On day one, introduce four words: *the, boy, can,* and *go,* one at a time. Each word should be written carefully on a separate 40" × 80" card.

Use the following techniques with each word.

Display the word card on the board.

1. *Say the word.* When introducing the word *the,* tell the children that most people do not pronounce this word carefully; instead they say "thu." Instruct the students to say "thē" so they can hear each sound. (The reason for asking them to pronounce it like this is so that they can move smoothly on to related words, such as *then, them,* and *these.* Once they have learned to spell all these words, students usually will get sloppy and revert to saying "thu," but this usually doesn't occur until they thoroughly know how to spell *then, them,* and *these.*)

2. *Have students repeat the word.*

3. *Spell the word:* "t.h.e. spells *thē.*"

4. *Ask students to repeat what you just said.*

   Talk about the sound of the *th.* Some young children have trouble making the sound because their tongues do not move out easily; it may take one-on-one work with a few before they can routinely move  their tongue out. Making the *th* sound involves two steps: (1) sticking out the tongue about one-half inch, with the teeth on top of it, and (2) blowing air over the tongue. For some students, several days of practice may be necessary to accomplish this. Practice this sound with all students, while reminding them that every time they hold their mouths in this way, they are ready to make the *th* sound.

5. *Have students watch your mouth* as you slowly say *th* and *e.* Ask them to repeat it slowly as you point to the "th" and then to the "e" on the word card.

6. *Have students repeat the phrase* t.h.e. says "the" *three times as you point to the letters.*

7. *Have students write the word three times as they say the letters.*

8. Tell individual students *to close their eyes, put their fingers in their ears,* and *spell the word.* By so doing they are removing visual and auditory distractions.

On the second day, go through the same lesson again, but *add "read" and "play."*

On the third day, *repeat* the procedures.

On the fourth day, after going over all six words, give each child a pad of plasticine clay and a toothpick to use as a stylus. *Have students write each word in clay.* This supplements the auditory approach with one that is tactile.

Give a trial test, circulating as students take it. If someone misses a word, tell her to circle it so that she knows which words she needs to practice more. Observing them work allows you to know which students are going to be slower learners. Do not give your first recordable spelling test until every student can spell at least five words correctly and earn a passing grade.

For the next spelling lesson, keep the original six words and add *with, us, to,* and *you.* Follow the same procedures as previously outlined. Sentences they can write are:

> *You can read to us.*   *Can you play with us?*
>
> *Can you go with us?*   *The boy can play with us.*

(Do not worry about the use of capitalization, periods, or question marks yet.)

By the third lesson, you can teach students to say, "The vowels are *a, e, i, o,* and *u* and sometimes *y* and *w.*" Say the phrase with them every day until they know it.

During their daily lesson, have students mark the vowels in each word:

> *go the boy read can play*
>
> v   v   vv   vv   v   vv

Give them a paper with a dotted-line word to trace. After tracing, have students mark each letter that is a vowel and trace over it with a red crayon (shown here as a bold line). Demonstrate this with a crayon.

In the next lesson, continue to use the words with which they have been working, but add the words *girl, help, like, mother,* and *not.* Sentences they will be able to write include the following:

> *Mother can read to the boy.*   *The girl can help mother.*
>
> *I like to read.*   *The boy and girl can play.*
>
> *The girl likes the boy.*

For the next lesson, add the words *did, not, see, will, work,* and *man.* Have students think of sentences they can make from these words.

By the time your students can spell all the words in the first column of the First 100 Most-Used Words list, and if they simultaneously have been doing the decoding activities from Chapter Eleven, they will be familiar with the sounds of most letters. They are also familiar with the words you have put on the word board, and they have added many words to their dictionary. They now are ready to begin writing their own sentences. As they arrive first thing in the morning, review the nouns they know: *boy, girl, mother, man,* and *you.* Ask them to write a sentence for each noun. Have each child read his favorite sentence to the class.

Teach the word family *be, me, we, he,* and *she.* Display this word family on a banner in the front of the classroom.

Review these words with students daily. You will find that they will pick them up without having to work on spelling them. For a spelling lesson, go on to the words in the second column of the word list; begin with the verbs *eat, going, make, said,* and *are.*

When students write their spelling words, ask them to put a dot under each sound they are able to hear. This will help them later as they attempt unknown words. For example:

but	could	at	am	ask	has	is	over
⋯	⋯	⋅⋅	⋅⋅	⋯	⋯	⋅⋅	⋯
ⓣⓗat	away	blue	from	just	old	ran	ride
⋯	⋯	⋯	⋯⋅	⋯⋅	⋯	⋯	⋯

This kind of practice helps students learn words quickly. They will use inventive spelling to attempt unknown words. For example:

She gav mother a nis gft.

At this stage, accept inventive spelling if you can figure out what the student is trying to communicate. If you cannot figure out what the child is trying to say, ask him. Then, using the "robot" technique, help the student spell the undecipherable words phonetically. If the student misspells a word she has been given in a spelling lesson, ask her to correct that word.

At this point, explain to students that every word has at least one vowel. Thus, even though we do not hear the vowel *i* in the word *girl,* it is there.

After five to six months of phonemic awareness activities, phonics activities, and spelling activities, most students are ready to begin learning some of the rules of our language. Teach the silent *e* first.

Some teachers tell students that "when two vowels go walking, the first one does the talking." Most LD kids do not understand what that phrase means. They do, however, grasp the concept that the *e* at the end of a word is a basketball player. The *e* reaches over, slam-dunks the first vowel, and says, "Say your name or I'll make a slam dunk again." Thus:

at	becomes	*āte*	*rid*	becomes	*rīde*
not	becomes	*nōte*	*tub*	becomes	*tūbe*

Show them that even if two vowels are side by side, the same thing happens; the second vowel bullies the first into "speaking":

pan	becomes	*pāin*	*bet*	becomes	*bēet* or *bēat*
her	becomes	*hēre*	*rod*	becomes	*rēad*

Update their spelling lists to reflect this new information.

kēep māke grēen nēed rīde

The *c/k* sound can be puzzling. A key rule is that if you hear the *c/k* sound as the initial sound in a word, the word usually begins with a *c*; if you hear it as the last sound, the word usually ends with a *k*.

cat   car   cake

Teach word families as you introduce the first word in that family:

make	down	went	run
take	town	sent	sun
lake	gown	tent	fun
wake	crown	rent	bun
rake	drown	spent	

Speaking Activities for Young Students with Learning Disabilities

Children love to put on plays. Take advantage of this fact and turn classic stories into plays. Do not use scripts at this stage. Instead, teach the lines to the students and demonstrate the use of expression—how they can make the material "come alive." If three students are cast for each role—cast 1, cast 2, and cast 3—all students get a chance to participate, provided you perform the play to enough audiences. A second advantage is that if someone is absent, you have two other people who are able to stand in.

One of the simplest classics is the "Three Billy Goats Gruff." The roles include the narrator, the big billy goat, the medium-size billy goat, the tiny billy goat, and the troll. No costumes are needed. Scenery is minimal— three tables laid end to end to be the bridge across the river. The troll lives below the middle table. If desired, masks can be made from paper plates.

Another oral language opportunity that students enjoy, and learn from, is a lesson on phone manners, including the proper way to answer the phone and how to take messages.

Handwriting Skills for Older Students with Learning Disabilities

Many students with LD are not ready to abandon printing at the mid-second- or early-third-grade level. If a student is barely reading, it is unwise to have him shift to cursive. He still has not mastered printing. Once a student can read fluently at the 2.0 level, he can be switched to cursive. In teaching letters and letter recognition, emphasize the basic shape of a printed letter and then introduce different styles of representing letters. With each introduction of a new letter shape, it is wise to reiterate the sound the letters make, no matter their shape or presentation.

After about the fourth grade, focusing on handwriting performance means that instruction in another area suffers. If a student is past the fourth grade and still has trouble with writing, it's time to teach coping techniques. At this point, focusing on handwriting isn't going to improve a student's ability to take notes or complete a written assignment quickly, nor will it help students who can't write more than half a page in about fifteen minutes due to motor difficulties. Teach students to type their answers. Have students practice taking notes on the computer during class and then help them organize them, or use the overhead to model how to take notes. Compare student work to show different perspectives on the lesson.

Students can learn cursive through tracing activities. You will have to explain the procedure. Make pattern sheets as shown on Worksheets 12.2 and 12.3 and laminate them to protect them. On each letter, the student colors the first segments, made with dots, with a red marker; colors the second, "dashed" segments, with a green marker; and colors the third, solid-line segments, with a blue marker.

WORKSHEET 12.2. CURSIVE TRACING: LOWER CASE.

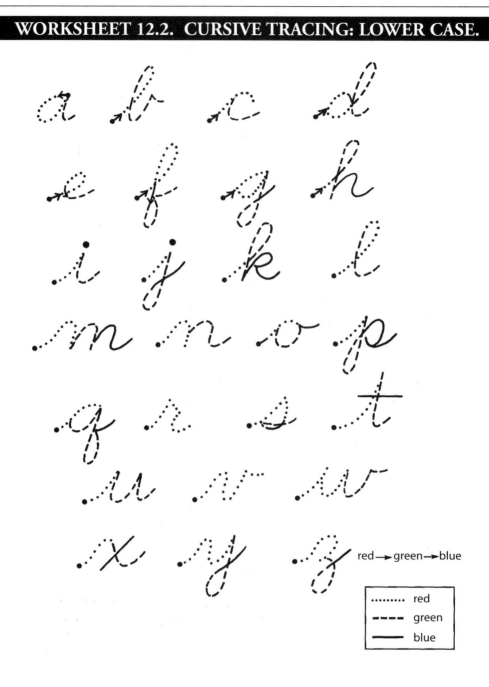

red → green → blue

··········	red
- - - - -	green
——	blue

WORKSHEET 12.3. CURSIVE TRACING: UPPER CASE.

red → green → blue

....	red
- - - -	green
——	blue

Once the student has practiced for several days forming each letter by tracing it, have him put the pattern on his desk and practice making each letter freehand. Then teach him how to join the letters so that he can write a two- to three-letter word without lifting his pencil. The value of cursive is that it is a faster way to write. Letters that have a tail that ends on the lower line are not usually troublesome. The ones that need special emphasis are those that have a tail in the air, such as the *b*. Teach students how to make these combinations: *ba, be, bi, bo, bu,* and *by*. Likewise, teach the *wa, we, wi, wo,* and *wu* combinations.

The Mechanics of Writing for Older Students with Learning Disabilities

Most LD students will pick up the idea of putting a space between each word just because the teacher reminds them to do so countless times during the first three grades. There are, however, a few hard-core cases where you must do something dramatic to teach this skill. Make a red square ($\frac{1}{2}"\times\frac{1}{2}"$) and require the child to place it between each word as she writes. Of course, on the first day, someone must sit with the student to make sure she follows the direction. Most students require only one session of practice. Whether due to the red color or just the annoyance of having to physically put that red square in each time, this method works to help students become aware of spaces between words.

Once students are reading fluently at grade 2.0, it is important to teach them to *proofread their work before submitting it*. LD students tend to be inactive learners, exhibiting failure syndrome; they believe that they can't be good students, so they just want to "hurry up and do" the activity and move on to something else. Knowing this, you must figure out some way to make them "want" to review their work or some way that requires that they do so before they switch to another activity.

Students need to be taught to *analyze a sentence*. This will entail explaining to them that a sentence is a complete thought. It also involves teaching them to identify nouns, verbs, and phrases. Once students have a knowledge of what nouns, verbs, and phrases are, they will be more equipped to analyze and proofread sentences. When teaching sentences, it is helpful to ask students to identify both sentences and sentence fragments so that they can see the differences. Read a sentence fragment. Say, "Raise your hand if these sentences communicate a complete thought. Clap your hands if they do not. *The girl at the bus stop* [fragment]; *Is the girl at the bus stop?* [sentence]."

It is important to realize that some students with LD will have continual trouble with the concepts of grammar and sentence structure. For students whose main disability occurs in the areas of language and sound recognition or order, as in the case of dyslexia, the structure of a sentence can be very confusing. Because these students tend to have trouble processing the smallest sounds in the language, as well as difficulties with adding sounds together to make words, you can imagine the confusion when sentences must be structured from a specific grouping of words to make "grammatical sense." In cases like this, a word processing program that accommodates these issues may help provide immediate visual feedback about the structure of a sentence, especially with regard to fragments and grammar.

After learning to analyze and recognize how a sentence is structured, students need to move on to *learning to write paragraphs.* Present the concept that a paragraph is a group of sentences about a single subject.

For the first lesson, ask, "What is a paragraph?" Even high school students have surprised me with how fuzzy their concept of this is. Ask students probing questions, such as, "How many sentences make a paragraph?" "What is a topic sentence?" and "How do we tell where a paragraph begins and ends?"

Using a textbook, have students show you where a paragraph begins and ends. Discuss with them the term *indent.*

Have students count the number of sentences in several paragraphs and list their findings on the board. Help them realize that three to eight sentences are common for a paragraph.

Ask students to read some examples of good paragraphs and have them identify the main idea of each paragraph and supporting detail sentences.

At the end of this chapter you will find samples that provide ideas for other activities that must be done in order to advance your students' knowledge about paragraph writing. Tailor the activities to the age, literacy level, and needs of your group.

Students need to learn how to write process paragraphs sequentially. For example:

Did you know that raisins are made from grapes? When the grapes are ripe, they are picked. Then, they are washed. Next, they are placed in the sun to dry. Finally, they are boxed and sent to market.

Students must learn to write nonsequential paragraphs as well. For example:

> *It is very important to take care of your teeth. They are needed for eating and talking. Brush them after every meal. Go to the dentist twice a year.*

When students begin to write paragraphs, remind them to indent; demonstrate this concept on the board. Give them a writing topic. You may choose to use pictures to direct their thinking. (The two Writing a Story activities at the end of this chapter are good ways to practice writing sequential paragraphs.) The following paragraph is an example of a nonsequential paragraph.

> *Lions live in groups called prides. The group is like a big family. There are usually two or three grown male lions and several females with their cubs. A mother lion carries her baby by the nape of the neck. The lions show affection for each other by rubbing against one another.*

Encourage students to put the main idea at the beginning of their paragraph. If you have students who put extraneous information in their paragraphs, point out several examples of this to heighten their awareness. Develop paragraphs at their level of reading. In each paragraph, they can locate the sentence that does not relate to the topic sentence.

The following paragraph includes extraneous information:

> *About a hundred years ago, some children were playing in the sandy bed of a dried-up river. One boy found a stick. One found a rock. Since the rock was somewhat different from others he had seen, he took it home. It turned out to be a "blue stone" diamond. Immediately, people began exploiting this land. Africa produces most of the world's diamonds.*

As students advance in their ability to write, there are many forms of writing they need to be taught, such as the personal letter, the business letter, the report, and the creative story.

Teach children to use the spell-check feature on their computers. Some students with dyslexia may never learn to spell all words correctly; it is best to teach them coping mechanisms for situations where a professional-level piece of writing is needed. They may need to be taught how to use the spell-check feature so that they don't choose the first word suggested by the program. Students will need to be taught how to prepare written work on the computer, and they will also need to be taught to have someone review their applications for jobs, college, insurance, and so on.

Letter Writing

The best way to teach letter-writing skills is by providing students with real opportunities to communicate in this format. Arrange to pair your students with those in another class, preferably in your school. Match each LD student with two regular classroom students to increase the odds of finding a compatible writing or recess partner for the LD student. Explain the letter format: where to place the date, the greeting, the body, and the salutation. Give the students a guide that illustrates these things. At first, the letters should be short, so that writing them doesn't seem a chore.

Encourage students to write about what they like and don't like to do. Remind them to always end the letters with some question to be answered, thus giving the respondent a reason to write back.

May 13, 2009

Dear Devin,

I really enjoyed yesterday. I like holidays. My family drove up to the mountains for a picnic. I got to fish in a stream. I didn't catch anything but it was fun anyway.

What did you do on Memorial Day?

Your friend,

Business letters are more fun if they are actually mailed, as there is a possibility of getting an answer. Discuss with students ways to enhance their chances of receiving a reply.

- Send a letter in care of the postmaster of the capital city of the state.

- Send only one letter to each state.

- Use home addresses for replies.

- Address the envelopes, stamp, and mail the letters.

This project is unsuccessful when students forget to mail the letters or lose them, or when parents won't give them a stamp. You may want to mail the letters for the students.

Return.............

address............

Date ....

Send to............

Address............

....

   My family is planning to visit your state on our vacation. We would certainly appreciate any materials (maps or brochures) you can send that would be helpful in deciding where to go and what to see.

Sincerely,

(sign with full name)

E-mails and Digital Communication

If students are reluctant to handwrite letters, or their disability precludes them from doing so, e-mails and other forms of digital communication can greatly assist in helping students express their ideas. Most schools will limit what students are able to access online, even down to allowing students to work in only one select area. Students can begin to compose letters to their classmates, for political or environmental purposes, or to ask a question about a product.

   The benefits of e-mails include faster gratification, the use of word processing elements, and freedom from manually writing a letter when a student has extreme difficulty with penmanship or coordination. For some, the computer keyboard allows for a much wider range of expression and faster composition. Some students may be able to type much faster than they can write. Closely monitor the content of students' e-mail messages. You should also give a lesson on e-mail and digital communication etiquette.

Report Writing

The following are some guidelines for teaching students to write reports:

- Ask for initial reports of only one page.

- Work with the students in class on the first three reports.

- Always give students a guide of points to cover on their topic.

- Show students how to make reports look neat by incorporating a title page, drawings, and a cover.

Here are two sample outline guides; they can be adapted for any animal or used for any state or country:

Hummingbirds	California
I. Description	I. Size
A. Size	A. Area
B. Color	B. Population
C. Special characteristics	II. Location
D. Flight patterns	III. Terrain
II. Habitat	IV. Climate
A. Where they live	V. Economy
B. What they eat	A. Natural resources
III. Reproduction	B. Products produced
A. Nests	1. Agricultural
B. Number of eggs	2. Manufacturing
	VI. Interesting places to see

Consider letting students do more than one report of each kind.

Journal Writing

Daily journal writing is a good idea if you give students a topic. Most LD students have difficulty generating their own ideas. Research has shown that students tend to write more when they are given a topic, particularly one that stimulates their thinking.

The following are some sample writing topics:

1. Your mom says you can have any small pet you want. What would you choose and why?

2. Which do you think makes a better pet—a dog or a cat? Tell me why.

3. You are going to build a tree house. Tell me how it will look.

4. Do you think nighttime or daytime is more dangerous? Tell me why.

5. If you could go anywhere you wanted, where would you choose to go and why?

Most teachers have children work in the journals in the morning. You can use journal writing effectively as an end-of-the-day activity by having students reflect on their science or social studies lesson that day.

Here are some examples of subject area tie-ins:

1. What was the Abilene Trail, and how was it used?

2. Today we learned that cotton is a *solid.* What makes it a solid?

When students work in their journals at the end of the day, you have time to give out homework and notes.

Have students leave their journals on top of their desks at the end of the school day so that you can read them. Read about five a day, and make positive comments on the journals. Positive comments motivate LD students to "risk" trying to express themselves.

Spelling Activities for Older Students with Learning Disabilities

Many kinds of spelling activities can be used with older LD students, those functioning at grade 2.5 and above. Give students a packet of spelling activities to do during the week. By Thursday they must submit proof that they have done two primary activities and four optional ones. Include in the packet a list of words for vocabulary development. Following is a sample word list and a list of activities. The activities are described in the next paragraphs.

Sample Word List

| large | friend | import | huge | people | export |
| remember | September | page | October | exit | paint |

Spelling Activities

- Syllabicate and color-code.
- Write a sentence using each spelling word.
- Complete a listening-for-sounds activity.
- Do configuration exercises.
- Do dot-to-dot letter practice.
- Put words in alphabetical order.
- Write word ladders on graph paper.
- Do missing letters exercises.
- Proofread and correct.
- Answer list of questions on activity sheet.

    1. *Syllabication and color-coding* activities have been shown to be very helpful to all students, and are particularly beneficial to the visual learner. First, the student breaks the words into syllables and writes them in large letters. Then, she colors consonants green and vowels red.

2. *Write a sentence for each spelling word.* Students with learning disabilities tend to write short sentences that begin with the word *I*. Most of their sentences sound as if they were written by a first grader. (*I have a friend* or *I can paint.*)

Help students grow. Tell them that they are allowed to begin only one sentence with the word *I.* Remind them that there are other people to use as subjects of their writing. Post a list:

mother	brother	sister	uncle
father	they	we	teacher

Review nouns, verbs, helping verbs, and phrases. Next, tell them that each of their sentences must contain a noun, verb, and a phrase.

Show them that if they cannot think of a sentence, the dictionary may give one. *Praise them* when they write a really good sentence. Ask them to read their outstanding sentences to the class.

3. The *listening-for-sounds activity* is a critical skill for students with learning disabilities at all grades through high school. Ask them to put a dot under every phoneme they can hear in the list below:

large   friend   import   huge   people   export

remember   September   October   page   exit   paint

Explain to students that the letter *g* normally makes the sound it makes in *go*, but when it is followed by *e, i,* or *y*, it may sound like a *j*.

Call attention to the first syllable of *remember*. Have them look at a dictionary and find other words that include the prefix *re*. You can do the same with the *im* in *import*—help them transfer the sound to other dictionary words that have the same sound. LD students do not make these transfers unless you point them out. They regard every word as being totally new in all its parts or syllables.

When you review his work, a student may argue with you. Some sounds are a bit subjective; discuss this with the students. You will all get better at listening for phonemes.

4. In *configuration* activities, the students' attention is called to the shape of each word as well as to the fact that some letters are tall,

some are short, and some fall below the line. Students must visualize the word's shape to place it in the correct configuration.

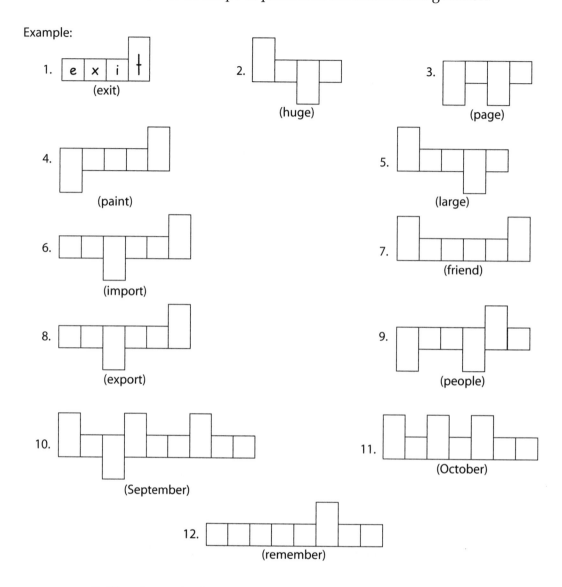

Example:

1. | e | x | i | t |
(exit)

2. (huge)

3. (page)

4. (paint)

5. (large)

6. (import)

7. (friend)

8. (export)

9. (people)

10. (September)

11. (October)

12. (remember)

5. The *dot-to-dot* letter-practice activity is particularly helpful in getting students with attention deficits to pay attention. In this activity, the student writes each word using dots. For example:

6. *Putting words in alphabetical order* is another way to get students to write words from their word list.

7. Supply students with half-inch-squared graph paper for them to do *ladders*. The student can write each word in the following way:

Example 1:

l				
l	a			
l	a	r		
l	a	r	g	
l	a	r	g	e

Example 2:

l	a	r	g	e
l	a	r	g	
l	a	r		
l	a			
l				

8. *Missing letters* is an activity that can be very beneficial to students, by calling their attention to, and requiring focus on, specific parts of each word. Graph paper can enhance the experience. For example:

l _ _ ge   imp_ _ t   r_ m _ mb _ r

lar_ _   _ _ port   _ _ mem _ _ _

9. *Proofreading and correcting* require students to look carefully at each word and compare it with their word list. This activity often appeals to the auditory learner as well as to the student who finds writing a laborious task. Instruct students to correct errors with a pencil other than blue or black.

1. larj	5. expart	9. inpart
2. frend	6. paj	10. September
3. remember	7. huj	11. exit
4. October	8. peaple	12. pant

10. The activity in Worksheet 12.4 solidifies the spelling concepts introduced in the lesson. Students' answers to these questions can help teachers gauge their progress.

284

Name _____   **Date** _____

1. List all the words in your word list that contain a **j** sound.

   _____   _____   _____

   (Circle the two letters that make the **j** sound.)

2. Find two words in the list that have almost the same meaning.

   _____   and   _____

3. If "ex" means **out** and "port" means **to carry**, what would the word **export** mean?

   _____

4. Here are three words:

   sample   **people**   **steeple**

   What do all of them have in common?   _____

5. There are two months on your word list.

   Write their names.

   _____   _____

   What do these words have in common?   _____

6. Take the "t" off of **paint** and you have   _____

   The new word means: **drink**   **lip**   **hurt**

Answers

1. huge large page
2. large, huge
3. to carry out
4. ple
5. September, October (ber)
6. pain (hurt)

Speaking Opportunities for Older Students with Learning Disabilities

Students with LD in the early grades tend to develop a fear of taking risks. They are often laughed at, ridiculed, or teased when they make errors. Teachers at all grade levels need to be aware of how serious this can be. No one likes to be the victim of teasing or ridicule. Such action is unkind at best. Teachers who see it happen have a duty to stop it.

It is probably unwise to force students at any grade level to speak to the class if they are uncomfortable doing so.

In the early grades, we should not ask a poor reader to read aloud to others. Instead, you or an aide should make time to listen to this student read one-on-one. If a poor reader wants to read aloud, set the stage for her. "Jan wants to read. She is doing a very brave thing. This material is kind of hard. If she comes to a word she doesn't know, who is going to help her?" *(the teacher)*. After the child has taken a short turn, say, "Jan has shown a lot of courage today." Have everyone clap for her effort and say, "Thank you for being so kind to her."

If a student makes an error and someone laughs, deal with the issue each time it occurs. "You are acting, Larry, as if you have never made a mistake. It is not appropriate for you to laugh at Melinda. You, like all of us, will make many errors in your lifetime, and you won't want people to laugh at you."

The media has covered numerous stories about students who became killers at their schools. When discussing the "why's," it is often mentioned that the students had acted violently after being teased or bullied. We need to discuss with students our concerns about this issue and work with them to prevent, or at least lessen the likelihood of, school violence.

Junior high students are probably the most self-conscious. Role playing and discussion in small groups with peers of their choice tend to draw these students into participation. These students usually like to do playlets; take advantage of this by assigning them such topics as telephone skills (business or personal) and manners. Most love to discuss relating to the opposite sex in social settings. In vocational exploration classes, they can benefit from role-playing ways to handle various job interview situations, how to react to criticism, and how to relate with coworkers under different stressors.

To form discussion groups, allow each student to choose a partner to work with. After everyone has a partner, let each pair choose another pair of students to work with, thus forming a group of four. Give them a written task to complete and circulate to give guidance to groups.

Divide the class into two parts and have them sit in circles: one group with the aide, the other group with you. Discuss an issue, such as "Can a boy and a girl just be friends?"

At the senior high level, students enjoy debating various topics. Some may like to be involved in researching the pros and cons of the issue; others may prefer the research to be done for them.

Sample Lesson: Recognizing Nouns

Objectives: Students will recognize that nouns are the names of people, places, or things. Students will recognize words that are nouns.

Directions

1. Get children's attention by telling them you are going to play a game. Raise your voice slightly and say, "It's a bird! It's a plane! It's Superman!" while pointing at imaginary things in the air.

2. Write: *Nouns are usually things we can draw.*

   Nouns are the names of people, places, and things.

3. Go around the room and point randomly to individual students. Ask each one to rapidly name a noun by saying, "It's a . . . table!" If someone cannot think of something, you can give a clue by pointing to something that has not been named.

Students think this is fun; they will enjoy the rapid-fire pace of the game if you do not let it lag. At the end of the game, students can use Worksheet 12.5 to record some of their responses in the correct column.

WORKSHEET 12.5. NOUNS ARE THE NAMES OF PEOPLE, PLACES, OR THINGS.

Name _____   Date _____

people

places

things

people	places	things
1. Mother	1. hospital	1. ruler
2. Daddy	2.	2.
3. sister	3.	3.
4. brother	4.	4.
5. baby	5.	5.
6.	6.	6.
7.	7.	7.
8.	8.	8.
9.	9.	9.
10.	10.	10.
11.	11.	11.
12.	12.	12.
13.	13.	13.
14.	14.	14.
15.	15.	15.

Sample Lesson: Recognizing Verbs

Objective: Students will recognize *helping verbs* and *doing verbs*.

Directions: Distribute a copy of Worksheet 12.6 to each student. Tell students that you are going to practice saying the helping verbs every day until they know them. Tell them that as soon as they can say them all from memory, you will give them a small reward and send a positive note home to the parent. Every day they will read the list aloud chorally. Starting in the second week, they will also read the list to a partner.

See Worksheet 12.6 on the next page.

WORKSHEET 12.6. HELPING AND DOING VERBS.

Helping Verbs	Doing Verbs
am	eat
are	sleep
be	help
been	wash
being	walk
can/can't	talk
could/couldn't	play
did/didn't	work
do/don't	go
does/doesn't	run
had/hadn't	sit
had/hasn't	fall
have/haven't	write
is/isn't	fold
may	jump
might	cut
must	draw
should/shouldn't	print
was/wasn't	underline
were/weren't	read
will/won't	circle
would/wouldn't	

Others:

_____

_____

_____

_____

Others:

_____

_____

_____

_____

Writing Activities

WORKSHEET 12.7. THE FIVE ELEMENTS OF A GOOD SENTENCE.

Directions: The five elements of a good sentence are a capitalized first letter, a noun, a verb, a phrase, and punctuation. Fix these ten sentences so that they have all five elements in them.

1. I am to _____

   _____

2. she could see _____

   _____

3. Mother doesn't like to _____

   _____

4. My friend went _____

   _____

5. We can go to _____

   _____

6. the dog was _____

   _____

7. Dad told me that I had _____

   _____

8. The teacher _____ us to _____

   _____

9. The Olympic Games were _____

   _____

10. _____ asked her to _____

    _____

WORKSHEET 12.8a.   WRITING A STORY: BEGINNING, MIDDLE, AND END.

Directions: Write a story with a beginning, middle, and an end. Use the pictures below to help you write your story.

My Accident

WORKSHEET 12.8b. WRITE YOUR OWN STORY.

Directions: Draw or cut out pictures of the beginning, middle, and end of your own story. Make sure you give your story a title.

Title of My Story

WORKSHEET 12.9. WRITING PARAGRAPHS.

Directions: Using the main idea given below, write at least three supporting details. Make sure you write complete sentences.

Winning a Million Dollars

Someone asked me, "What would you do if you won a million dollars?"

_____
_____
_____
_____
_____
_____
_____
_____
_____
_____
_____
_____
_____
_____
_____
_____
_____
_____
_____

Using a cluster can be helpful in organizing your ideas. Here is a sample cluster:

give some to my parents

buy a new home and car

If I won
a million dollars,
I would:

travel around the world

save the rest of the money

WORKSHEET 12.10. HOW TO RECOGNIZE QUESTIONS: CHART OF SINGLE WORDS.

? ? ? ?

? Words That ?

? Signal ?

? Questions ?

<u>What</u>   <u>Who</u>   <u>Where</u>
<u>When</u>   <u>Why</u>   <u>How</u>

Are   Has
Can   Have
Do   Is
Does   May
Did   Will

WORKSHEET 12.11. HOW TO RECOGNIZE QUESTIONS: USING QUESTION MARKS.

Name _____ **Date** _____

Directions:

1.   Underline the first word of each sentence.

2.   Look at the chart (Worksheet 12.10) of the words that signal questions.

3.   Is that underlined word on the chart? If the answer is yes, put a question mark (?) at the end of the sentence. If the answer is no, put a period (.) at the end of the sentence.

- What time does your plane leave _____

- Why are you always late _____

- My bed needs to be made _____

- Is the dog outside _____

- The nurse gave me a shot _____

- I want to go with Mother to the store _____

- Have you told her you can't come to her party _____

- May I use your book _____

- How did you get the answer to that question _____

- They took a walk in the park _____

- Where did Father go _____

- Will you help me clean my room _____

- She does not like that kind of pie _____

- Can you wink one eye at a time _____

WORKSHEET 12.12. ANSWERING SIX IMPORTANT QUESTIONS.

Directions: Read the story below. Using the information given, answer each question with a complete sentence.

Tom felt bad all day. His stomach hurt. As soon as school was out, he hurried home and went to bed. Tom's mother kept coming into his room to look in on him because she was worried about him.

1. **Who** was sick?

_____

_____

2. **What** was wrong with him?

_____

_____

3. **When** did he go to bed?

_____

_____

4. **Where** was he when he got sick?

_____

_____

5. **Why** did his mother keep looking at him?

_____

_____

6. **How** long was he sick before he went to bed?

_____

_____

Chapter 13

Teaching Mathematically Challenged Students

This chapter details various ways to improve the math skills of "at-risk" and LD students. These students sometimes have difficulty learning a skill through traditional methods of instruction. All the techniques described in this chapter have been classroom tested, with good results.

Diagnosing a Student's Difficulties

There are many reasons a student may experience difficulty with math. Let's discuss a few of the possibilities.

Lack of readiness. Young children come to school with varying degrees of readiness to learn math. Some children can accurately count to twenty, recognize some or all of the mathematical symbols, and even count actual sets of objects. They have had preschool experiences with blocks, figures, and various shapes. They can look and tell whether the "square block" will go through the "round hole." Many can already write the numbers. Other young children have not had the benefit of preschool nor a wide range of experiences, and are not "ready."

If you have a class of young students with LD, check their IEPs. You may find their mental age to be less than their chronological age. You may have five- or six-year-old students with mental ages lower than age three. Such children are not ready for formal math teaching; for them, experiences with blocks, shapes, and sizes—such as fitting lids on the correct size pan—are of the appropriate level. The curriculum needed will resemble that of nursery school; these children are not ready to sit at desks and work on math problems.

Visual perceptual deficits. Many learning disabled students have visual perceptual deficits. The psychologist's report should give an age-equivalent visual perceptual score. It is not uncommon to have a nine-year-old with a visual perceptual score of age five. It is common to observe that

- The student has difficulty when writing numbers, often reversing them. This can be ameliorated by daily board work, practicing a single number until it is no longer reversed. Write the number about a foot high, and as the student traces over it, call his attention to how it feels to write it.

- Students do not grasp the meaning of the words *set* or *group*. They do not see objects in a picture as a set until someone colors a border around the set and talks to them about the items "inside the border."

- Students cannot accurately count without physically moving manipulatives from one side of their desk to the other as they count. Students with this problem will need a patient adult at their side to make sure they are counting correctly.

- Students don't see four lines as forming a square. They must have colored-paper forms they can feel or must have the square directly on top of the rectangle to see the difference between the two forms.

- Older students cannot line up columns of numbers; they may need graph paper in order to keep columns of numbers straight.

Poor spatial sense. Some students have difficulty with concepts such as *over* and *under* or *more* and *less.* If this is the case, you will need to devote extra time to building these concepts.

Poor memory. This is a big challenge for many. Students frequently do not become automatic in memorization of facts, and we see them having to count on their fingers or making slash marks on paper even as teenagers and young adults. Short-term memory scores below the 10th percentile suggest that the student may need to use a calculator or a times table chart. With assistive technology, students with poor memory may be able to learn more math than they would if left to decipher every problem without these devices.

Math anxiety. Students who have trouble with math often develop an emotional overlay. They just "freeze up" when they see a math problem. Some say they feel as if they are becoming sick to their stomach. If this occurs, help them calm down. Take the pressure off with sympathetic comments, such as "Just take your time" or "I understand you may feel worried. Don't get uptight. I'll help you."

Teachers find assessment devices valuable for identifying which skills students will need to learn. The math section of the Wide Range Achievement Test or the test shown on the following pages can be used as assessment devices. It is helpful to watch as students take a test in order to see how they go about solving the problems and how they react when they are uncertain. When a student misses a problem on a test, assigning one or two similar problems may provide more information about a potential trouble area. When using the assessment test on the following pages, proceed to Math Assessment 2 only if the student does well (75 percent or better) on Math Assessment 1. These worksheets can serve as pre- and post-tests.

Analyze missed problems. Where did the student's understanding break down? For example, students may do fine on the simple subtraction problems but not understand when to borrow on more complex ones.

Teach unknown skills. Use known skills to design homework or seatwork assignments.

Teaching Techniques

Levels of Understanding: Concrete, Representational, and Abstract

Understanding always proceeds in the same way—we must begin at the *concrete level*. For instance, in math, students will never be able to manipulate fractions with any understanding until they have spent numerous hours manipulating physical pieces representing fractions. From this concrete manipulative stage, understanding moves to the *representational* or *pictorial level*, where students can look at symbols or pictures and understand how to move things around to get proper or improper fractions. The last stage is the *abstract level*, where the student understands so well that he can manipulate concepts in his head. He can understand relationships such as equivalent fractions; he can deal with problems that involve whole and fractional numbers in the same problem.

Name_____

Date_____

Math Assessment 1

3	6	12	25	47
+ 4	+ 2	+ 54	+ 35	+ 59

9	6	39	60	82
- 6	- 2	- 15	- 48	- 57

There are 4 cats playing.
One runs away.
How many cats are left playing? _____

You have 6 books.
Someone gives you 3 more.
How many books do you
have now? _____

What time is it?

_____   _____

Use real coins.

• Show student 2 dimes, 3 nickels,
  and a penny.
  How much money do you see?

  _____

• Show a quarter, dime, and nickel.
  How much money do you see?

  _____

Name _____

Date _____

Math Assessment 2

$3 \times 2 =$

$4 \times 8 =$

$$62 \times 3$$

$$48 \times 2$$

$$95 \times 41$$

$2\overline{)9}$

$3\overline{)12}$

$5\overline{)80}$

$8\overline{)1872}$

What does the
6 in <u>6</u>7 stand for?

_____

What does the
3 in 4<u>3</u>21 stand for?

_____

How long is this line?

▬▬▬▬▬▬▬

What fraction of each figure is shaded?

_____

_____

$$\begin{array}{r} \frac{2}{3} \\ + \frac{3}{4} \\ \hline \end{array}$$

$$\begin{array}{r} \frac{2}{3} \\ + \frac{3}{4} \\ \hline \end{array}$$

- There are 3 teams. If 7 kids play on each team, how many players are there?

_____

$$\begin{array}{r} \frac{1}{2} \\ - \frac{9}{12} \\ \hline \end{array}$$

$$\begin{array}{r} \frac{1}{2} \\ - \frac{1}{12} \\ \hline \end{array}$$

- A bottle holds 32 ounces. How many 8-ounce cups does it contain?

_____

Name _____

Date _____

Math Assessment 3

368
974
671
+ 85

$1285 + 963 + 9 =$

$1\frac{7}{8}$
$+2\frac{5}{8}$

$6\frac{1}{4}$
$+4\frac{1}{2}$

627
- 392

8012
- 3809

4013
- 2978

6
$-3\frac{1}{4}$

$8\frac{1}{3}$
$-4\frac{3}{4}$

635
× 28

801
× 50

$\frac{3}{8} \times \frac{2}{3} =$

$2\frac{1}{2} \times \frac{2}{3} =$

$15\overline{)96}$

$63\overline{)2142}$

$\frac{3}{4} \div \frac{1}{2} =$

Our school is going on a field trip. There will be 420 riders in all. If each bus holds 60 riders, how many buses will be needed?

_____

You have a plane to catch at 10:25. You are told to be at the airport an hour early. It takes 45 minutes to get to the airport. What time should you leave home?

_____

Recently I was in a high school special education math class. The skill being taught was addition of like fractions. Students were being asked to add $\frac{3}{4} + \frac{3}{4}$ and then express the fraction correctly. All students were confused. The teacher asked one girl for her answer. When she said, "Three twos," he threw up his hands in frustration. The teacher was teaching at the abstract level of understanding when most of his students needed to be working at the concrete manipulative level. The teacher was frustrated. The students were frustrated.

In talking with the student later, I could see that she had no experience using manipulatives to solve math problems. She did not understand that $\frac{3}{4}$ meant something had been divided into four pieces and she had three of them. She also did not understand that each piece was equal in size. As for her answer of $\frac{6}{4}$ when she added $\frac{3}{4}$ and $\frac{3}{4}$, she said someone had told her that when she saw problems like this, she "should add the top but not the bottom numbers." The words *numerator* and *denominator* were not in her vocabulary.

$$\frac{3}{4}$$

$$+ \ \frac{3}{4}$$

$$\frac{6}{4} \ = \ \frac{3}{2}$$

When asked how she reduced to $\frac{3}{2}$, she responded that she had copied the answer from her boyfriend's paper. (He sat next to her.)

The point to be made here is that we cannot expect students who are functioning at the preoperational or concrete level to do advanced calculations requiring knowledge at the abstract level. This particular student needed to start at the concrete level with cutting activities until she could cut circles and squares into halves, thirds, fourths, and so on. If successful at this level, she could progress to the next level and finally to the abstract level.

Incorporating Reading into the Math Curriculum

One of the traps teachers fall into when teaching math to students with LD is that they concentrate on computational skills, often omitting word problems because of the reading difficulties their students have. Instead of eliminating them, teachers should present daily oral story problems using concrete objects. For example, read this problem: "Three children are playing." (Ask three children to come to the front.) "Two more children come to play." (Two more go up.) "How many children are playing now?" Have students draw a picture and determine the answer:

$$🕺🕺🕺 + 🕺🕺 = 🕺🕺🕺🕺🕺 \text{ or } 5$$

Make up and present two or three story problems daily. Use simple problems at the beginning so as not to confuse or intimidate students. For example: "Graham finds four stacks of books on a table. Each stack has five books in it. How many books are there in all?" (Put books in the stacks on a table; let Graham count them while others watch. Also show them $5 + 5 + 5 + 5 = 20$.)

If you begin teaching story problems as soon as students can accurately count, they do not develop anxiety over them. If you have older students who are fearful of story problems, tackle the problems together. You might draw pictures on the board while they work on paper. Using your students' names in problems adds interest.

Make arrangements to take your class to a supermarket when teaching lessons on weight, shopping, or careers. Focus attention on centers within the store, using one adult to supervise each center. One group of students can witness what goes on in the bakery or deli department, while another observes the meat department and talks with the butcher. Another might watch the cashier, another a shelf stocker. Students will get far more out of this firsthand experience if they have a booklet of questions to ask each person they observe. In determining the questions, consider what you want students to think about—for example, How are cookies sold (by the pound or by the dozen)? Does the butcher have a scale? (Include a picture of it.) Is the scale for weighing vegetables like the scale for weighing meat?

When you return to school, guide children in painting a mural on wide butcher paper that depicts the different centers at the supermarket. Use the mural as a prop to remind students of their experiences in the different centers when doing story problems. Write story problems using items that were handled in the store. Have students stand in front of the mural, using empty cookie bags, plastic jars with their labels, and drawings of fruits, vegetables, meat, and dairy products to connect the story problems to real life.

Teaching Specific Skills

Counting Symbols and One-to-One Correspondence

Many activities can help teach counting:

- Teach young ones numeral songs and finger plays, such as "One, Two, Buckle My Shoe." Students can use gestures to demonstrate the counting aspect of the words.

- Read books that involve counting—for example, *Over in the Meadow.*

- Draw a number line on the playground blacktop and have students hop and count.

- Play "Mother, May I?" In the beginning use low numbers ("two giant steps" or "five baby steps").

- Use counting as a signal— students are to be quiet by the time you reach five.

- Once they can count orally to five, introduce the number symbols 1–5. Give tracing papers like the one shown here.

- Put a small stack of blocks on each desk. Say, "Show me four blocks" or "Put two blocks beside your book." Another day, do the same activity with crackers or other small objects.

- Put numbers on 4"× 6" index cards; also make cards with corresponding numbers of dots. Shuffle the cards and ask a child to arrange the numbers in correct order and match with correct number of dots.

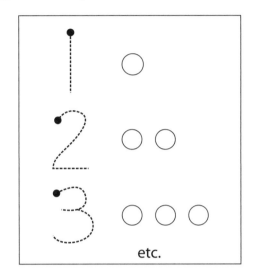

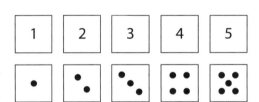

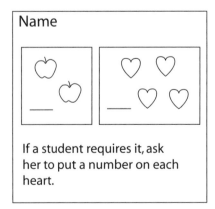

- When students understand 1–5, add a number every few days until they understand 1–10.

- Make pencil-and-paper counting cards.

- When students can count to twenty, have them draw a number line showing 0–20; ask them to show you various numbers on the line. ("Show me 0," "Show me 20," "Show me 8," and so on.) Keep doing these drills until each student can find any given number efficiently without hesitation. Once they can, teach them to visualize 0–20 with their eyes closed. Stand at the back of the room and tell them to "point in the air to . . ." You can tell by where they are pointing if they are able to "see" the numbers in their head. At that point, say, "Put your finger on 6. Go forward three numbers. What number are you on?" (They say 9.) "Now go backward one. What number do you see?" (They say 8.)

Beginning Addition

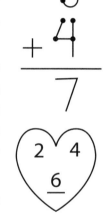

- Work with numbers that make sums under 10. In the beginning, students can use "touch points" to add correctly. (If you have not seen the "touch math" system, ask lower-grade teachers to teach you.)

- Use manipulatives, such as small blocks, to teach the associative property of adding. Put numbers inside a heart; tell students, "These numbers are in love." With manipulatives show them that 4 + 2 = 6, but if you reverse it, 2 + 4 = 6. "Two and four belong to a family called six."

- Begin using flash cards to drill sums up to ten: list the fact on the front, the answer on the back. Let students work in pairs to teach these to each other.

- Use manipulatives. Give each student eight blocks and have them group the blocks into three (3) and five (5). Ask them to move one block from the 5 group over to the 3 group. Ask if they still have eight blocks in all. Surprisingly, some LD children have trouble with this concept and will need to recount to be sure that 4 + 4 = 8. Demonstrate the ways to make 8 by moving blocks.

$$\begin{array}{r} 1 \\ +7 \\ \hline 8 \end{array} \qquad \begin{array}{r} 2 \\ +6 \\ \hline 8 \end{array} \qquad \begin{array}{r} 3 \\ +5 \\ \hline 8 \end{array} \qquad \begin{array}{r} 4 \\ +4 \\ \hline 8 \end{array}$$

- When students show a readiness to do problems with three or four entries, show them how to group pairs (activity reinforces their drill on basic facts). Be sure to do story problems and to teach that the plus sign means "put the numbers together."

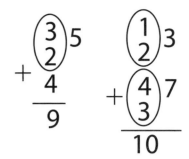

- When you are ready to teach the addition of larger numbers, have the child "shove" the bigger number into her head (touch her head, say the first number), hold up enough fingers for the second number, and count. Some children will not be able to start at nine and add seven. They will have to start at one and count to nine and then go on from there. This is a maturation deficit. You can help them by switching to a number line. They can then place their finger on 9 and move up seven spaces.

Counting and Understanding the Numbers 0–100

When students are proficient at counting 0–20, begin teaching them to count and write numbers to 50 using the chart shown in Worksheet 13.1. The numbers at the top of the worksheet are important at this stage as a model for the directionality of numbers, so that the students do not turn numbers backward. As you guide a small group of students through writing their numbers, help them realize that all the teens begin with a 1, all the twenties begin with a 2, thirties with a 3, and so on. When you have students recite the numbers 0–50, teach them to point to each digit in the number. For the number 34, ask the child to touch the 3 as he says "thirty" and then to point to the 4 as he says "four." Once students can write and say the numbers 0–50, add one more line each week, until they reach 100. This skill requires *daily* practice until mastered. Once mastered, spend time having students locate a given random number by pointing to it. Overemphasize the "forty" in 46 to help them locate the row of numbers that starts with 40.

After students can count to 100, use number strips with students and go through the process of helping them visualize the continuum. Just as you did with 0–20, do "Show me" drills for 1–100, asking students to "visualize" and "point in the air" to the approximate location of any given number.

WORKSHEET 13.1. COUNTING CHART: 0–100.

0	1	2	3	4	5	6	7	8	9
100									

Recognizing and Counting Coins

- Obtain drawings of coins that are transparent for use in an overhead projector. These can be found in math supply catalogues or, in some schools, in the school resource room. Begin by teaching students to recognize the penny and nickel and to distinguish between them. Point out first that they are different colors. Give each child a real penny and nickel to look at. Give the students copies of Worksheet 13.2 and guide them to look carefully at and draw the front and back of the nickel on the two blank circles at the bottom of the sheet. Talk about what the words and images symbolize. Ask them to take special note of their values on the backs—one cent and five cents.

- Have students work in small groups to count various amounts of change involving only nickels and pennies. Some may need to draw the coins in the following manner in order to count them.

- After a few days using only pennies and nickels, add a dime. Again, have them draw both sides of the dime and note the words "one dime."

  Spend several days having students work in small groups counting varying amounts of change in this manner.

- When you introduce the quarter, have students note the words, but instead of trying to make twenty-five marks on that circle, they need to start counting at 25 and move up. Hound students until they demonstrate on three consecutive days that they know that two quarters equal 50¢, three equal 75¢, and four equal $1.00.

Place Value: Ones and Tens Place

Use the following lesson to demonstrate place value. You will need

1. An enlarged 0–100 counting chart with the numbers filled in.

2. Ten dimes, ten pennies, and one dollar.

WORKSHEET 13.2. COINS.

Let the students hold the pennies. As you count, ask the students to lay a single penny on each space until you reach 10. At this point, have a child scoop up the ten pennies and trade them for a dime, which is placed on the "10" rectangle. For 11, show them that there is one dime and one penny on the chart, making 11, which is 10 + 1. Write:

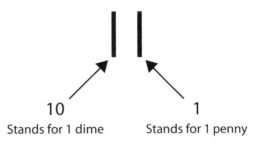

10 | 1
Stands for 1 dime | Stands for 1 penny

As you go on, have students repeat the formula: 12 is one dime and two pennies; 13 is one dime and three pennies, and so on.

When you reach 20, instruct someone to scoop up the ten pennies and trade them for another dime. Show them that 10 + 10 = 20 and that everything on this row will start with the word "twenty." Have them observe that 24 means 20 + 4, which you write with the 2 to represent the two dimes (10 + 10), and the 4 to represent four pennies (1 + 1 + 1 + 1). Proceed through the number chart, periodically stopping to ask a child to tell you what a number means and to write it in expanded notation (for example, 60 + 7 = 67). At 100, ask students to give you all the change; replace the coins with the dollar. Do this activity with them for two or more days until you feel that they understand it.

Expanded notation is important. Give a different number each day for math review and instruct students to break down the number (85 = 80 + 5). This skill may help them do problems in their head. Explain that if they are trying to add 16 + 24, they can break the numbers into: 10 + 20 = 30, then add 6 + 4 = 10, for a total of 30 + 10, or 40.

Counting by Fives

Once kids can count by tens, begin teaching them to count by fives in preparation for learning to tell time. Some children will pick up fives quicker by looking at the 0–100 counting sheet and noting the zigzag pattern of counting by fives.

Time—by the Hour

Following are some preliminary steps that help prepare students to tell time:

1. Make sure students understand the concept of "clockwise." With them facing a clock, have them move their whole arm clockwise. Do this several times.

2. Have students say, "The short hand is the hour hand." Teach them to identify its general location: "The short hand is between the 2 and the 3, so it is after 2 o'clock, but it's not yet 3 o'clock."

3. Ask students to note that all hands on the clock are moving; that all move "clockwise"; and that the second hand moves very fast, the minute hand moves fast, and the hour hand moves slowly. Help them realize that just before the next hour comes up, the hour hand is very close to the number indicating the new hour.

4. Take several weeks to call students' attention to the clock and ask, "Tell me the hour." Firmly plant this skill in their minds before teaching them to count the minutes.

Time—by Hour and Minute

If you have been asking students daily what hour it is at various times of the day and have taught them to count by fives, they are ready to learn how to count the minutes shown by the minute hand and to write time.

Go to a thrift store and get several mechanical clocks. Broken clocks are cheaper and work just fine as long as students can turn the hands backward and forward to watch what happens. If you tell the manager they are for school, they often cost almost nothing.

Draw a big clock on your overhead and explain that there are five little notches between the 12 and the 1 and that they represent five minutes. Show the hands of the clock on the 10:00 hour, with the minute hand on the 12. Say: "This is exactly 10:00." Tell the students to notice that the minute hand is on the 12. Show them that you indicate time by writing the hour, a colon, and two zeroes. Have them write it on their paper (which shows a series of clocks). Move the minute hand slowly to the 1 and say, "Now, it's past 10:00. It's 10:05." Write this under the second clock. Make a point of writing the 0 before the 5. Have the students do the same, and draw how the hands should look on their clock.

Circulate, and instruct them to make the hour hand short and the minute hand so that it lays on top of the 1. Move the minute hand slowly to the 2, and write 10:10 under the next clock and draw the position of the hands. Continue this procedure until you get to 11:00. Be sure students note that when the minute hand is on 10:30, the hour hand is halfway between 10 and 11, and that as the minute hand moves toward 10:50, the hour hand is very near the 11.

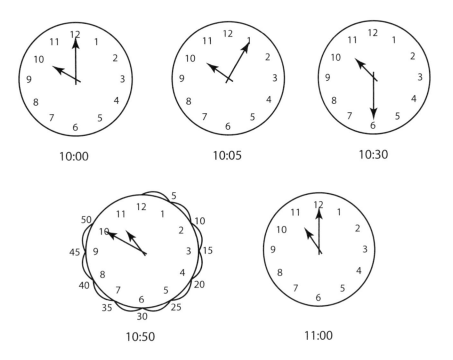

10:00   10:05   10:30

10:50   11:00

The next day, give the students their papers back and go through the process again, showing them with a clock how the hands move and counting off the minutes, "Five, ten, fifteen, …" This time have the students just check the accuracy of their drawings with yours.

Give students at least one problem a day that requires telling time: "Show me 6:10." Using a real clock, have students move the hands to show 6:10 and then draw on their paper what they see on the clock.

Other facts students need to know include

• 60 minutes (not 100) in an hour

• 24 hours in a day; 12 hours of AM, 12 hours of PM (teach them the meaning of AM and PM)

• Seven days in a week

• Approximately thirty days in a month

• Twelve months in a year

Beginning Subtraction

There are some critical concepts to be taught here:

1. Students need to talk aloud. This is absolutely essential if they are to be accurate later in this skill. Have them touch the number at the top of a subtraction problem and say, "I have seven blocks. What happens when I take away four?" In the beginning have them use manipulatives—blocks, dried beans, M&Ms, and the like.

2. Be sure the students learn the names of and differences between the minus and plus signs. Explain that *plus* means you are "putting things together," whereas *minus* means you are "taking them apart."

3. Review with them that when you are subtracting, the bigger number is written on top.

4. Give them one or two word problems a day.

Doing and Undoing: Plus and Minus

This is a fun concept to teach and is an essential one both in mathematical terms and in vocabulary development terms. Bring to your classroom a small suitcase and stand in front of the students, packing it. The kids will be "all eyes," not knowing what's going on. Ask: "What did I do?" *(pack).* Then, without a word, unpack it, then ask: "Now what did I do?" *(unpack).* Continue with: "We can add, which is putting things together (doing), and we can subtract, which is taking things apart (undoing)." For some reason, seeing such a demonstration solidifies the concepts for students.

1. During these lessons, ask students to observe:

Add			**Subtract**	
little	**3**		big	**8**
+ little	**+ 5**		− little	**− 3**
big	**8**		little	**5**

2. Teach them to learn or write families of facts:

   $4 + 3 = 7$ (doing) $7 - 3 = 4$ (undoing)

   $3 + 4 = 7$ (doing) $7 - 4 = 3$ (undoing)

3. Put up a mathematical bulletin board to help students learn to look at the wording of story problem questions and find the clue words that will guide them as to what to do. A sample of such a board follows. Post only addition and subtraction examples initially. Add multiplication and division as you study those processes.

Sample Bulletin Board

CLUES FOR SOLVING MATH STORY PROBLEMS

Addition (putting sets together)

• How many in all?

• How many altogether?

• Find the sum.

• What is the total?

D
O
I
N
G

Subtraction (taking sets apart)

• How many are left?

• Find the difference.

• How many more/less

• Compare two numbers:

• How much bigger?

       heavier?

       older?

U
N
D
O
I
N
G

Multiplication (putting equal sets together)

• How many in all?

• How many altogether?

• Find the product.

D
O
I
N
G

Division (taking equal sets from the whole)

• Find the quotient.

• What would one unit be?

• If shared equally?

• If divided equally?

U
N
D
O
I
N
G

Building Numbers

Youngsters need many experiences with manipulatives* when building numbers. Using small blocks, we want to have them build numbers, such as 8, in as many ways as they can—for example, 5 + 3, 6 + 2, 4 + 4.

Later we want them to use manipulatives to "show" that they understand that 37 means three groups of ten and seven ones.

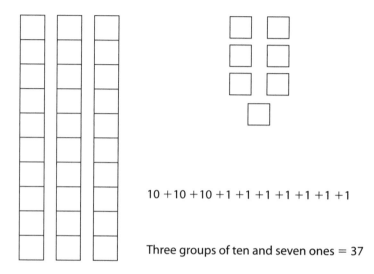

10 + 10 + 10 + 1 + 1 + 1 + 1 + 1 + 1 + 1

Three groups of ten and seven ones = 37

* Note: The school resource room may have manipulatives for building numbers—1s, 10s, 100s.

When students thoroughly understand place value in the tens and ones columns as demonstrated by *doing* (building a number) and *undoing* (looking at a number such as 42 and telling you it contains four groups of ten and two ones), they are ready for you to introduce the hundreds column.

After students build numbers on paper, divide the class into small groups to use craft sticks as another manipulative. Bind sets of ten sticks with a rubber band and give several sets to each child. You can do this activity with as many as five students at a time. Write numbers on index cards (39, 42, 28, 51, 32, and so on) and assign each child a different number. Ask children to use bound sets of ten and individual craft sticks to "build" their assigned numbers.

2 sets of 10

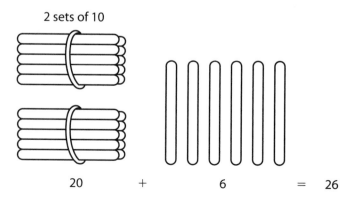

20   +   6   =   26

Addition and Regrouping

To teach addition with regrouping, have students work in pairs. Give each member of the pair bundles of tens, as well as individual sticks totaling less than ten. Have each pair write a number sentence for the total; for example, five bundles of ten plus six ones is written 10 + 10 + 10 + 10 + 10 + 1 + 1 + 1 + 1 + 1 + 1 = 56.

Next give each child one or more tens, and ones that combined will total more than ten. Tell them to put all their sticks together and write a number sequence to show how many there are. Sentences may vary. For example, most will write a sentence like this:

$$10 + 10 + 10 + 1 + 1 + 1 + 1 + 1 + 1 + 1 + 1 + 1 + 1 + 1$$
$$= 30\ 11\ (\text{or } 30 + 11 \text{ or } 3011).$$

Some students may figure out that the total is forty-one. Present the problem of "thirty eleven" to the class. Ask students to count beginning with thirty. Allow them to proceed into the forties. Ask them if there was a "thirty eleven." Ask the class how they might solve this problem of figuring out what to call these sticks. Give them time to think about it while manipulating the sticks. If no one can solve the problem, have them undo the bundles and count all the sticks, starting with one. When they arrive at forty-one, ask them how they can group the sticks to show four tens and one unit. If they need a hint, hold up a bundle of tens, but don't say anything. When they bundle the tens, ask what happened to the eleven units.

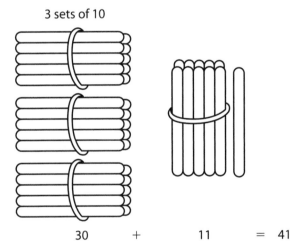

3 sets of 10

30   +   11   =   41

More and Less

The first time you introduce the concepts of more and less, bring out a big candy bar and a small one. Show them side by side. Ask your students which one they would choose. They will answer, "The big one." Ask them why; 90 percent will say "because it is more." Review the terms *more* and *less*.

When asked to use the symbols $<$ and $>$ LD students are sometimes confused. To help them, put two numbers on an overhead. Ask, "Which is more?" Put two dots next to that number. Put one dot by the smaller number. Then connect the dots.

$$33\!:\; \cdot14 \qquad\qquad 33\!>\!14$$

unconnected dots   connect to show "more"

Practice having them say "Thirty-three is more [or greater] than fourteen."

Simple Story Problems

Understanding simple story problems is really a reading comprehension skill. In the beginning, use simple problems in which the numbers and vocabulary are easy to understand. Instruct the students to read to the first period and then stop and draw a picture of what they read. Ask them to proceed through the next sentence and do another drawing. In the beginning it is very important to go over story problems daily and to relate them to the question clues that are on your bulletin board.

Worksheet 13.3 lists six sample questions with the numeric fields left blank so that you can reuse the questions by filling in different amounts each time.

Note: By your insisting that they write a whole answer, students get spelling practice (example: 8 cars). Ask students to draw pictures to illustrate their answers.

As students master these kind of questions, you can add two-step problems like these:

You go to the store and buy paper for $.79 and a pen for $.59. How much will your purchase cost? _____

If you hand the clerk $2.00, what will your change be? _____

You are giving a party for yourself and five friends. If you get four cookies for each child to eat, how many cookies will you need? _____
How many dozen is that? _____

Subtraction With and Without Regrouping

When students begin working with larger numbers, it is extremely important that you train them to "talk to themselves" so that they subtract accurately.

Model the talking, and then have students repeat and write problems on paper. After several days working mixed problems—some that involve borrowing, some that do not—let several students go to the board as a motivation for practicing.

WORKSHEET 13.3. SAMPLE WORD PROBLEMS.

Word Problems

1. You have _____ toy cars. You get _____ more. How many toy cars do you have now? _____ _____

(drawing space)

2. On a plate, there are _____ doughnuts. You and _____ friends will share them. How many will each of you get?

_____ _____

3. A package of gum holds _____ slices. You give one to your mom and _____ to a friend. How many slices of gum are left for you?

_____ _____

4. There are seven days in a week. If it is _____ weeks until your birthday, how many days are left until your birthday?

_____ _____

5. It is _____ P.M. now. What time will it be in _____ more hours?

_____

6. A bottle of soda holds _____ ounces. How many _____-ounce cups will fill it? _____ _____

①

$$\begin{array}{r} 72 \\ -18 \\ \hline \end{array}$$

"I have <u>2</u>, can I take away <u>8</u>?
No. I'll have to borrow from the 7."

②

"Let's see. I'll change the <u>7</u> to <u>6</u> and move the 1 over in front of the <u>2</u>.
Hm. Now I have <u>12</u>.
Now, can I take away 8?
Yes, that leaves <u>4</u>."

③

"I have <u>6</u>, can I take away <u>1</u>?

Yes, that leaves 5.
My answer is <u>54</u>."

$$\begin{array}{r} {}^{1} \\ {}^{6}\cancel{7}2 \\ -18 \\ \hline 54 \end{array}$$

④ "If I undo this by adding the <u>54</u> to <u>18</u>, will I get <u>72</u>? Yeah! I know I'm right."

Rounding Numbers to the Nearest 10 or Nearest 100

Students can learn to round to the nearest 10 or nearest 100 only if they use manipulatives until they can visualize the numbers in their mind's eye.

Using the templates in Worksheets 13.4 and 13.5, you can make number strips that will help students learn to round to the nearest 10 and later to the nearest 100. These skills will be essential when students begin learning to estimate later on.

Recognizing and Spelling Number Words

As students show a readiness to learn larger numbers, teach them how to spell them as well. This is a skill that is used to write checks once students are old enough to do their own banking. Have students use the guide in the box to practice looking at number words and writing them as numbers. For example, 43 is written as *forty-three*.

After students move on to bigger numbers, teach them to spell these; for example, 756 is written as *seven hundred fifty-six*.

1–one	11– eleven	30–thirty
2–two	12– twelve	40–forty
3–three	13– thirteen	50–fifty
4–four	14– fourteen	60–sixty
5–five	15– fifteen	70–seventy
6–six	16–sixteen	80–eighty
7–seven	17–seventeen	90–ninety
8–eight	18–eighteen	100–one hundred
9–nine	19–nineteen	1,000–one thousand
10–ten	20–twenty	1,000,000–one million

WORKSHEET 13.4. NUMBER STRIP 1 TO 100

Laminate. Cut apart strips. Attach strips to each other.

0	1	2	3	4	5	6	7	8	9	1	Attach next strip here match 1 + 0 to make 10
0	11	12	13	14	15	16	17	18	19	2	Attach next strip here 2 + 0 = 20
0	21	22	23	24	25	26	27	28	29	3	Attach next strip here 3 + 0 = 30
0	31	32	33	34	35	36	37	38	39	4	Attach next strip here 4 + 0 = 40
0	41	42	43	44	45	46	47	48	49	5	Attach next strip here 5 + 0 = 50
0	51	52	53	54	55	56	57	58	59	6	Attach next strip here 6 + 0 = 60
0	61	62	63	64	65	66	67	68	69	7	Attach next strip here 7 + 0 = 70
0	71	72	73	74	75	76	77	78	79	8	Attach next strip here 8 + 0 = 80
0	81	82	83	84	85	86	87	88	89	9	Attach next strip here 9 + 0 = 90
0	91	92	93	94	95	96	97	98	99	100	

WORKSHEET 13.5. NUMBER STRIP FOR ROUNDING TO NEAREST 100.

	50		150		250	Attach
0		100		200		

	350		450		550	Attach
300		400		500		

	650		750		850	Attach
600		700		800		

	950		1050		1150	
900		1000		1100		

Place Value—Through Thousands

As a trick to get students primed to count by thousands, call a student to the front, stick out your hand, and say, "Give me five." Next say, "Give me five more." By then you'll have everyone's attention. Then ask the student, "How many did you give me in all?" He'll answer, "Ten." Ask students, "How many did he say he gave me?" They'll say "Ten." Say to the student, "Stick out your hand, so I can give you those ten hundreds back." As you slap his hand, count 100, 200, 300 … until you get to ten hundred; the students may repeat "ten hundred." Wag your finger in a motion meaning "no" and say, "One thousand." Write this on the board: *Ten hundreds equal one thousand.*

Draw this figure on the board:

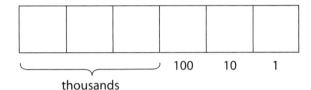

Write a few big numbers into the squares and read them to the students. Use numbers like 12,850. Draw a circle around the 12, explaining that it is the number of thousands. Use 150,017. Draw a circle around the 150 and explain that it is 150 thousand. Some student almost always says, "I wish I had that much money." Now is your opportunity to tell them how they can end up with that much by saving and investing.

Continue daily practice having them read and write large numerals such as seventy-five thousand, three hundred forty-two. Talk about the use of the comma to separate thousands from hundreds.

Teach expanded notation: 75,000 + 300 + 40 + 2 = 75,342. Or show them the same addition problem in columns:

$$
\begin{array}{r|c|c|c}
75 & 0 & 0 & 0 \\
& 3 & 0 & 0 \\
& & 4 & 0 \\
+ & & & 2 \\
\hline
75, & 3 & 4 & 2
\end{array}
$$

Linear Measurement

Introduce students to some of the tools used for linear measurement—the steel tape, the yardstick, the ruler.

Let students begin to do measuring activities with rulers that are only divided into inches. When they are proficient in measuring with these, introduce rulers that measure to the half inch.

Make sure they learn that

- 1 foot is 12 inches long.
- 1 yard is 36 inches or 3 feet long.

Teach them to convert inches to feet. Measure students in inches and have them figure how tall they are when their height is converted to feet and inches.

Show them a yard of material. Stretch it from your nose to fingertips to demonstrate that a yard equals three feet.

Ask them to measure the room, their desk, or lines drawn on paper.

Teach them to spell *yard, foot,* and *inch.*

You may want to make number squares and strips for inches, feet, and yards.

unit

12 units   1 foot

36 units   1 yard

Make these manipulatives out of construction paper or oak tag and laminate them.

Have students line up the inch squares on the ruler and write the number sentence:

12 inches = 1 foot

Next have them line up 36 inches on the yardstick, writing:

36 inches = 1 yard

Finally, have them line up 3 feet on the yardstick, writing:

3 feet = 1 yard

Simple Multiplication Techniques

Post the multiplication section of your bulletin board. There are several critical concepts students must know in order for them to understand multiplication.

Have students notice that the types of questions asked are the same in both addition and multiplication problems. Students should understand that both addition and multiplication are ways of "putting things together."

Multiplication is a way to add equal sets more quickly.

Addition		**Multiplication**
equal sets	unequal sets	always equal sets

2	4	
2	3	
2 or	+ 8	
+ 2	‾‾‾‾	
‾‾‾‾	15	
8		

$$4 \times 2 = 8$$

If you can add equal sets, why learn multiplication? It is a shortcut when you are dealing with large numbers, such as 757×45. No one would relish adding 757 groups of 45!

Technique 1

Remember that you need to begin at the *manipulative* or *concrete* stage in developing a skill. Dried pinto beans and rubber bands can serve as inexpensive manipulatives.

Have students lay out four rubber bands in a row and draw a picture of them on their paper.

Then tell students to put two beans inside each rubber band and to draw the beans on their paper.

Ask: "How many beans are there in all?" (*eight*)

Show how to write the problem: 4 × 2 = 8

Ask: "What does the four mean?" (four groups)

Ask: "What does the two describe?" (two beans in each set)

"Oh! Four *groups* with two beans *in each set* mean you have eight beans in all?"

Put problems on the board, using facts that yield small products. Have students find solutions for several problems. Distribute manipulatives and have them solve the same problems by drawing solutions. Circulate to see if they have caught on.

Technique 2

Give each child a piece of colored paper and an index card on which associative facts are written, such as:

6 × 2 = 12

2 × 6 = 12

Ask children to make a poster to illustrate that

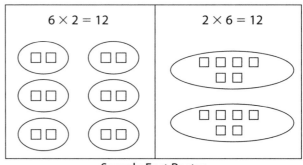

Sample Fact Poster

these facts are true. Have each child illustrate a different fact. Make a colorful bulletin board with students' work. The sets are encircled with roving (heavy yarn).

Technique 3

Using a multiplication-table matrix, the child fills in the squares to complete each line: 2, 4, 6, 8, 10, 12, 14, 16, 18, 20. The class says the numbers in unison. Drill these until they are memorized.

Begin working with the 2s and 3s. When these are memorized, move on to the 4s and 5s. (Note: The 5s were learned when "time" was taught.)

Later, move on to the 6s and 7s, and finally, the 8s and 9s. Show students that there is a trick for the 9s.

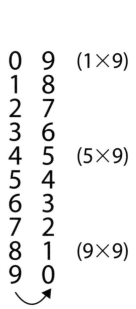

Simple Division Techniques

Post the division section of your bulletin board.

Have students count out twelve pinto beans. Tell them to separate the beans into groups with four in each group and to draw a picture of their answer.

Show how to set up the problem in two ways:

$$4 \overline{) 12} \quad \text{and} \quad 12 \div 3 =$$

When absolutely certain they have mastered the skill of dividing numbers that come out evenly, with no remainder, begin teaching division problems that do have remainders. Teach students to this point:

$$\begin{array}{r} 3\,r\,1 \\ 3 \overline{) 10} \\ -9 \\ \hline 1 \end{array}$$

Doing and Undoing (Multiplication and Division)

Make sure students can tell you that addition and multiplication are used to "put numbers together," whereas subtraction and division are used to "take things apart." Explain the terms *total, sum, difference, product,* and *quotient.*

Addition	Multiplication	Subtraction	Division
2 8 5 +6 —— (sum or total)	350 ×12 —— 700 350 —— (total)	9017 −3879 —— (difference)	(quotient) 3)12

Discuss and have them practice "fact families" through doing or undoing:

$9 + 7 = 16$	$4 \times 5 = 20$
$7 + 9 = 16$	$5 \times 4 = 20$
$16 - 7 = 9$	$20 \times 5 = 4$
$16 - 9 = 7$	$20 \times 4 = 5$

Liquid Measurement

This is best covered with firsthand experiences.

Bring in cartons of all sizes—gallon, quart, pint, cup.

Working together at the classroom sink, allow pairs of students to fill cartons with water to answer such worksheet questions as

- How many cups in a pint?
- How many pints in a quart?
- How many quarts in a gallon?

This activity is messy. Cover the floor by the sink with an old bedspread and the cabinet top with plain newsprint. Once students understand standard measurement, you can introduce the metric system.

Fractions

Put together packets of manipulatives for students to use.

Some tips:

- Make circles with a diameter of six inches. Represent each of the following sizes of fractions with a different colored paper, such as:

halves – pink	thirds – white
fourths – blue	sixths – tan
eighths – yellow	

- Label and mark divisions on each circle before laminating it. Mark halves with $\dfrac{}{2}$, fourths with $\dfrac{}{4}$, and so on.
- Laminate the circles before cutting them into fractional parts so that they will last for several years. Make extra circles of each color because, over several years of handling, you will need to replace some pieces.

Each student packet will need at least three circles of each size so that when working with a partner, students have enough manipulatives to represent the problem.

You will find that these manipulatives will get quite a workout—they will be used for a long time.

Sequence of Instruction

Step 1: Teach students to respond to such directions as "Show me **three** fourths" or "Show me **seven** thirds."

Step 2: When step 1 has been mastered, quiz the students: "Do you have a whole pie?" (*no*) "What would you need to make a whole pie?" (*one fourth more*) Have students demonstrate with their manipulatives that

$$\frac{3}{4} + \frac{1}{4} = \frac{4}{4} \text{ or } 1$$

Practice working with manipulatives and equation writing for several days, having students tell you what portion is missing to complete a whole. Make sure they understand that when the numerator and denominator are the same number, the pie is whole.

Step 3: Teach adding and subtracting like fractions. At this point, students will start to discover improper fractions on their own as they use their manipulatives. Show them how to write their answer in whole numbers and as fractions for such problems as

$$\frac{3}{4} + \frac{3}{4} = \frac{6}{4}$$

Do not teach reducing proper fractions yet.

Step 4: Teach students to experience equivalent fractions through manipulation of their fractional pieces.

On the first day, have them work with the halves, fourths, and eighths to discover that $\frac{2}{4}$ and $\frac{4}{8}$ are the same amount as $\frac{1}{2}$.

Have them write $\frac{4}{8} = \frac{2}{4} = \frac{1}{2}$

Once they discover that 2 is half of 4 and that 4 is half of 8, ask them if they can figure how many sixths would be the same as half. Then let them verify that using their manipulatives.

Write $\frac{1}{2}$. Ask: "If you had manipulatives representing tenths, how many tenths would be equal to half?" $\frac{?}{10}$

On the second day, quickly have them review the previous day's lesson.

Have them experiment with equivalencies for $\frac{2}{3}$ and $\frac{1}{3}$.

Step 5: Make certain all students show an understanding of all concepts covered up to this point before doing this step.

At various times, each student will be ready to learn how to reduce fractions to their lowest terms. Many students cannot figure out what number to use to reduce a given proper fraction. Give them a "Try 2, 3, 5, 7" guide to follow:

> Try a 2.
>
> If a 2 won't work, try a 3.
>
> If a 3 doesn't work, try a 5.
>
> If a 5 won't work, try a 7.

If none of these work, the fraction probably cannot be reduced.

Demonstrate talking through the process.

$$\frac{4}{8} = \frac{2}{4} = \frac{1}{2} \qquad \frac{3}{9} = \frac{1}{3} \qquad \frac{20}{25} = \frac{4}{5} \qquad \frac{21}{28} = \frac{3}{4}$$

a. The fraction is $\frac{4}{8}$.

I'll try dividing it by 2.

> 2 into $\underline{4}$ = 1
> 2 into $\overline{8}$ = 2

The fraction is now $\frac{2}{4}$.

I'll try it again.

> 2 into $\underline{2}$ = 1
> 2 into $\overline{4}$ = 2

The reduced fraction is $\frac{1}{2}$.

So, $\frac{4}{8} = \frac{1}{2}$

b. The fraction is $\frac{21}{28}$.

I'll try 2.

> 2 into $\underline{21}$ (no)
> 2 into $\overline{28}$ (yes)

So I can't use 2 because it has to work for both numerator and denominator.

I'll try 3.

> 3 into $\underline{21}$ (yes)
> 3 into $\overline{28}$ (no)

So I can't use 3.

I'll try 5.

> 5 into $\underline{21}$ (no)
> 5 into $\overline{28}$ (no)

I can't use 5.

I'll try 7.

> 7 into $\underline{21}$ = 3
> 7 into $\overline{28}$ = 4

Bingo!

$$\frac{21}{28} = \frac{3}{4}$$

Estimating

Estimating is a very useful skill. Practicing may alert you to potential overcharges on your purchases.

Many people play estimating games at the grocery store and become so good at it that they come very close to predicting the total on their basket of groceries.

To play this game, round up or down based on the dollar. If the item is under 50¢, don't count it. If it's between 50¢ and $1.00, count it as $1.00. Likewise, an item that costs between $2.00 and $2.50 is counted as only $2.00, and an item over $2.50 as $3.00.

Bring in cans and packages of groceries once a week and use them in an estimating activity. Be sure each item has a price. Have students see how close they can come in this game.

More Complex Story Problems

Technique A: Use upper-grade texts as a source for one-step story problems. Have students underline the question and try to match it with the appropriate mathematical process by looking at the bulletin board.

For students to feel successful at the skill, be certain that the question asked matches up with the wording on the bulletin board.

Technique B: Sometimes students feel threatened by big numbers. Should this be the case, it sometimes helps to have them think in smaller numbers.

Example for B

> *A bride and groom ask 156 people to come to their wedding. Twenty people say they cannot attend. How many people will be at the wedding?*

The students need to ask themselves if the answer will be more or less than 156. If they seem mystified, suggest that they just remove the last digit from each number; thus 156 becomes 15, and 20 becomes 2. Read the problem back with the simpler numbers in place of the original as follows: "A bride and groom ask fifteen people to come to their wedding. Two people say they cannot attend. How many people will be at the wedding?"

Student: "Thirteen."

Teacher: "How did you figure that out?"

Student: "Fifteen take away two is thirteen."

Teacher: "Let's do the same process with the bigger numbers."

Many students learn to multiply accurately by one digit, but make errors when asked to multiply by two or more digits.

In this problem, you can remind them that 45 is 40 + 5. If they have already taken care of the 5, they can simply multiply 40 × 134 and add it to the 670 to get the answer.

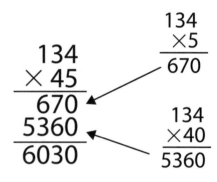

More Complex Division

LD students benefit from being allowed to use a handheld calculator to do more complex long-division problems. Long division requires so much concentration that students with math deficits rarely are successful.

After a student obtains an answer, she needs to double-check her computation by putting the numbers into the calculator again to be sure she gets the same answer.

Relating Fractions to Decimals

Show students that if they have a fraction, they can find the answer by dividing the numerator by the denominator.

Example:

Express the fraction as a decimal.

$$\frac{1}{8} \qquad \frac{1}{8} \quad \begin{matrix} \text{numerator} \\ \text{denominator} \end{matrix}$$

Divide the numerator by the denominator. Insert a decimal behind the one, and add zeroes. Use a calculator to check your answer. The calculator will say .125.

$$
\begin{array}{r}
.125 \\
8{\overline{\smash{)}\,1.000}} \\
\underline{8} \\
20 \\
\underline{16} \\
40
\end{array}
$$

Making Change

Have the classroom aide work with two students at a time. Provide coins for them to practice making change to give to a customer.

Purpose: to demonstrate that there may be more than one way to give change for a given amount.

Start with 50¢—find three ways to make change

80¢—find three ways

40¢—find two ways

75¢—find three ways

20¢—find two ways

Example:

50¢ might be 2 quarters

or 5 dimes

or 1 quarter and 5 nickels

Summary

In this chapter we have looked at ways to teach some math skills—but not all math skills. Some programs for teaching math offer books with matching manipulatives. Other programs focus on kinesthetic techniques. The activities offered in this chapter are designed to present basic math skills, and new methods, computer games, and board games are becoming available to reinforce these math concepts. Have fun, and if one technique doesn't work, you can always try another.

WORKSHEET 13.6. SAMPLE OF DAILY MATH SHEET.

Sample of Daily Math Sheet (grade level 3)

1. Write eight hundred twenty-seven as a numeral. _____

2. Write 3,614 in words.

_____

_____

3.
$$658$$
$$112$$
$$347$$
$$+723$$

4.
$$658$$
$$-387$$

5.
$$327$$
$$\times\ 4$$

6.
$$2\overline{)13}$$

7. You have three quarters, 2 nickels, and 6 pennies. How much money do you have? _____

8. Nine couples are dancing. How many people are dancing in all?

_____

9.
$$\frac{7}{8}$$
$$-\frac{3}{8}$$

Draw a picture to represent your answer to this problem.

Daily Score _____ number right
$$\frac{}{10}$$

Chapter 14

Adolescents and Adults with Learning Disabilities

George Burns (1896–1996)

American comedian and actor
Believed himself to be dyslexic

Contributions:

The Arts: Made the world laugh through his use of dry wit and comic timing in vaudeville, radio, TV, and movies

---

In this chapter, we will explore the characteristics and changing needs of students with learning disabilities as they become adolescents and adults. We'll look at what goes on at junior high, senior high, and even college. We'll discuss ways we can assist LD individuals make the transition from the school setting to the work world and to greater independence.

Understanding the Changing Needs of the Adolescent

School Changes

The average thirteen- to fifteen-year-old spends little time thinking about school. On becoming a teenager, the adolescent's vistas expand rapidly. The child moves from the nurturing environment of the elementary school into the middle school or junior high. In grade school he probably stayed in the same room most of the day with one teacher. Now he may move from room to room, and he must relate to more adults and more classmates because the class composition is not usually the same for each subject.

Some students will embrace these changes. I know of students who found that the rotation of teachers was freeing. If the student didn't like the teacher or didn't fit in with the current class, there were more options for change. Changes at the secondary level are not always traumatizing, although some students may feel insecure because of the number of changes they have to navigate initially.

Instruction at the secondary level is given primarily through the lecture method. Auditory processing and memory issues are often the causes of the student's learning disability, so a teacher may sound nonsensical to her. Teachers may seem aloof or uncaring, as they are often responsible for one hundred or more students a day. I that there is no place where she can perform adequately; she does not feel that she "belongs."

Not able to follow the lecture, the student checks out mentally: "It's so boring!" "I wonder if this teacher even knows my name?" "I can't do this." "Maybe if I just sit quietly I can squeeze by." Then the progress report comes—three F's. Oops!

The student who is in a self-contained special day class in junior high may enter with even lower achievement scores and a far greater satchel of failures. Social maladjustment may prevail in this classroom, ranging from quiet, withdrawn, or depressed students to loud, aggressive, assaultive, and acting-out students. Have you ever noticed how the self-contained rooms are generally not centrally located but are almost always in an outlying area? Research studies have shown that students with learning disabilities are less socially acceptable to teachers and classmates than their nondisabled peers. It is not surprising that such students feel isolated and often drop out of school as soon as they can. The percentage of these students who earn a high school diploma is higher than in the past, but we still have a long way to go to ensure that all students with learning disabilities earn a diploma.

Physical Changes

The predicament of young teens is that their bodies are no longer familiar. Teens spend a lot of time looking in the mirror to acquaint themselves with their new physique. Their bodies are undergoing tremendous changes because the hormonal system has come into play. There is usually a distracting interest in the opposite sex. Almost overnight, teens become very concerned about what their peers think of them. They become obsessed with clothing, and "must" wear whatever is the current mode of dress for the group to which they want to belong.

The teenager is a sensation-oriented creature, and often that desire for thrills leads young people into a collision course with danger. In fact, the brain undergoes a growth spurt during the teenage years, as accelerating hormones create new abilities to reason. But because their brains are not fully mature—they are only beginning or partially through the growth spurt—teenagers often have trouble exercising all the reasoning and judgment skills most adults have. Lacking mature judgment, they may skip school, joyride, run away, smoke, use alcohol or abuse drugs, shoplift, draw graffiti, and engage in sexual intercourse. Many times teenagers are eager to try these "adult" behaviors; they are testing their limits, and they don't always see the dangers that adults do. What adults find alarming, the teenager finds exciting and new.

Teenagers aren't always capable of understanding the consequences of their behaviors. This means that the teen may not be able to anticipate trouble when experimenting with risk-taking behaviors or experiences. The experimentation that is so common in youth is not always countered by reason and the limits that the adult brain may recognize. In fact, teenagers may accuse their parents or teachers (or any other *old* people) of being illogical: How could anything happen when they drive that fast? Don't we adults know that they know how to drive? Adults can see the consequences of driving recklessly, but teenagers may not yet have achieved that level of reasoning skill. For some people, the ability to reason and understand consequences or abstractions doesn't fully mature until the early twenties.

In terms of emotions, the teen finds that people expect more of her, yet she does not feel more confident. Her unfamiliar changing body may be more difficult to manage, so she may feel and appear awkward. For the student with LD, the normal changes of adolescence may be compounded by a feeling of inferiority. Entering junior high with achievement scores two or more grades below where they should be, this student often is unable to read the texts. However, there is the tendency to program LD students into classes with other LD students and to supplement their schedules with nonacademic electives, such as shop, art, or physical education.

Efforts to Engage the Junior High Student in the Educational Process

Departmentalization (School Within a School)

One plan that seeks to break down anonymity while allowing teachers to teach their "specialty" is the school-within-a-school approach. Faculty members (a math teacher, a science teacher, a language arts and reading teacher, and so on) are assigned to teams. Each team serves around 150 students. The math teacher, for example, may teach two seventh-grade classes, two eighth-grade classes, and one ninth. Within a junior high school, it is common to find from three to six "teams" or "families" or "pods" (the term varies by the individual school using the plan). Each team, usually with its own counselor, is housed in an area of proximity so students get to know other students on their team. Teachers can discuss with each other the needs of "their" 150 students. Students are then assigned to a faculty team.

This approach has much to recommend it. In elementary school, students may have one teacher with thirty other classmates. Now their world grows to five or six teachers, and includes changing classes and associating with a somewhat larger group, but they don't have to go all over the campus, get lost, use lockers, and feel completely overwhelmed. There is more of a feeling of belonging because they have six or so teachers who share the responsibility to help them. Teachers meet as a team once a week to share information, but still have contact with other members of their department at departmental meetings once a month. Special education students may be assigned to only one or two of the pods. This targeted placement makes it easier for special education staff to give services to students.

Personal Efforts of Individual Teachers

Mr. _____ saved my life. I was headed nowhere but he took me under his wing and turned my life around. He always came by my desk sometime during class to speak to me one on one. At first, he'd come tell me he was just glad to see me at school. I had been truant a lot and my parents were at their wit's end. Later, he would invite me to come in at lunch or after school and he'd give a bit of extra help on things I didn't understand. He'd sometimes share his lunch with me. One time he invited me to go with him—just me—to see the local college campus.

• • •

Ms. _____ was my guardian angel. She cared whether I did my work and stayed on me to get it done. She always noticed when I had new clothes. She really cared about me. Bit by bit I began to think maybe I could do the work.

These student testimonials tell us how important it is to go out of our way to personalize our relationship with students. A joke, a laugh, a compliment, a little extra help—any of these can make all the difference in a person's life.

Teachers sometimes say they do not have time to do this. Such small gestures don't usually take much time, but show you are thinking about your students. Some teachers become so focused on trying to beat facts into students that it is almost as though the subject they teach were the important part of the education equation and the student were incidental. Teachers who think about individual students during off-duty time and take them into consideration when planning a given lesson have the capacity to redirect these children's lives.

Curriculum for the Junior High School

Adapting the regular seventh-grade course of study for the individual student with LD requires much thought because the curriculum cannot be one-size-fits-all. Whether the student is assigned to a regular class or a special class, you must write goals that move her from where she is actually functioning toward meeting that seventh-grade curriculum standard.

For example, let's say that in *math,* a standard for the seventh-grade year is that students will be proficient in completing multiplication and division problems with decimals. By December, the students will be able to perform decimal multiplication problems that have two digits multiplied by one digit (example, 3.2 × .3), getting eight out of ten problems right in three out of four trials.

By March, the student will be able to perform decimal multiplication problems that have three digits multiplied by two digits (example, 4.25 × .17), getting seven out of ten problems right in three out of four trials.

In May, the student will be able to perform simple decimal division problems (example, 4.8 ÷ .2), getting eight out of ten problems right in three out of four trials.

In *language arts,* the standard might be that students will be able to write a persuasive paragraph.

By December, the student will write a three- to four-sentence persuasive paragraph once a week under teacher-supervised guided practice.

By March, the student will write a three- to five-sentence persuasive paragraph once a week, receiving teacher oral feedback and correcting all errors.

In May, the student will independently write a three- to five-sentence persuasive paragraph with fewer than four errors in spelling, capitalization, and punctuation.

When writing daily lesson plans, you will want to carefully consider each student's current level of functioning. You should modify a student's daily work considering the difficulty of the task, time allowed to complete the task, and the amount and quality of work expected (some students will be assigned less). Students also need to understand their goals and know what to do to meet them.

Modifications may include shortening the assignment to the most important questions or providing extra testing time. With a student who has memory problems, a history test may be given as an open-book or a multiple-choice test. For a child who can't read or spell, a test may be given orally. When reading disability is the issue, you may use a digital copy of grade-appropriate material and have the student listen to the material with a headset.

What motivates LD students? Novelty, firsthand experiences, and a choice of projects help maintain their enthusiasm:

- Make a garden out of an unused sand pile.

- Plan and build a wheelchair ramp.

- Shadow a city official for a day.

- Act out a teacher-written historical play.

- Break into groups to research and report about an event associated with the Civil War. Topics could include the plight of the slaves versus the needs of plantation owners, the architecture of the Civil War South, or the battles.

Students with LD learn best when they are actively doing work. The longer the teacher talks, the less students listen and learn.

To function effectively in today's rapidly changing world, students should know how to locate information, how to think about the ways they learn, how to monitor their own progress, how to increase their retention of information, and how to live with and work cooperatively with others.

Basic Skills

Students with learning disabilities have a tremendous need for basic skills training in junior high school. Typically they know most of the consonant sounds but remain confused about vowel sounds and rules. Very few seem to have ever heard of the vc/cv rule for syllabicating longer words; they are still prone to "guess" a word rather than "sound it out." (The material in Chapter Eleven is applicable to junior high reading teachers.)

Even if you are not grounded in phonics, it is sometimes helpful if you write any troublesome words on the board and share with your students how they might break down any unfamiliar words by syllables. Teaching word chunks (*help* + *ful*) is another useful strategy.

The student with learning disabilities needs to learn to do problem solving. Story problems may be a mystery because of deficits in reading skills. Students at the junior high level may still have trouble with very basic story problems. (Consult Chapter Thirteen for ways to remediate in this area.) Some students have a very limited understanding of the number system. It helps to teach students to visualize number concepts with drawings or manipulatives.

Spelling and writing skills are important. In order to learn skills, most LD students must do things more times than other students do. Give writing assignments of a shorter nature. Break a long report into smaller pieces by requiring just one paragraph a day. Have students write every day.

Strategies to Increase Metacognition and Learning

Teach students how their textbooks, and the information inside, are organized. Prior to teaching a chapter in science or social studies, take the students on several tours of the learning features in the chapter. First, walk the students through the chapter, having them read the chapter headings aloud, carefully examining pictures and charts for the information in them. Next, have them go through the chapter, writing down and defining all key terms (look for words in bold print and use the text or glossary to define them). As you know, key terms and charts are often the subject of later test questions.

In another lesson, have students walk through the chapter again, matching the key terms they found with chapter headings.

Next, have them read any study questions found at the end of the chapter. You may want to put these questions on a photocopy so that students can underline key words (usually nouns) in the questions and write notes on the photocopy.

By the time students have done this much previewing, they are somewhat familiar with the important concepts covered in the chapter and where the information about the concepts might be located.

These activities, plus some sort of graphic organizer, open-book tests, and discussions will enhance the ability of students with LD to compete with other students.

Teach students to read summaries, introductions, and the chapter headings to get main ideas for each chapter. Students can also make questions out of each chapter heading. An example for this section would be: What strategies are used to increase metacognition and learning?

When students answer each question, they begin to actively look for the main ideas of each section.

The Art of Counseling Adolescent Students

In talking with colleagues and junior high students, we find that teenagers relate best to their peers and invariably turn to their peers for advice. If, however, a teenager comes to you, there are some guidelines to follow. Be aware that lawsuits can be filed both for errors of commission (what you do) and for errors of omission (what you ought to have done but didn't), so you will want to protect yourself.

When you find yourself in a room alone with a student, it is wise to keep the door open. If it appears that the student is going to confide very intimate information, often signaled by the remark, "If I tell you something, promise not to tell," it is wise to say to the student, "No, I'm sorry, I cannot make that promise. There are many confidences I am able to keep. However, I must tell you that there are some kinds of information I must tell." Tell the student that you are willing to listen to her concern and that you will do all you can to help her with her problem, but if she is going to share her problem with you, she has to have enough trust in you to accept your handling of the problem.

When a problem is confided, it is best to let the student talk at length about it. Don't interrupt; do write down clarification questions so that you can ask them later. Explain to the student that you are writing notes to refer back to when she is finished talking. These notes will make you a more active listener.

Sometimes a student does not need or want help with her problem. She just wants to tell someone. The pressure she is feeling may be alleviated by this catharsis. So when a student has finally finished talking, you may want to say, "Why did you want to tell me about this?" and if appropriate, "What do you hope I can do to help you?"

Sometimes it is appropriate to help a student look at her fears and get them out in the open. "If _____ happened, what would be the worst scenario that you could foresee? Could you handle that? How?" You do need, however, to ask the other side: "If _____ happened, what would be the best scenario you could see? Are there ways we can act to move toward achieving the best scenario? How can I help?"

Occasionally, as a counselor, you may see something in a situation that the student did not mention. You can say one of the following:

• • •

"I wonder if _____?"
"Have you ever considered _____?"
"Is it possible that _____?"
"If I understand correctly, you feel _____."
"Perhaps you feel this way because _____."
"You feel _____, but your parents [friends, teacher] may feel _____."

• • •

It is best to help students come to their own understanding about themselves and their situation. It is important to respect the decisions students come to—unless the situation involves a life-threatening problem like suicide or abortion. (It is critical that you know your obligations according to your state's laws.)

Teachers sometimes overhear conversations or intercept notes such as the one in Figure 14.1. In this particular case, the teacher shared the note with the counselor and parents, and when the child was found to be suicidal he was given professional help.

Teaching Students to Be Their Own Advocates

Around the age of fourteen, students need to be trained to talk about their problem and to be their own advocate.

Step 1: Talk about "What is a learning disability?" During this first discussion, students are generally very quiet because they do not want to expose themselves. Share with them the names of some famous people who are or were learning disabled.

Start with the more recent ones, such as Tom Cruise, who claims to have a reading disability. See if they know who Cher is; she is dyslexic. So is Henry Winkler (who was "the Fonz"), and he also has problems with math. Tell them how Thomas Edison's teacher told his mother that school was a waste of time for Tom because he was so "addled"; then

FIGURE 14.1.

Sign of Potentially Suicidal Behavior.

MR. _____ IS A JERK

I AM NOT A WIZE KId. I'M Not
A Calculator. I AM 13 year old KI D.
Who is strugling i'n a math class.
I AM USE TO GETTINg F's on my Quize's Now.
BECAUSE I STIKE
STINK. I Wish I was Like
MY FRIED
I WISh I could gett
BETTER At math But I can't CAUse I'M
A slow learnen. MY WHOLE LIFE sucks
Now!

explain that Thomas Edison invented the electric light bulb, so people no longer have to use candles by which to read. Have students understand that several geniuses, such as Albert Einstein, Winston Churchill, and Woodrow Wilson, were learning disabled.

You may want to talk to your students a bit about how the brain works (see Chapter Two), explaining to them about their learning styles, the action of chemicals on the brain (neurotransmitters and neuroinhibitors), and how we can increase learning and improve memory by using better techniques of study. Most students have little or no information on this topic. They often listen and ask good questions.

Step 2: At some point, most learning disabled students will think of themselves as "dumb." Some will actually voice that belief. We need to teach all students to use positive *self-talk*. In an informal setting (circle or outside), explain to students that self-talk is potentially motivating or destructive. Explain that you want them to begin thinking of themselves in more positive ways. To demonstrate, present some situations and ask them to decide if they are motivating or destructive.

> "I can't play baseball because I can't hit the ball."
> "I am not able to hit the ball, but I can encourage my teammates."
> "I will hit the ball more often if I keep my eye on the ball."

> "I am never going to do art again."
> "Ugh. I don't like the way this tree looks, but I did a great job drawing that fence."
> "I am going to ask my art teacher to show me how to make that road look like it is moving away from the house into the distance."

> "I hate math."
> "I make a lot of careless mistakes. I think I'll ask my teacher if I can use the calculator to check my math or to do my math."
> "I got this one wrong. I think I'll ask _____ to show me where I went wrong."
> "If I keep trying, I can learn to do this."

Have students practice changing their self-talk. Do a brief exercise daily so they get practice. You begin . . .

> "I hate . . . my car, but it will look better if I clean it."
> "I hate . . . [a vegetable], but if I try a bit each time it is served, I can learn to eat some of it."

Somewhere along the line, we want to talk with students about the fact that we sometimes have no control over what happens to us, but that we do have control over our behaviors in regard to what happens to us. Help students look at the roles of courage and persistence in determining success.

Step 3: We want to help students analyze their strengths and weaknesses and begin to verbalize these to other people. We want them to be able to ask for help when they need it. For example:

> "I have a good personality and people like me. I'm pretty good at math, but I need help with reading."
>
> "I can look at things and see how they work. I can fix things. But my memory is limited. I have trouble remembering. I should try writing a list each day of all the things that I need to remember."
>
> "I have no sense of time. I know it's important to meet deadlines and get to places on time. I think I need to have a pocket organizer so I can keep a calendar of deadlines. It will buzz to remind me of appointments."

Step 4: Require students to practice asking for help. Teach them to be their own advocate. For example:

> "I'm learning disabled. I need . . . Could you help me . . . ?
>
> "I have a memory problem. I need to tape-record your lecture."
>
> "Can you help me identify exactly what material I need to study for the test?"

One of my former students shared a story with me. One day when she was in seventh grade, her science teacher was angry because he had given a test and everyone in the class had failed it. As he passed back papers, he put each student on the hot seat with "And what's your excuse?" When he reached her, she looked up sweetly and calmly said, "I'm sorry I didn't do very well. I really wanted to, but I'm dyslexic, and I can't read the book." The teacher thought she was pulling his leg, but checked her records and found out she was telling the truth. He called her in during conference time, apologized, and asked, "How can I help you?" Had she just suffered in silence, she would have continued to fail. She later received her diploma from junior college.

Step 5: Teach students strategies for learning. This includes mnemonics training, note-taking strategies, and visualization training.

Step 6: Teach students strategies for smart test taking. For example, on multiple-choice timed tests, they should first answer all the questions they are sure of and mark questions needing further scrutiny with a ? in the margin. For puzzling questions, they should try to eliminate as many choices as they can. Explain to them that if there are four answers to a question and they can eliminate one as being incorrect, their chance of getting the question right is 33 percent. If they can eliminate two answers, their chance of being right rises to 50 percent. Tell students that very few things in our world happen *all* the time. Likewise, the word *never* generally eliminates an answer. Students also should be told to watch the clock. Five minutes before the test ends, they should check to be sure they have marked an answer to every question, even if they are guessing. They may pick up some extra points by guessing.

Transition IEPs

The Individuals with Disabilities Education Act (IDEA) requires that an "individualized transition plan" be written as part of the IEP for every student with learning disabilities beginning at age fourteen. The purpose of the transition plan is to prepare the student for the years beyond the secondary school—for postsecondary education, employment, and independent living.

The process brings the parent, student, and school into communication. Beginning with the student's current levels of functioning, the team, the parent, and the student explore the student's interests, aptitudes, and post-school goals. The plan outlines a series of activities in which the student will participate, such as vocational or career education, work-experience programs, and community-based instruction.

Among students with LD, 58 percent will go into some sort of employment from high school, 28 percent will elect to go to college, and 32 percent will enroll in a vocational training program (Wagner and others, 1993).

Some transition programs help prepare the student to meet entry-level requirements, help locate jobs for them, and provide job coaching at the employment site.

Two laws designed to assist students are the Tech Prep Act (an amendment to the Carl D. Perkins Vocational and Applied Technology Education Act of 1990) and the School-to-Work Act of 1994. Under these laws, LD students may be eligible for vocational assessment, support services, counseling, and career development planning.

Understanding the Needs of the High School Student with Learning Disabilities

Curricular demands rise again in high school. If the student with LD is in a content-area regular class, there is a great need for the special educator to be involved. She needs to collaborate with the regular teacher, who is not trained to work with these students, on ways to

1. Present the information meaningfully to the student, adjusting for deficits in language processing and short-term memory

2. Modify the assignments or testing situation expected of the student, addressing deficits in reading and writing skills, and the need for freedom from distractions and for additional time

3. Give help in completing the assignments, thus teaching study skills

4. Refer students to assistive technology, such as word processors, text readers, and digital text, and to such Web sites as www.ncld.org and www.ldonline.org for more help

5. Give encouragement when the student feels overwhelmed

If these things are not routinely done, it is inevitable that students will do poorly or drop out of school.

High school students with learning disabilities still need instruction in the basic skills of reading, writing, vocabulary development, and mathematics. Special attention is crucial for these students.

Work-Study Program

Many high school students benefit from the opportunity to be in a work-study program where they receive on-the-job coaching and lessons at school geared toward meeting their needs at work. In some schools, this may be set up as a "career center" that allows students to take courses focused toward a specific career.

Parents are informed at the time of the first transition interview of the existence of these work-study and career-center programs. In California, for example, "Project Workability" encourages employers to hire special needs students. The project pays the student's salary for the first hundred hours of work and provides staff to help work out problems that may arise.

Students with learning disabilities often continue to need survival skills in the areas of behavior control, people-pleasing behavior, study skills, and test-taking skills. High school students need to understand their disability. Even if this subject was dealt with in junior high, it is still a good idea to discuss it again in high school, especially in the last year of school.

At this point students are more open to advice about getting their first jobs. They will benefit from having employers come to class to role-play interviews and give them pointers on how to act, what to wear, and what to say. After they have role-played with three different employers, they are much more confident about going for a job interview.

Students pay attention when employers talk about

- Dependability
- Punctuality
- Preparedness
- Appropriate dress
- Getting along with others
- Willingness to do what is asked

Continuation Schools and Independent Study Programs

Some students with learning disabilities cannot make it in the regular high school program, but will be able to complete an alternative high school program. Most continuation schools have smaller classes, allowing more one-on-one contact between student and teacher. Some have on-campus nurseries so that students who are young parents can nurse their baby, see their baby, and learn to care for their child.

Some students cannot handle being around other students, but will complete work if allowed to do it at home. Students in an independent study program meet weekly with a teacher, review completed assignments, and receive new ones to do at home.

Life and Social Skills

Students need to learn how to make a budget, how to handle personal banking, and how to interact appropriately with other people in a variety of settings—a wedding, a funeral, at work, when meeting someone new, and so on. They need instruction on the use of a credit card and explanation of the true cost of items bought on credit. LD students should be given instruction on consumer issues: what's a good buy and where to get purchasing advice should they need it. They need instruction on time management; getting along with a roommate, spouse, or family; and where to go to meet people for social purposes. By age sixteen, most students show a definite interest in these topics.

Most schools are not doing a very good job of meeting the LD high school student's needs. As you can see in Figure 14.2, achievement hovers between fifth- and sixth-grade level by the end of high school.

Understanding the Needs of the Young Adult with Learning Disabilities

Do you remember the decisions you faced upon finishing high school? The LD student faces all these concerns and more.

FIGURE 14.2.

Cumulative Deficit and Academic Plateau.

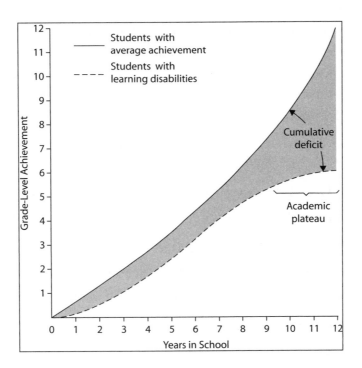

Source: *W. N. Bender,* Learning Disabilities: Characteristics, Identification, and Teaching Strategies, *4th ed.* *(Boston: Allyn & Bacon, 2001). Reprinted by permission of Allyn & Bacon.*

Five years after graduating from high school, 60 percent of LD students still live at home with their parents. They often need the help and advice of their parents. About 75 percent of LD high school graduates will obtain jobs. This figure is not significantly different from that of their nondisabled peers. The difference is that, generally, LD individuals still work in entry-level positions earning minimum wage, or work only part-time. They are often dissatisfied with the job they have. They also report more periods of unemployment (Sitlington, Frank, and Carson, 1992).

Research by Okolo and Sitlington (1986) found that there were three reasons why students with mild learning disabilities were underemployed. These same three reasons hold true for today's students:

1. They lacked interpersonal skills.

2. They lacked job-related academic skills.

3. They lacked specific vocational skills.

Services Available to Students Going to College

Section 504 of the Rehabilitation Act of 1973 mandated that services be provided for all individuals with handicaps to assist them in becoming economically self-supporting. Today more than five hundred colleges and universities offer services to students with disabilities. Students with LD, for example, may apply to take entrance exams under modified circumstances (for example, alone in a quiet room, with extra time).

Once admitted to a college, students with LD benefit from program accommodations:

- Assistance with registration and strategic placement in classes with empathic instructors
- Extra tutorial assistance (at no cost to the student)
- Recorded lectures or textbooks and assistance with note-taking
- Provision of notes by the instructor
- Access to word processing equipment, calculators, and computers
- Access to a learning lab where they are taught specific study strategies
- Proofreading services
- Typists to help with papers
- Waivers for some courses, such as math
- Permission to reduce course load without loss of full-time student status
- Highlighted texts
- Alternative modes of testing and arrangements for testing
- Assistance with time management and personal organization
- Psychoeducational testing and therapy
- Support groups
- Social skills training

As always, the effectiveness of student support services is largely dependent on the individuals providing such services. Thus the parents of LD students who are going on to college need to seek out those institutions that demonstrate their commitment—those with sympathetic faculties. Visit campuses. Talk to personnel in the Student Services office.

Occasionally a person will reach college with a learning disability that has never been recognized. Sarah was such a student. She squeaked by in high school, but finally realized that she had a terrible problem in math. At the age of twenty-five, she requested assessment, but her request was met with resistance. Finally, after threatening to file an appeal with the Office of Civil Rights, she was assessed and identified.

Vocational Rehabilitation Services for the Learning Disabled

Some individuals with learning disabilities are accepted for training through various vocational rehabilitation services, such as Goodwill or state departments of rehabilitation. Again, the effectiveness of this approach is dependent on the knowledge and dedication of the staff.

Vocational rehabilitation services may include a combination of services from the following list:

- Books and tuition for trade school or college

- Transportation

- Job training

- Reader, interpreter, or note-taking services

- Tools or other equipment needed for a job

- Initial stock or supplies in a small business

- Medical services if needed

- Training in job-seeking skills

- Job placement

- A "job coach" on the work site to help the student learn the job

- On-the-job follow-up to monitor employee and employer satisfaction

Adult Education Opportunities

Years after leaving high school, some LD individuals realize that they need to do something to improve their job situation. Many communities offer adult education classes for adults of any age who want to learn basic skills or enroll in a vocational program. Attending these classes can be a good way to meet new friends and study partners. Many of these classes are held in the evening. Students can learn more about these classes by contacting their local school district.

Chapter 15

The Role of the Family

During the preschool years, the family plays a major role in the child's cognitive and social development.

The home is the child's first school, and family members are its faculty. The first five years of a child's life are called the "formative years." For years, we have weighed the importance of nature versus nurture. A child is born with a genetic code that defines, in part, her temperament and potential, but studies show that environment is also critically important to a child's development.

The Role of Parents—as Parents

Parents who are warm, attentive, flexible, supportive, and accepting, and who invest time in talking with the child, reading to the child, and teaching manners will find this attention is reflected in higher competencies throughout the child's life.

We know that when a child is born, the brain has trillions of cells. We also know that if these cells are not stimulated, they are pared away. We know that the optimal time for development of many cognitive functions, such as language development, occurs before age three. We also know that when this development does not take place during the optimal period, the child rarely catches up.

The Home Environment

Parents create the environment in which the child will grow up. Even babies are sensitive to the atmosphere of the home. They sense tension and show anxiety. If there is yelling or frequent fighting, they may become fearful. Their world does not seem to be a safe place.

Learning disabled children need more supervision, so the decision as to whether both parents should work is a hard one. Where will the child receive the best care? If both parents are going to work, they face the challenge of finding quality child care. Every child benefits from receiving positive attention from either one or both parents.

Parents have tremendous responsibilities for decisions about their children's lives. One decision on which they need to agree is how much television their children will watch and what kind of programming they will allow. The same is true of computer and Internet use.

Television

There are interesting statistics on TV watching in children. Children who watch more than ten hours of TV per week show lower school achievement (Williams, Haertel, and Walberg, 1982). A study by Williams (1986) of children in one Canadian town, before and two years after the introduction of TV to their town, found that the children showed a decline in reading fluency and creative thinking, and an increase in verbal and physical aggression. It is estimated that by the age of eighteen, the average child has witnessed 13,000 killings and over 101,000 violent episodes on TV (Huston, Watkins, and Kunkel, 1989).

The National Center for Education Statistics (2003) reports that when parents restrict television viewing, expect their children to make good grades in school, and talk with the child about future educational plans, the children are more likely to stay in school.

Siblings

If a child has siblings, it is not unusual that the siblings will feel jealous of the additional attention the learning disabled child receives. While one parent is paying attention to this child, it is helpful if the other parent steps in and becomes involved with the other siblings.

Inevitably, there will be occasional squabbles. The child with learning disabilities should not be coddled or overprotected. With rare exceptions, that child needs the same parameters the other siblings are given and similar consequences when guidelines are violated.

Providing Worthwhile Activities

A playhouse and outdoor play equipment are great for four- to eight-year-olds. Young children need objects to stimulate them, such as toys, books, and audio- and videotapes. (See Chapter Four for a list of toys that are suggested for the early ages.)

If the amount of TV is restricted, as many experts advise doing, parents must consider what activities their children will pursue to occupy those extra hours. An activity-filled house is likely to become the neighborhood gathering place and will demand more parental supervision, but at least those parents will be able to supervise what their children are doing.

It is healthy for children to spend time without playmates at times and to learn to amuse themselves when alone. You can take them to the library where helpful librarians can guide them in the selection of worthwhile fiction and nonfiction books. Most children will pick up books and read if they find an interesting topic. Hobbies can be developed with some help from parents (the child's own or others). Drawing materials appeal to both boys and girls.

Look into after-school programs, such as dance lessons, singing lessons, art lessons, and sports, which will develop physical skills. For the LD child, soccer is one of the best sports because good sportsmanship is encouraged, and every child gets to play the same number of minutes. It is not wise to overschedule the child with activities every day of the week, however. The child will need extra help and time with schoolwork. If you can afford private tutoring, look for a patient, nurturing tutor. Listen to the child. If she indicates that she is unhappy or uncomfortable, you may have the wrong tutor.

Above all, know where your child is, what he or she is doing, and that he or she is being directly supervised by a responsible adult. I remember one case where a fourteen-year-old had her mom drop her off several times at the church for youth group. Arriving early to pick the daughter up one evening, the mom went in, only to learn from the adult in charge that her daughter had never attended the youth group.

The Role of Parents—as Teachers

Supervision of Homework

Parents of students with learning disabilities need to supervise homework through to completion. I encourage parents to ask the teacher(s) to call them immediately if their child does not turn in homework. Because these children often have trouble remembering assignments, most will need an agenda or assignment notebook. Ask the teacher or a peer helper to write down all assignments and due dates.

If your child comes home with the "I don't have any homework" story, it should be understood that he still has homework with you. Listen to him read for fifteen minutes. One pleasant way to do this is to have the child read aloud while you prepare dinner. If something does not make sense, say, "Oops, please read that again; I didn't understand that." As the reading progresses, discuss what is going on in the story. When his "I don't have homework" is repeated two nights in a row, make a contact by phone or e-mail with the teacher.

What should you expect in terms of homework? Homework is generally given Monday through Thursday nights, but teachers may not send home work every evening.

For grades 1–2, homework should consist of some reading, spelling, and math. If the child applies herself to the tasks, it should take no more than fifteen to twenty minutes to complete. Following are some time guidelines for homework in the other grades:

- Grades 3 and 4: thirty to forty-five minutes

- Grades 5 and 6: about an hour

- Junior high: about an hour and a half

- Senior high: up to two hours

Addressing Homework Problems

If the child has an attentional problem, it may help to *break the homework session into smaller increments, with a short break or reward* following the completion of each task.

If the child complains the homework is too hard, *contact the teacher to ask whether that might be true.* You will need to work with the teacher to make adjustments.

If the student has more homework than he can do in the time suggested in the previous list, talk with the teacher(s). Perhaps unfinished classwork is being sent home. In this case, *consider asking the teacher to prioritize the most important assignments or questions.*

The Homework Environment

Parents should provide their child with the tools needed to do homework, including crayons, colored pencils, glue stick, ruler, and dictionary.

Homework is ideally done in a quiet place, free of distractions and with good lighting and comfortable furniture. The TV should be turned off. If there are several children in the family, it may work to gather them at the kitchen table and have everyone do his or her homework there. As each finishes, review what was done before dismissing each to go elsewhere. If this proves too distracting for the child with LD, it would be best to set up a desk and necessary supplies for her to work in a quiet part of the home.

When the child sits down to do homework, *review the directions with him and be certain he knows what to do.* Ask him to explain to you what he is to do so that you can be sure he understands.

Always try to help the student with things she does not understand, but be wary if you are having to supervise her work every minute. Many LD students have learned how to "con" parents into doing the work for them.

Be lavish in praise: "I like the way you are being so neat" or "That's a great sentence."

Some parents reward children with money for completion of assignments, but limit this to no more than 50¢ a day for homework. Other parents use a similar technique with middle or high schoolers, adapting the currency to fit. The parents may give their child money to go to the basketball game on Friday with his friends if the child completes all his homework during the week.

Helping at School

You would be wise to spend some time each month in your child's classroom in elementary school. This reinforces to the child that she is important and that education is important. It also can build rapport between you and the teacher and allow you to see what's going on in your child's classroom. If asked, many employers are willing to allow parents to take a couple of hours a month to do this.

The Role of Parents—as Advocates

You are the most important advocate for your child, as you will be with him throughout his school career. IDEA supports the right to be intensively involved in the educational planning for your child.

Although most school personnel are well-intentioned people, many are overworked, and, unfortunately, some are poorly trained or inexperienced. Be aware of your child's specific needs and be assertive in asking for things that might help your child.

Become knowledgeable about learning disabilities. Join an organization such as the Learning Disabilities Association, or look for advocacy information through the Reading Rockets organization. You may also want to join your school district's Special Education Parent-Teacher Association (SEPTA).

Attend your child's IEP meetings, ask questions, and offer solutions. Obtain copies of all paperwork and keep these records readily available. When attending IEP conferences, you should insist on a full understanding of what services are available to help your child.

If you and the teacher work hand in hand and have regular contact, your child probably will make steady progress in his skills. If you receive a poor progress notice, call for a special IEP review. Let your child know he can learn. Teach him to persevere. Do not make the child overly dependent by babying him and doing everything for him. Help your child take advantage of the vocational opportunities available through the school system. Insist that he make use of the computer, and become familiar with the ways it could support him in learning. You are the most important advocate in your child's life!

Tips for Helping Your Child

1. Use encouraging statements, such as "Keep trying. You can do it!"

2. Expose the child to all kinds of social situations. Before you go out together, give the child some idea of what will happen—tell him to watch your behavior for clues on how to act.

3. Talk with the child after exposing her to a social situation. "What did you see?" "What did you learn?" Compliment her for what she did right. "You were very good for the first half hour." (Longer than that is hard for all children.) "Next time I would like for you to . . ." Take a writing pad and pencil if you anticipate that the situation will exceed an hour.

4. Talk, talk, and talk some more with your child. Read to him from such books as *Treasure Island* or from the Harry Potter series. Reading develops his vocabulary and his imagination.

5. Take your child to the library. Try to make it a fun routine, especially if the library has a story hour or special speakers when you're there.

6. Limit TV viewing to less than an hour daily and avoid programs that are violent, even cartoons.

7. Make the home environment nonstressful, pleasant, and calm. It's good for you, too.

8. Stay on good terms with your child's teachers and the school. Make contact with your child's teachers every two weeks to ascertain how the child is doing. Try to help for an hour a week in your child's class.

9. Know where your child is and what she is doing. Let your house be the place the neighborhood kids want to be. Supervise children carefully.

10. Supervise homework.

11. Arrange for your child to participate in a weekly activity, such as dance, sports, or choir. If money is tight, churches or community centers often provide activities that are free.

12. With your partner, decide what the parameters for your child will be.

13. Assign chores. Have your child help you set the table, take out the garbage, and keep his room clean and neat.

14. Set up an allowance system. Buy fewer things at the store for your child. Teach her to plan, save, and buy. (It will be cheaper for you in the long run!)

15. Send siblings to timeout when they squabble. Talk with each privately to clarify behavioral expectations.

16. Enforce a bedtime of no later than 8:30 PM. Children need the sleep, and parents need time to unwind.

17. Do not be afraid to set and enforce limits—for example, "You may go play when your chores are done." When an infraction occurs, devise a consequence that fits.

18. In the morning, give your children a good breakfast and start another great day!

Chapter 16

Education in the New Millennium

As educators and parents, we want our children to have the best future possible. We know education will play a large part in their future.

Present trends and conditions are likely to affect education in the twenty-first century in several ways. There will be

- Continued and expanded mainstreaming, with fewer students served in special education resource classes

- An increase in the use of assistive technology

- A renewed sense of the importance of education—greater participation by the business sector and parents in the activities of the school

- Reduction in the number of students at a given school, resulting in reduced class size or improved adult–student ratios

- Expanded curricular offerings

- Changes in teacher education

- Improvement in teachers' salaries and better working conditions

Increased Mainstreaming

We have been encouraged to try to serve children with special needs in the "least restrictive environment" since the passage of the Education of All Handicapped Children Act of 1975 (P.L. 94-142). The Regular Education Initiative of 1986 also voiced this principle. During the period from 1975 to 2000, regular teachers have become more accustomed to working with children who have learning disabilities and other special needs. They have developed new ways to plan lessons that include students who are functioning at multiple ability levels.

We want to minimize labeling of students and maximize healthy interpersonal relations among peers. Both of these goals are best achieved when students can be maintained in the regular classroom. In most classrooms there is a good amount of change in the daily schedule, with students regularly leaving the classroom for such subjects as art, music, and computers. Small groups of students may come and go throughout the day—some to the resource room or to speech therapy, music, the computer lab to learn keyboarding skills, and adaptive or regular physical education classes.

Another trend of the 1990s was inclusion. Inclusion opened up more opportunities for students with learning problems. More students are served in their least restrictive environments.

Now that we have reached the twenty-first century, the majority of students with learning disabilities remain in the classroom, and only those who are emotionally impaired, severely physically impaired (so that they cannot be serviced in a traditional classroom), or exceptionally learning impaired remain in special education classes for the entire school day. Students with dyslexia, language disorders, autism, auditory processing disorders, and many more may leave the traditional classroom just for supplemental instruction. The child with LD will most likely be mainstreamed like their peers.

Increased Use of Technology

In the 1990s, Congress passed several pieces of legislation designed to encourage the use of technology to help individuals with disabilities. These included

- Part G of the Education for All Handicapped Children Act of 1986 (P.L. 99-457)

- The Individuals with Learning Disabilities Act of 1990 (P.L. 101-476)

- The Technology-Related Assistance of Individuals with Disabilities Act of 1998 (P.L. 100-407)

As a result of these legislative advances, we saw the following efforts put in place for the twenty-first century:

- Most classrooms in the nation were equipped with one or more computers, some software, a television, a listening center with earphones, an overhead projector, and a tape recorder.

- Teachers received instruction on how to use computers in the classroom.

- Efforts had begun to evaluate in statistical terms the effectiveness of specific interventions with students who have learning disabilities (Swanson, Hoskyn, and Lee, 1999).

- Districts were encouraged to evaluate which forms of assistive technology might help a given learning disabled student maximize his or her skills or potential. This suggests the use of assistive technology—encompassing any device or equipment that can improve or maintain functional capabilities—will increase in the twenty-first century.

In my own experience, I have found that students seemed to enjoy drill work more when doing it on the computer. They reported that they liked the game format, color, and sound. They particularly appreciated word processing programs, which allowed them to make corrections without having to rewrite the entire paper. I found that most of my students showed good on-task behavior (interest) when using the computer. Extra computer time was one of the most requested rewards.

It has been noted that students with learning disabilities produce more written work when they are allowed to do it on the computer (MacArthur, 1988). These children often show a special facility with the computer (Edyburn and Majsterek, 1993).

Class Size

Educators, parents, and employers have all expressed concern because U.S. children have not measured up academically to our expectations of them. In 1983, the results of a comprehensive study were published in a book titled *A Nation at Risk.*

Parents blamed educators. Educators said that class size was too high. In California, they have reduced regular class size in kindergarten through grade 3 to a maximum of twenty students; it has led to significant improvement in student achievement. Because we know that students with learning disabilities benefit when they get more one-on-one help, it seems probable that with more paraprofessional help in the regular classroom (working directly with individual students), we would see a decline in special education enrollment.

Class size in special education classes is another issue that needs attention. In some places, districts have chosen to place more than twelve students in a given special day class. The higher the number of students rises, the more likely it is that the children are just being "warehoused." Because of the extreme neediness of each child, the teacher and aide end up spending more time preventing misbehavior than teaching.

The same is true with schools generally. In California, we have some elementary schools with enrollments of eight hundred to a thousand students. The sense of anonymity generated by such large populations affects both staff and students negatively. In small elementary schools of three hundred students, the staff know each student, and there is a feeling of community.

Teacher Preparation Trends and Issues

When you talk with school district administrators, there is a prevailing theme of needing more and better-trained teachers. This has led to requirements for more training both before and after certification. In addition to a four-year college degree, most states require additional coursework throughout the teachers' careers. Before being credentialed, candidates must pass several tests to prove they are proficient in basic subject matter. Some of those who can pass the many tests are not necessarily good teachers. Many leave the profession after less than five years.

We need to increase regular education teachers' knowledge of the needs of special education children and of the techniques for teaching these students so that teachers feel more competent in working with them. If we make these changes in teacher preparation, by the time students receive their credentials, they would be better prepared and more experienced professionals, thus reducing the costly turnover rate we see currently in the profession.

As a result of new information coming out of research on reading disabilities, specifically on the new appreciation of the role that phonological awareness plays, we may reasonably expect changes in the training of special education teachers. Both colleges and districts will need to give training in special techniques required to teach reading-impaired children, such as the Lindamood Auditory Discrimination Program, the Fernald-Keller (VAKT) approach, and the Gillingham-Stillman approach.

Professional Salaries and Working Conditions

It is likely that we will see a demand on the part of teachers for meaningful salary improvement. Teachers remain severely underpaid considering the amount of training required to qualify for the credential and the amount of responsibility assumed. Whereas the student school day is six hours long, the teacher workday is much longer because of meetings, record keeping, lesson and activity planning, and required continuing education.

Conclusion

There is no greater national treasure than our children, for they are the leaders of tomorrow. If they become wise, productive, and well-balanced people, we and the nation will benefit from their productivity.

- Wouldn't it be comforting to know that every child has a competent, caring teacher?

- Wouldn't it be wonderful if every student in elementary school could get the help he or she needs as it is needed and without being labeled?

- Wouldn't it be great if school psychologists had time to work with troubled families?

- Wouldn't it be helpful if our teachers and school professionals had additional training on learning disabilities and the techniques used to overcome them?

All this is possible. Yes, it is a matter of money. It is a matter of time. It is a matter of priorities. But let's look at the payoffs. Fewer special day classes! Better self-esteem! Fewer juvenile delinquents! More productive and more capable adults! *Let's continue to work to improve education!*

References

Adams, M. J. (1990). *Beginning to read: Thinking and learning about print*. Cambridge, MA: MIT Press.

Ames, L. B. (1968). Learning disabilities: The developmental point of view. In H. R. Mykleburst (ed.), *Progress in learning disabilities*. Vol. 1. New York: Grune & Stratton.

Ashtari, M., Kumra, S., Bhaskar, S., Clarke, T., Thaden, E., Cervellione, K., Rhinewine, J., Kane, J., Adesman, A., & Milanaik, R. (2005). Attention-deficit/hyperactivity disorder: A preliminary diffusion tensor imaging study. *Biological Psychiatry*, *57*(5), 448–455.

Barberesi, W., Katusic, S., Colligen, R., Weaver, A., & Jacobsen, S. (2007). Long-term school outcomes for children with attention-deficit/hyperactivity disorder: A population-based perspective. *Journal of Developmental and Behavioral Pediatrics*, *28*(4), 265–273.

Barnett, W. S. (1995). Long-term outcomes of early childhood programs. *Future of Children*, *5*(3), 25–50.

Bauminger, N., Shulman, C., & Agam, G. (2003). Peer interaction and loneliness in high-functioning children with autism. *Journal of Autism Developmental Disorders*, *33*(5), 489–507.

Belmonte, M., Allen, G., Beckel-Mitchener, A., Boulanger, L. M., Carper, R. A., & Webb, S. J. (2004). Autism and abnormal development of brain connectivity. *Journal of Neuroscience, 24*, 9228–9231.

Bender, W. N. (2001). *Learning disabilities: Characteristics, identification, and teacher strategies*. (4th ed.) Boston: Allyn & Bacon.

Bradley, L., & Bryant, R. (1985). Rhyme and reason in reading and spelling. In *International Academy for Research in Learning Disabilities*. Ann Arbor: University of Michigan Press.

Brandeis University. (2007, May 10). New research sheds light on memory by erasing it. *ScienceDaily*. Retrieved April 21, 2008, from www.sciencedaily.com/releases/2007/05/070509073522.htm.

Braun, J., Kahn R., Froehlich, T., Auinger, P., & Lanphear, B. P. (2006). Exposures to environmental toxicants and attention deficit hyperactivity disorder in U.S. children. *Environmental Health Perspectives*, *114*(12), 1904–1909.

Brooks-Gunn, J., Han, W.-J., & Waldfogel, J. (2002). Maternal employment and child cognitive outcomes in the first three years of life: The NICHD study of early child care. *Child Development*, *73*(4), 1052–1072.

Brown, A. L. (1980). Metacognitive development and reading. In R. J. Spiro, B. C. Bruce, & W. F. Brewer (eds.), *Theoretical issues in reading comprehension*. Mahwah, NJ: Erlbaum.

Bryan, J. H., & Bryan, T. S. (1983). The social life of the learning disabled youngster. In J. McKinney and L. Feagans (eds.), *Current topics in learning disabilities*. Vol. 1. Norwood, NJ: Ablex.

Bryan, T., Donahue, M., & Pearl, R. (1981). Learning disabled children's peer interactions during small group problem solving task. *Learning Disability Quarterly*, *4*, 13–22.

Bryan, T. S. (1991). Social problems and learning disabilities. In B.Y.L. Wong (ed.), *Learning about learning disabilities*. Orlando, FL: Academic Press.

Bryan, T. S., & Wheeler, R. (1972). Perceptions of learning disabled children: The eye of the observer. *Journal of Learning Disabilities*, *5*, 485–486.

Cantwell, D. P., & Baker, J. (1991). Association between attention deficit hyperactivity disorder and learning disorders. *Journal of Learning Disabilities*, *24*, 88–95.

Cone, T. E., Wilson, L. R., Bradley, C. M., & Reese, J. H. (1985). Characteristics of LD students in Iowa: An empirical investigation. *Learning Disability Quarterly*, *8*, 211–220.

Copeland, A. P., & Reinger, E. M. (1984). The selective attention of learning-disabled children: Three studies. *Journal of Abnormal Child Psychology*, *12*, 455–470.

Courchesne, E., Carper, R., & Akshoomoff, N. (2003). Evidence of brain overgrowth in the first year of life in autism. *Journal of the American Medical Association*, *290*, 337–344.

Courchesne, E., Karns, C. M., Davis, H. R., Ziccardi, R., Carper, R. A., Tigue, Z. D., Chisum, H. J., Moses, P., Pierce, K., Lord, C., Lincoln, A. J., Pizzo, S., Schreibman, L., Haas, R. H., Akshoomoff, N. A., & Courchesne, R. Y. (2001). Unusual brain growth patterns in early life in patients with autistic disorder: An MRI study. *Neurology*, *57*, 245–254.

Courvoisie, H., Hooper, S., Fine, C., Kwock, L., & Castillo, M. (2004). Neurometabolic functioning and neuropsychological correlates in children with

ADHD-H: Preliminary findings. *Journal of Neuropsychiatry Clinical Neuroscience, 16,* 63-69.

Curran, L., Newschaffer, C. J., Lee, L. C., Crawford, S. O., Johnston, M. V., & Zimmerman, A. W. (2007). Behaviors associated with fever in children with autism spectrum disorders. *Pediatrics, 120*(6), 1386–1392.

Dearing, E., McCartney, K., & Taylor, B. A. (2001). Change in family income-to-needs matters more for children with less. *Child Development, 72*(6), 1779–1793.

Deruelle, C., Rondan, C., Gepner, B., & Tardif, C. (2004). Spatial frequency and face processing in children with autism and Asperger syndrome. *Journal of Autism and Developmental Disorders, 34*(2), 199–210.

Deshler, D. D., Schumaker, J. B., & Lenz, B. K. (1984). Academic and cognitive interventions for LD adolescents: Part 1. *Journal of Learning Disabilities, 17,* 108–117.

Donofrio, A. F. (1977). Grade repetition: Therapy of choice. *Journal of Learning Disabilities, 10,* 349–351.

Douglas, V. I., Barry, R. G., O'Neill, M. E., & Britton, B. G. (1986). Short-term effects of methylphenidate on the cognitive and academic performance of children with attention deficit disorder in the laboratory and in the classroom. *Journal of Child Psychology and Psychiatry, 27,* 191–211.

Draper, K., Ponsford, J., & Schönberger, M. (2007). Psychosocial and emotional outcomes ten years following traumatic brain injury. *Journal of Head Trauma Rehabilitation, 22*(5), 278–287.

DuPaul, G. J., Barkley, R. A., & McMurray, M. B. (1991). Therapeutic effects of medication on ADHD: Implications for school psychologists. *School Psychology Review, 20,* 203–219.

Dykman, R. A., & Ackerman, P. T. (1991). Attention deficit disorder and specific reading disability: Separate but overlapping disorders. *Journal of Learning Disabilities, 24,* 96–103.

Eckert, M. A., Leonard, C. M., Richards, T. L., Aylward, E. H., Thomson, J., & Berninger, V. W. (2003). Anatomical correlates of dyslexia: Frontal and cerebellar findings. *Brain, 126*(2), 482–494.

Edyburn, D., & Majsterek, D. (1993). Technology applications for individuals with LD: What can we say today? *LD Forum, 19,* 3–5.

Fagerheim, T., Raeymaekers, P., Tønnessen, F. E., Pedersen, M., Tranebjaerg, L., & Lubs, H. A. (1999). A new gene (DYX3) for dyslexia is located on chromosome 2. *Journal of Medical Genetics, 36*(9), 664–669.

Flowers, J. M., Wood, F. B., & Naylor, C. E. (1991). Regional blood flow correlates of language processes in reading disabilities. *Archives of Neurology, 48,* 637–643.

Galaburda, A. (1991). Anatomy of dyslexia: Argument against phrenology. In D. D. Duane and D. B. Gray (eds.), *The reading brain*. Pankton, MD: York Press.

Gessel, L., Fields, S., Collins, C. L., Dick, R. W., & Comstock, R. D. (2007). Concussions among United States high school and collegiate athletes. *Journal of Athletic Training, 42*(4), 495–503.

Goldberg, J. (2002). Clonidine and methylphenidate were effective for attention deficit hyperactivity disorder in children with comorbid tics. *American College of Physicians Journal*. Retrieved Nov. 15, 2007, from www.acpjc.org/Content/137/2/issue/ACPJC-2002-137-2-070.htm.

Gruen, J. (2005). Annual meeting of American Society of Human Genetics. [Press release]. Yale Child Health Research Center, Yale School of Medicine.

Hale, S., Bookheimer, S., McGough, J. J., Phillips, J. M., & McCracken, J. T. (2007). Atypical brain activation during simple and complex levels of processing in adult ADHD: An fMRI study. *Journal of Attention Disorders, 11*, 125–139.

Hough, L. (2007, Spring). Science says. *Ed.* Retrieved Apr. 21, 2008, from www.gse.harvard.edu/news_events/ed/2007/spring/features/science.html.

Huston, A. C., Watkins, B. A., & Kunkel, D. (1989). Public policy and children's television. *American Psychologist, 44*, 424–433.

Hynd, G. W., Marshall, R., & Gonzalez, J. (1991). Learning disabilities and the presumed central nervous system dysfunction. *Learning Disability Quarterly, 14*, 283–286.

Hynd, G. W., & Willis, W. G. (1988). *Pediatric neuropsychology*. New York: Grune & Stratton.

Isaacson, R. L., & Spear, L. P. (1984). A new perspective for the interpretation of early brain damage. In S. Finger and C. L. Almli (eds.), *Neurobiology and behavior*. Vol. 2: *Early Brain Damage*. Orlando, FL: Academic Press.

Johnson, C. P., Myers, S. M., & the Council on Children with Disabilities. (2007). Identification and evaluation of children with autism spectrum disorders. *Pediatrics, 120*, 1183–1215.

Jorge, R. (2005). Pathophysiological aspects of major depression following traumatic brain injury. *Journal of Head Trauma and Rehabilitation, 20*(6), 475–487.

Keilitz, I., & Dunivant, N. (1986). The relationship between learning disability and juvenile delinquency: Current state of knowledge. *Remedial and Special Education, 7*, 18–26.

Koponen, S. (2002). Axis I and II psychiatric disorders after traumatic brain injury: A thirty-year follow-up study. *American Journal of Psychiatry, 159*(8), 1261–1264.

Kuhl, D., & Dewitz, P. (1994). *The effect of handwriting style on alphabet recognition*. Paper presented at the meeting of the American Educational Research Association, New Orleans.

Levin, E. K., Zigmond, N., and Birch, J. W. (1985). A follow-up of fifty-two learning disabled adolescents. *Journal of Learning Disabilities, 18,* 2–7.

Lindamood, C. H., & Lindamood, P. (1984). *Auditory discrimination in depth.* Austin, TX: Pro-Ed.

MacArthur, C. A. (1988). The impact of computers on the writing process. *Exceptional Children, 54,* 536–542.

Maddux, C. D., Green, C., & Horner, C. M. (1986). School entry age among children labeled learning disabled, mentally retarded and emotionally disturbed. *Learning Disabilities Focus, 2,* 7–12.

Magnuson, K. A., Meyers, M. K., Ruhm, C. J., & Waldfogel, J. (2004). Inequality in preschool education and school readiness. *American Educational Research Journal, 41,* 115–157.

Manis, F. R. (1985). Acquisition of word identification skills in normal and disabled readers. *Journal of Educational Psychology, 77,* 78–90.

Mann, V. (1991). Language problems: A key to early reading problems. In B.Y.L. Wong (ed.), *Learning about learning disabilities.* Orlando, FL: Academic Press.

Mastropieri, M. A., & Scruggs, T. E. (1991). *Teaching students ways to remember.* Cambridge, MA: Brookline Books.

Mayo Clinic. (2007, Sept. 24). Medication for ADHD may help students succeed at school. *ScienceDaily.* www.sciencedaily.com/releases/2007/09/070918144259 .html.

McKinney, J., & Feagan, L. (1983). Adaptive classroom behavior of learning disabled students. *Journal of Learning Disabilities, 16,* 360–367.

Medway, F. J. (1985, Jan.). To promote or not to promote. *Principal,* pp. 22–25.

Medway, F. J., & Rose, J. C. (1986). Grade retention. In T. R. Kratochwill (ed.), *Advances in school psychology.* Vol. 1. Mahwah, NJ: Erlbaum.

Michigan State University. (2007, Dec. 6). Even low lead exposure linked to ADHD. *ScienceDaily.* www.sciencedaily.com/releases/2007/12/071203204513.htm.

National Assessment of Educational Progress. (2005). *NAEP 2004 Trends in academic progress: Three decades of student performance in reading and mathematics: Findings in brief* (NCES 2005-463). Washington, D.C.: U.S. Government Printing Office.

National Center for Education Statistics. (2003). *National assessment of adult literacy (NAAL): A first look at the literacy of America's adults in the twenty-first century.* Washington, D.C.: U.S. Government Printing Office.

National Reading Panel. (2000). Teaching children to read: An evidence-based assessment of the scientific research literature on reading and its implications for reading instruction. Bethesda, MD: National Institute of Child Health and Human Development. Available at www.nationalreadingpanel.org/publications/summary.htm.

Nöthen, M. M., Schulte-Körne, G., Grimm, T., Cichon, S., Vogt, I. R., Müller-Myhsok, B., Propping, P., & Remschmidt H. (1999). Genetic linkage analysis with dyslexia: Evidence for linkage of spelling disability to chromosome 15. *European Child and Adolescent Psychiatry, 8*(3), 56–59.

Okolo, C. M., & Sitlington, P. (1986). The role of special education in LD adolescents' transition from school to work. *Learning Disability Quarterly, 9,* 141–155.

Parker, H. C. (1992). *The ADD hyperactivity handbook for schools.* Plantation, FL: Impact Press.

Pellicano, E., Jeffery, L., Burr, D., & Rhodes, G. (2007). Abnormal adaptive face-coding mechanisms in children with autism spectrum disorder. *Current Biology, 17,* 1508–1512.

Pierangelo, R., & Jacoby, R. (1996). *Parents' complete special education guide.* Paramus, NJ: Center for Applied Research in Education.

Pressley M. (1982.) Elaboration and memory development. *Child Development, 53,* 296–309.

Reiff, H. B., & Gerber, P. J. (1990). Cognitive correlates of social perception in students with learning disabilities. *Journal of Learning Disabilities, 23*(4), 260–262.

Rogers, J. M., & Read, C. A. (2007). Psychiatric comorbidity following traumatic brain injury. *Brain Injury, 21*(13), 1321–1333.

Runyan, M. D. (1991). The effect of extra time on reading comprehension scores for university students with and without learning disabilities. *Journal of Learning Disabilities, 24,* 104–108.

Semrud-Clikeman, M., & Hynd, G. W. (1990). Right hemispheric dysfunction in nonverbal learning disabilities: Social, academic, and adaptive functioning in adults and children. *Psychological Bulletin, 107*(2), 196–209.

Share, D. L., & Stanovich, K. E. (1995). Cognitive processes in early reading development: Accommodating individual differences into a mode of acquisition. *Issues in Education: Contributions from Educational Psychology, 1,* 1–57.

Shaw, P., Eckstrand, K., Sharp, W., Blumenthal, J., Lerch, J. P., Greenstein, D., Clasen, L., Evans, A., Giedd, J., & Rapoport, J. L. (2007). Attention-deficit/hyperactivity disorder is characterized by a delay in cortical maturation. *Proceedings of the National Academy of Sciences, 104,* 19663–19664.

Shaw, R., Grayson, A., & Lewis, V. (2005). Inhibition, ADHD, and computer games: The inhibitory performance of children with ADHD on computerized tasks and games. *Journal of Attention Disorders, 8*(4), 160–168.

Shaywitz, B., Fletcher, J., & Shaywitz, S. (1995). Defining and classifying learning disabilities and attention deficit hyperactivity disorder. *Journal of Child Neurology, 10,* 550–557.

Shepard, L. A., & Smith, M. L. (1986). Synthesis of research on school readiness and kindergarten retention. *Educational Leadership, 44*, 78–86.

Sitlington, P., Frank, A., & Carson, R. (1992). Adult adjustment among high school graduates with mild disabilities. *Exceptional Children, 59*, 221–233.

Smith, C. R. (1994). *Learning disabilities: The interaction of learner, task, and setting.* Boston: Allyn & Bacon

Sparks, B. F., Friedman, S. D., Shaw, D. W., Aylward, E. H., Echelard, D., Artru, A. A., Maravilla, K. R., Giedd, J. N., Munson, J., Dawson, G., & Dager, S. R. (2002). Brain structural abnormalities in young children with autism spectrum disorder. *Neurology, 59*, 184–192.

Spencer, T. J., Sallee F. R., Gilbert D. L., Dunn, D. W., McCracken, J. T., Coffey, B. J., Budman, C. L., Ricardi, R. K., Leonard, H. L., Allen, A. J., Milton, D. R., Feldman, P. D., Kelsey, D. K., Geller, D. A., Linder, S. L., Lewis, D. W., Winner, P. K., Kurlan, R. M., & Mintz, M. (2008). Atomoxetine treatment of ADHD in children with comorbid Tourette syndrome. *Journal of Attention Disorders, 4*, 470–481.

Stanovich, K. E. (1988). Explaining the differences between the dyslexic and the garden-variety poor reader: The phonological core variable difference model. *Journal of Learning Disabilities, 21*, 590–604.

Stanovich, K. E. (1993). Does reading make you smarter? Literacy and verbal intelligence. In *Advances in Child Development and behavior.* Vol. 25. Orlando, FL: Academic Press.

Swanson, H. L., Hoskyn, M., and Lee, C. (1999). *Interventions for students with learning disabilities: A meta-analysis of treatment outcomes.* New York: Guilford Press.

Swanson, H. L., & Malone, S. (1992). Social skills and learning disabilities: A meta-analysis of the literature. *Psychology Review, 21*(3), 427–443.

Tallal, P., Miller, S. L., & Merzenick, M. M. (1996). Language comprehension in language learning-impaired children improved within acoustically modified speech. *Science, 271*, 77–83.

Torgeson, J. K., Wagner, R. K., & Rashotte, C. A. (1994a, Oct. 24). Genetic flaw: Closing in on the cause of dyslexia. *Newsweek*, p. 66.

Torgeson, J. K., Wagner, R. K., & Rashotte, C. A. (1994b). Longitudinal studies of phonological processing and reading. *Journal of Learning Disabilities, 27*, 276–286.

University of California, Los Angeles. (2007, Apr. 20). Researchers unlock key to memory storage in brain. *ScienceDaily.* Retrieved Apr. 21, 2008, from www.sciencedaily.com/releases/4007/04/070419140914.htm.

U.S. Department of Education. (2007). *Nation's report card shows record gains: Achievement gap continues to narrow as student population becomes more diverse.*

Washington, D.C.: U.S. Government Printing Office. www.ed.gov/nclb/accountability/achieve/report-card2007.html.

Vaughn, S., Hogan, A., Kouzekanani, K., & Shapiro, S. (1990). Peer acceptance, self-perceptions, and social skills of learning disabled students prior to identification. *Journal of Educational Psychology, 82*(1), 101–106.

Wagner, M., Blackorby, J., Cameto, R., Hebbeler, K., & Newman, L. (1993). *The transition experiences of young people with disabilities: A summary of findings from the National Longitudinal Transition Study of Special Education Students.* Menlo Park, CA: SRI International.

Williams, P. A., Haertel, G. D., & Walberg, H. J. (1982). The impact of leisure-time television on school learning: A research synthesis. *American Educational Research Journal, 19,* 19–50.

Williams, T. M. (1986). *The impact of television.* Orlando, FL: Academic Press.

Wolf, M., & Bowers, P. G. (1999). The double-deficit hypothesis for the developmental dyslexias. *Journal of Educational Psychology, 91*(3), 415–438.

Further Reading

Abramson, M., Willson, V., Yoshida, R. K., & Hagerty, G. (1983). Parents' perceptions of their disabled child's educational performance. *Learning Disability Quarterly*, *6*, 184–194.

Ackerman, P. T., Dyksman, R. A., & Gardner, M. Y. (1990). Counting rate, naming rate, phonological sensitivity and memory span: Major factors in dyslexia. *Journal of Learning Disabilities, 23*, 319–327.

Alley, G., & Deshler, D. (1979). *Teaching the learning disabled adolescent strategies*. Denver, CO: London Publishing.

American Psychiatric Association. (2000). *Diagnostic and statistical manual of mental disorders* (DSM-IV-TR) (4th rev. ed.) Washington, D.C.: American Psychiatric Association.

Ames, L. B. (1968). Ready or not: How birthdays leave some children behind. *American Education, 10*, 30–33.

Ariel, A. (1992). *Education of children and adolescents with learning disabilities*. New York: Macmillan.

Barkley, R. (1990). *Attention deficit hyperactivity disorder: A handbook for diagnosis and treatment*. New York: Guilford Press.

Begley, S. (1994, Aug. 24). Why Johnnie and Joanie can't read. *Newsweek*, p. 52.

Behrman, R. E., & Vaughan, V. C. (1983). Attention deficit disorder. In *Nelson's textbook of pediatrics* (12th ed). Philadelphia: Saunders.

Busch, B. (1995). Attention deficits: Current concepts, controversies, management, and approaches to classroom instruction. *Annals of Dyslexia, 43*, 5–25.

Chapman, N. H., Igo R. P., Thomson, J. B., Matsushita, M., Brkanac, Z., Holzman, T., Berninger, V. W., Wijsman, E. M., & Raskind, W. H. (2004). Linkage analyses of four regions previously implicated in dyslexia: Confirmation of a locus on chromosome 15q. *American Journal of Medical Genetics. Part B: Neuropsychiatric Genetics, 131B*(1), 67–75.

Cook, R., Tessier, A., & Klein, D. (1992). *Adapting early childhood curriculum for children with special needs* (3rd ed.). New York: Macmillan.

Cosden, M. A., Gerber, M. M., Goldman, S. R., Semmel, D. S., & Semmel, M. I. (1987). Microcomputer use within micro-educational environments. *Exceptional Children, 53,* 399–409.

Deshler, D. D., & Schumaker, J. B. (1988). An instructional model for teaching students how to learn. In J. L. Zins & M. J. Curtis (Eds.), *Alternative educational delivery systems: Enhancing instructional options for all students.* Washington, D.C.: NASP.

Edgars, E. (1985). How do special education students fare after they leave school? *Exceptional Children, 51,* 470–473.

Gardner, H. (1983). *Frames of mind: The theory of multiple intelligences.* New York: Basic Books.

Gray, C. (2000). *The new social story book: Illustrated edition.* Arlington, TX: Future Horizons.

Gray, C., & White, A. (Eds.). (2002). *My social stories book.* London: Kingley.

Hanley, J., & Sklar, B. (1976). Electroencephalographic correlates of developmental reading dyslexias: Computer analysis of recordings from normal and dyslexic children. In G. Leisman (Ed.), *Basic learning processes and learning disability.* Springfield, Ill.: Thomas.

Haywood, H. C., & Switzky, H. N. (1986). The malleability of intelligence: Cognitive processes as a function of polygenic experiential interaction. *School Psychology Review, 15,* 245–255.

Jenkins, J. R., Larson, K., & Fleisher, L. (1983). Effects of error correction on word recognition and reading comprehension. *Learning Disability Quarterly, 6,* 139–145.

Klorman, R. (1991). Cognitive event: Related potentials in attention deficit disorder. *Journal of Learning Disabilities, 24,* 130–140.

Knowlton, H. C., & Clark, G. M. (1987). Transition issues for the 1990s. *Exceptional Children, 53,* 562–563.

Lavoie, R. (2005). *It's so much work to be your friend: Helping the child with learning disabilities find social success.* New York: Touchstone.

Malouf, J. (1987–1988). The effect of instructional computer games. *Journal of Special Education, 21,* 27–28.

Moody, K. C., & Holzer, C. E., III. (2000). Prevalence of dyslexia among Texas prison inmates. *Texas Medicine, 96*(6), 69–75.

National Archives and Records Administration. (2008).*Title 34: Education.* http://ecfr.gpoaccess.gov/cgi/t/text/text-idx?c=ecfr&tpl=/ecfrbrowse/Title34/34tab_02.tpl.

Outhred, L. (1989). Word processing: Its impact on children's writing. *Journal of Learning Disabilities, 22,* 262–263.

Pennington, B., Gilger, J. W., Pauls, D., Smith, S. A., Smith, S. D., & DeFries, J. C. (1991). Evidence for major gene transmission of developmental dyslexia. *Journal of the American Medical Association, 266,* 1527–1534.

Pierangelo, R., & Giuliani, G. (1998). *Special educators' complete guide to 109 diagnostic tests.* Paramus, N.J.: Center for Applied Research in Education.

Radius, M., & Lesniak, P. (1997). *Student team manual.* Sacramento: California Department of Education.

Rief, S. F. (1993). *How to reach and teach ADD/ADHD children.* Paramus, N.J.: Center for Applied Research in Education.

Sabornie, E. J., & Kaufman, J. M. (1986). Social acceptance of the LD adolescent. *Learning Disability Quarterly, 9,* 55–61.

Salvia, J., & Ysseldyke, J. E. (1988). *Assessment in special and remedial education* (4th ed.). Boston: Houghton Mifflin

Schumaker, J. B., & Deshler, D. D. (1992). Validation of learning strategy interventions for students with LD: Results of a programmatic research effort. In B.Y.L. Wong (Ed.), *Contemporary intervention research in learning disabilities: An international perspective.* New York: Springer-Verlag.

Sharpe, R. (1994, April 12). To boost IQs, aid is needed in the first three years. *Wall Street Journal,* pp. 33–35.

Vaughn, S. R., Levin, L., & Ridley, C. A. (1986). *PALS: Problem solving and affective learning strategies.* Chicago: Science Research Associates.

Zuckerbrod, N. (2007, Nov. 15). One in ten schools are 'dropout factories.' *USA-Today.* www.usatoday.com/news/education/2007-10-30-dropout-factories_N.htm?csp34.

Index